The Roots of Love

A guide to Family Constellation:
Understanding the ties that bind us and the path to
freedom

By

Svagito R. Liebermeister

The Roots of Love

A guide to Family Constellation:
Understanding the ties that bind us and the path to freedom

ISBN 978-1-905399-23-9

Cover Design by Carsten Abelbeck and Doris Schneider

Cover painting by Meera Hashimoto
(For more information on her work visit www.meera.de)

Edited by Subhuti

PERFECT PUBLISHERS LTD
23 Maitland Avenue
Cambridge
CB4 1TA
England
www.perfectpublishers.co.uk

"One birth has been given to you by your parents, the other birth is waiting. It has to be given to you by yourself. You have to father and mother yourself."

Osho

Contents

Acknowledgments

I wish to express my gratitude to Osho, my spiritual Master, who has been the greatest source of inspiration to me personally and in my work as a therapist. He has helped me find the courage to question conventional attitudes, gain deeper insights into life and appreciate the element of mystery that pervades all aspects of human experience.

I am grateful to Bert Hellinger for having created the Family Constellation approach to therapy, especially new perspectives it has opened for me, both personally and professionally.

I am grateful to my mother, who taught me unconditional love and to my father, who taught me respect for freedom. I am grateful to my beloved partner and wife, Meera, who shares my journey with me and who is always ready to awaken my joy and sense of adventure.

I also want to thank Savita, who started this book project with me and Subhuti, who completed it. Without their help and encouragement, I would not have even begun to write and without Subhuti's ability to keep the tone of my writing light and 'to the point', this book would not have come out as well as it did.

I feel grateful to all my teachers and partners in Family Constellation work, especially to Suravi, who does a great job in helping to spread this form of therapy in Spain and to all my students and group participants, whose trust and love has touched me deeply. They have enriched my life, my work and helped my understanding to grow. Many of their case histories have been included in this book, but I have changed their names – and in some instances their countries – to protect their privacy.

Introduction

Everybody has a mother and a father. It is such a universal and self-evident fact that we mostly take it for granted and sometimes even forget about it. Yet these are two of the most significant relationships in our lives. Through our parents we came into physical form and into the world, through them we came into life. As the mystic Osho puts it:

"Half of your being consists of your mother and half of your being consists of your father. You are here because of them; if they were not here you would not be here. All that is happening to you is, in a way, because of them... One has to become aware of this."

Each of us, knowingly or unknowingly, is deeply connected to his parents, feeling either love towards them or resentment against them, perhaps wanting to remain close to them, or, conversely, doing our best to get away from them. Rarely, is there anyone who is simply indifferent towards them.

'Family' is considered either as the root of all misery, or as the foundation of a healthy society and the dynamics of family relationships have been the subject of scientific studies for decades.

Family Constellation is a relatively recent form of therapy developed by Bert Hellinger, a German therapist and it has quickly gained worldwide interest. At the core of this approach is the discovery of basic laws that govern families systems and which are the same in all cultures.

This book is for people who want to understand the basic insights of Family Constellation. It can be used as a handbook. In it, I discuss the main points in simple language and place them in a wider context that goes beyond therapy. I summarise Bert Hellinger's discoveries, add my own insights and introduce meditation as a parallel and complementary approach that connects people to Family Constellation in a deeper and more profound way.

The case studies I use as examples are drawn mostly from my own practice, which spans several countries and are clearly marked in the text.

This book can be used as a training manual for people who want to facilitate Family Constellation sessions and is also offered to those who want to look for deeper understanding in their personal and family relationships.

In part one, I discuss the laws that govern the relationship between parents and children, applying these laws to the original family into which we were born.

In part two, I examine the uniqueness of the man-woman relationship and how we can relate to our partners in a more healthy way.

Part three points out what factors need to be considered when leading Family Constellation sessions.

In part four, I describe a way of combining Family Constellation with meditation, with the understanding that this method is not a way to 'fix' people, but a stepping stone to come closer to one's true nature, to discover what guides our behaviour… and what lies beyond.

Also in part four, I bring Hellinger's work together with the insights of Osho, an Indian mystic who has developed many different meditation techniques. Osho's basic approach to psychotherapy, including methods like Family Constellation, is that it is a useful method of unburdening the mind so that we can move more easily into the silence and stillness of meditation.

Specific Expressions

There is a certain vocabulary that accompanies Family Constellation, the meaning of which will become more evident as we progress through the book. However, it will be helpful to cover a few basic points here:

When we refer to a **family member** in a constellation session, we are referring to the representative who is 'standing in' for that person. Actual family members are usually not present during a session.

The **client** is the one who is receiving the constellation. It is his family relationships that are being examined.

The leader of the constellation is referred to as the **therapist** or **facilitator.** I use these terms inter-changeably.

A **representative** or **stand-in** means a person who is placed by the client in a constellation to represent one of his family members, or himself.

A **solution sentence** is a statement given to a representative, or to the client, usually by the facilitator, to say to another person in the constellation.

The word **destiny** is used to indicate the way life has taken shape for someone... with all its good and difficult aspects.

A **movement** is either a physical movement by a representative, or an inner emotional stirring, or feeling.

The expression **entanglement** means the emotional involvement of a person in the life of another member of his family or social group.

When we refer to someone being "**small**," or "**big**," we do not mean physical size, but indicate a psychological attitude, as explained in the book.

Since we are bound by the fact that the English language has no personal pronoun to refer to both men and women, we at times use "he" and "him," and at other times "she" and "her," to include both sexes.

Part One

Understanding Family Constellation

Chapter One

Family Systems: How They Work

Over a hundred years ago, Sigmund Freud, the founder of modern psychology, discovered that the relationship with our parents in childhood affects each tiny detail of our psychological development. In particular, he saw how the relationship with our mothers, as much as it nurtured and provided for us, could also lead to neurosis, confusion and despair.

For a while, mother alone was held responsible for the downside of our psychological life. Since there was truth in it, it became fashionable to make her accountable for every small event that didn't go our way. In therapy circles, blaming parents, especially the mother, became the standard way to account for unhappiness.

Then, in the 1960s, pioneering psychiatrists such as R.D. Laing, Thomas Szazz and others explored the dynamics of the whole family, not just the parents, showing how neurotic and psychotic behaviour is often the outcome of conflicting messages experienced early in family life. Treating disturbed children and unhappy adults as part of their entire family system soon found its way into mainstream psychotherapy.

When you think about it, it makes sense. Just as in quantum physics it has been determined that each part of a complex system of atomic particles is affecting and being affected by every other part, the same is also true for all kinds of larger systems, including global weather patterns, animal food chains and the human family.

The laws and influences governing family systems were further developed by Virginia Satir and others and then in the 1990s an innovative German psychotherapist, Bert Hellinger, attracted worldwide attention by presenting an entirely new approach to working with families and organisations. Now in more than 25 countries, consultants, therapists and other practitioners of family and organisation constellations are working with the Hellinger approach.

A classically-trained psychoanalyst, Hellinger brought together several different elements of psychological observation and family systems theory and integrated these with his personal experience of how South African Zulu tribes deal with family relationships. He'd observed this during his years as a missionary. Out of these diverse elements, he created a brief, intense form of therapy called Family Constellation, or Systemic Constellations.

In his new method, Hellinger also adopted and modified elements of psychodrama, originally developed by Jacob Moreno, and family sculpture, created by Virginia Satir.

Psychodrama makes visible the emotional issues of the client's early life in a theatrical way, where a group of participants, including the client himself, play out family roles as if onstage, trying to illustrate and resolve the client's problems and often projecting better solutions and more positive outcomes than what is actually happening in the family right now.

Satir, who is often referred to as "The Mother of Family System Therapy," also used participants to act out family scenes, but in a more symbolic way. She was the first to observe that the distance between people as well as their postures indicated something about their relationship to each other. Satir started by working with the client's actual family, but when some family members didn't turn up one day, she had to pull in strangers to represent them and in this way discovered that other people in their position could, and did, feel what the actual family member would have felt.

Hellinger refined Satir's insight by using *only* representatives to 'stand in' for the original family members and gave these representatives freedom to follow what they feel from inside themselves, without being influenced by the client's personal interpretation.

Hellinger also drew on the work of Eric Berne, a Canadian-born psychiatrist who was the founder of transactional analysis. Berne observed that everyone goes through life following a secret 'life script,' created long ago in childhood, which can be brought into the light of day, consciously acknowledged and then changed.

However, Berne didn't go beyond a person's personal life, whereas Hellinger found that a script can be taken over from a person from an earlier generation and embraced as one's own. Having discovered the hidden life script, both Berne and Hellinger then introduce 'solution sentences' to help a person get out of the confinement of a certain script.

It's important to realise that, even though Hellinger's work owes much to other forms of therapy, Family Constellation is far more than the sum of its parts. It is an organic system in itself and one of the deepest and most powerful therapies ever devised. In a single session, lasting perhaps as little as 20 minutes, it reveals deep truths about our families and ourselves that can heal, transform, liberate and radically change our lives for the better.

What is a Constellation?

The technique of a Family Constellation session is deceptively simple. Someone who wants to examine his family dynamic is brought together with a group of people from whom he selects individuals to represent different family members, including one to represent himself. Without giving them any explanation or instructions, the client positions these people to 'stand in' for original family members by arranging them in the room in any way he feels like.

What we have here is a portrait of a family: a configuration that expresses something about the degree of intimacy, pain, love, or sense of abandonment, each family member feels in relation to each other.

Very quickly, within the group, the stand-ins begin to feel things that the original family member actually felt, a phenomenon that has been corroborated many, many times by reports from actual family members. It is not uncommon for stand-ins to report a body sensation that turns out to be an accurate representation of a disability belonging to the family member they are representing; someone whom they do not know anything about.

On one occasion, the stand-in for a client's grandfather felt a strong pain in his right leg and after inquiring we learned that his grandfather had sustained a leg injury during the war. On another occasion, a stand-in feeling a pain in his throat discovered that the relative he was standing in for had died from strangulation. Frequently, a spontaneous utterance made by a stand-in exactly replicates the kind of thing the original person might say.

These synchronicities are so commonplace in the Family Constellation set-up as to be no longer remarkable, although how they happen exactly evades rational understanding. It appears that a certain field of energy exists where random people can have access to the feelings and perceptions of the people they represent. It is like stepping into the energy field of a family system and instantly being able to perceive certain truths about the relations within that system. This phenomenon is known by different commentators as a 'morphogenetic field', an 'informing field' or a 'knowing field.'

During the course of the session, the stand-ins change position and are given brief sentences to say, usually simple one-liners, which reveal deep truths about the relationships between the family members they are representing. As the process unfolds they find different positions in relation to each other where, ultimately, everyone feels more at ease.

The client remains a passive observer for most of the session, but in many cases gets positioned within the constellation towards the end, replacing the person who was representing him. However much he directly participates, the overwhelming conclusion from such sessions is that the client experiences new understanding and relief in relation to certain worries, problems or tensions regarding his family.

In other words, Family Constellation is very effective in producing positive results for the client within a very short time.

We Are Part of a Collective

Through experimenting with this work, we come to understand that we are not just isolated individuals who have popped out of nowhere. We discover we are an integral part of the family system to which we belong – whether we like it or not. We are also deeply steeped in the culture and society in which that family raised us and we have been directly affected by such cultural influences.

One-to-one therapy tends to isolate the client. It takes him through the relationships that have moulded his life while working with him on his own, as an individual. Family Constellation looks at the whole picture. As in holistic medicine, which looks on the body-mind as one dynamic system, Family Constellation seeks to address the individual as part of a family system that functions as an organic unity.

When in a session the therapist alters the position of other members of the family, or changes the way they speak to each other, it is easy to see the way the individual is affected. For example, when a person's deceased younger brother, who might have been positioned at the back in the constellation where nobody could see him, gets moved to a focal point in the centre of the family, we immediately notice the effect it has on all family members, not only on the stand-in for the client.

People may visibly take a deep breath, feel anxious, or may start weeping. In this way, everyone participating in these Family Constellation sessions becomes more aware of the way in which each of us is part of a collective to which we are emotionally tied and we begin to see that falling in tune with the larger system to which we belong will help us live in greater harmony with ourselves and those around us.

The work of Family Constellation gives us a chance to understand the way in which, truly, no man is an island. No one is an isolated entity without ties. It is an illusion to imagine we somehow landed on this planet discontinuous from our parents and unconnected to the generations that preceded us. We are all related, especially to members of our family and our ancestors, whether we even *know* these people or not. Family Constellation helps us experience this for ourselves.

It helps us to open our hearts to those who came before us and have been influencing our life, without us knowing it and this in turn helps us to get rooted in the life force that has been transferred to us down through the generations.

Who Can Benefit from Family Constellation?

We all come from one sort of family or another and, though we may not be aware of it, we all have something unresolved in our relationship to our family. So everybody who has a mother and a father has something to gain from this therapeutic approach.

Anyone who takes the opportunity to assemble their family members in a constellation through the Hellinger work will find that it accurately represents their relationships with each other and reveals hidden significance to the one who is arranging them.

But family difficulties may not be the only issue for a Family Constellation session. You may have a problem which appears to have nothing to do with your family. Perhaps, you can't find a love partner, or are having difficulty continuing a relationship. Or you may be struggling with a job you dislike, or be having trouble making a living. You may even have an illness you sense may have psychosomatic origins. Or perhaps there is nothing specific going on, but you feel that your life is empty and meaningless.

Family Constellation can look at anything that brings emotional or practical upheaval in our lives, because most of these psychological problems can be traced back to unresolved family issues. The problems that pull us away from living a joyful life don't come out of the blue. Just by understanding that my personal difficulties are part of some larger disharmony that involves all the people with whom I grew up, and those who came before, allows me to relax.

Setting up a Constellation

Let us say a client comes to a Family Constellation therapist with a health problem, such as a repeated flare-up of psoriasis, a common skin disease that often has its roots in buried psychological issues. The client wants to observe some aspect of her original birth family that she feels might shed light on it.

To create her constellation, the therapist begins by collecting a group of people that is slightly bigger than the significant members of the client's family of origin. At the start of the session itself, the client is invited to choose somebody to represent her father, someone for her mother, somebody to stand in for herself and then maybe some other important members, who belong to the family system. She may be asked to add more people later on. Who is important will be discussed later in the book.

The client then takes each person with both hands and according to her intuition, moves them to a space within the room. She does so without saying anything, placing each person at any spot in the room that feels right to her, facing in any direction. These representatives are not given any particular posture or gesture and they don't say anything. Each person simply stands in whatever position they have been placed.

This is the classic way of doing a constellation. It is a spontaneous configuration, using the space in the room, reflecting the way in which the client feels the members of her family relate to each other

In individual sessions, where no other people are present, the therapist uses different means to represent family members; cushions, chairs, or pieces of paper. Some people even use shoes. But when the family system is set up within the context of a workshop, actual people stand in for its members.

The client, once she has set up her family, now sits down and watches what goes on as a passive observer. The stand-ins have been positioned and a certain relation between the individual family members has started to come to light.

The function of the therapist, or facilitator, is to understand the root of the problem that is being brought to light by this configuration of the client's family system. He can then initiate a movement towards resolution, in the course of which he may ask the representatives how they feel in their positions, as well as help them find a new and more harmonious place within the system.

Since my purpose here is to explain the basic format, I will not take this example any further. There will be many opportunities throughout this book to see how such sessions develop.

A One-Session Method

A constellation is best done when there is a real motivation or urgency from the client to understand or gain insight. Even though many clients do not know their real issue and will be surprised when it emerges, it is usually helpful for them to have an idea of what they would like to get from a constellation.

Family Constellation is practiced in a single session rather than a sequence of sessions. The therapist, or facilitator - we use these terms inter-changeably - looks at a particular dynamic in the family, helps the client to understand and absorb whatever resolution or change has occurred and then brings the session to an end, leaving the experience to work on the client in its own way and its own time. The same client may want to do another constellation at a later date, when something inside his consciousness has moved on, but this, too, will stand alone as an individual session.

Those who participate as stand-ins representing family members do not need to have had any previous experience, nor does anyone need to know anything about the client's history ahead of time. Apart from the fact that we normally choose people to represent someone of the same sex, it otherwise does not make any difference who represents whom.

There are no practical steps for the client to take after a session. Whatever impact the session has made on him will continue to work silently, of its own accord, from within the unconscious part of his mind. It is enough that he has contacted something deep inside himself.

After the constellation, having understood something from within his family dynamic, the client may feel motivated to conduct aspects of his life in a different way, but this will be a spontaneous response, not an intellectual decision or plan. If there is going to be a change, it will steal up on him from some deeper place within his being.

It's the depth of the revelation that initiates change. When you realise the plums you were about to eat are actually nothing but stones, you don't put them in your mouth and bite on them. Similarly, when you understand something that changes your personal gestalt, you find you cannot do things in the way you did before.

You may have had certain family conflicts brought dramatically to your attention; you may have a new understanding about them and, as a result, be aware of the right action to take.

Much depends on how deeply you are able to perceive and receive what happened in your constellation session. During a session, for example, something may have come to light about the relationship between you, your ex-wife and your daughter. Afterwards, you may say to yourself, "Okay, it's time to take more responsibility for my child." It feels right that you, as her father, should now give more support to your daughter.

It is important to remember that Family Constellation therapy does not "work through" issues in a conventional psychological manner, eventually arriving at a specific conclusion or resolution. This form of therapy has a different concept, even though many clients begin with the idea that something should be "solved" for them. What is important is that we come in contact with a certain truth or reality about ourselves and our family entanglement. We see something that is meaningful and this in itself is the benefit. Of course, many times within a session there will be a movement, things change and people move closer to a point of reconciliation, but not always.

People tend to think that only a feeling of harmony and peace is important, which is an understandable but simplistic attitude. Maybe to remain with a difficult situation, rest with it and let understanding and insight ripen in their own time is more valuable than finding a quick solution. Even if a therapist concludes a constellation when seemingly nothing has changed, in the long term this may be the outcome that is needed. Hellinger himself has often told a client, "I cannot do anything for you," which seems harsh, but which may be the only way, at this moment, to move the client's issue towards future resolution.

So, in general, real change happens after a session, not during. In other words, you find yourself coming out of old, fixed beliefs and ideas about yourself, feeling more natural, free and authentic and then bigger forces of life move you onwards. Inner growth is a natural happening, not one's own deliberately planned 'doing.'

A Typical Family Constellation Session

Max, an Austrian of about 40, has difficulty in making contact with people. He feels himself to be withdrawn and is unable to express what is going on inside him. In the pre-session interview, I learn that his mother's father died when his mother was only three or four years of age.

When asked to choose stand-ins for himself and his parents from a group of about 25 participants, Max places them all looking in one direction, his mother and father side by side and himself in front of them with his back to them. The mother begins to stare intently at her son, while the boy looks down towards the floor with a sad face.

I ask the representatives how they are feeling and the mother reports that her son is most important to her and that she is not much aware of her husband. The stand in for Max reports that he cannot see his parents and feels very sad.

I now bring in a man to represent the dead grandfather and position him lying on the ground in front of the son. The mother keeps looking at her son, while the son is drawn to his grandfather and lies down next to him. The mother now starts showing some degree of discomfort and unease, while her son looks relaxed and comfortable next to his grandfather.

I invite the son to stand up and the mother to lie down in his place next to her father. She feels good there and her son now moves towards his father, taking a deep breath of relief and embracing him.

I ask everyone to stand up and let the mother face her father, which makes her burst into tears and ultimately she embraces him. Then we place everybody in a new constellation, which can be called the resolution constellation: first the grandfather, then the mother next to him on his left, then the father and finally the son.

At this point, I invite the client to take his place in the constellation and his representative sits down. I ask him to look at his grandfather and bow down to him with respect, saying to him "Dear grandfather, I honour you!" Then he looks at his mother and says to her: "Dear mother, your father has a place in my heart. I am only your child and I cannot replace your father. Please look at me as your son and please allow me to go to my father." Then he moves towards his father, hugs him with a lot of affection and a sense of relief and says to him: "Dear father, please keep me with you!"

Let us examine what happened here:

The mother's intent look at her son indicates that he represents an important person from her past or that she expects her son to do something in her place. The son looking at the ground indicates that he is looking at a dead person - this has been verified in many constellations, that a person looking at the ground is really looking at someone who has died. Both observations are supported by the feelings of the representatives. It seems that the son is doing something for his mother.

From knowing that the mother's father died at an early age, we can assume that Max may be looking at his grandfather. As I will explain in the following chapters, Max carries his mother's feeling, bearing the pain of an early loss that she may never have allowed herself to feel wholeheartedly, while at the same time identifying with his grandfather. By representing his mother's own father, he becomes emotionally tied to his mother in an unnatural way, unable to move away from her even though he is a mature adult. As a result, he will have difficulty connecting with his own father and be unable to find his strength as a man... all of which may be contributing to his present problem.

Initially, this is just an unproven hypothesis and has therefore to be tested by seeing how the representatives respond and this is done by bringing the 'missing' person - in this case the grandfather - into the constellation. If there is no visible effect on other representatives, the hypothesis would probably be wrong. If there is a strong effect, as in this case, then most likely it is right.

In this case, the identification of Max with his grandfather becomes clear when his own representative feels drawn towards him. When this comes to light, the solution to the problem is also apparent: the mother has to complete the unfinished relationship with her father, facing the pain of losing him and her son has to leave this pain with her and come closer to his father.

At each step in the resolution process, the relief of each person involved and especially of the client is visible to everyone present. Max looks as if a great burden has been lifted off his shoulders.

These are all welcome signs that we have accurately understood the problem and are moving strongly in a direction of resolution, relaxation and relief. Knowing the underlying causes of such family entanglements is the key to resolving them and these we will examine in the following chapters.

Chapter Two

Conscience: the Compelling Force

When we look at what guides our behaviour, what tells us what is 'right' or 'wrong,' what to do and not do, we often refer to an inner sense described as conscience. It is a mechanism of the mind that knows which values should be followed and which must not to be followed.

How do we get to know these values? We learn them from a certain social group: a nation, a tribe, clan or sect, into which we are born and to which we belong. Within this social group, the main instrument for passing on these values to us is the family, especially our parents.

Belonging to a social group ensures our survival. Wanting to belong to a group is an ancient instinct dating back to our days as primitive nomads, when alienation from the tribe meant certain death, so the instinct to belong is deeply ingrained in us and regarded as essential by almost everyone.

Our willingness to learn and conform to the values dictated by our social group is intimately connected with the instinct for survival. We are born in a state of helplessness and ignorance and our parents want us to survive, so they are eager to make sure we grow up in the right way, develop the 'right' attitudes and do the 'right' thing. They want us to 'fit in' and be accepted as new members of their group.

Have you ever wondered why your parents were so concerned about what the neighbours might think if you did something bad, like throw sweet wrappers over the wall, or scream too loudly while playing in the yard, or leave broken toys in their driveway? Can you remember the alarmed expression on your mother's face?

It wasn't just fear of your immediate neighbours that made her so worried. It has its roots in the age-old survival instinct that was motivating her conscience. Her underlying fear was of social isolation and rejection – both for herself and her child - which, in the unconscious layers of our collective memory, means death.

You may recall experiencing something similar, if you were unfortunate enough to be rejected or excluded from a social clique at school – it can be a very traumatic experience, far bigger than the occasion seems to warrant, because it stirs these ancient roots.

Conscience is like a social barometer: if we are feeling relaxed, innocent and comfortable, we know we are following the rules and our right to belong is assured. If we are feeling guilty, we know we went against the rules. Since we want to belong to many groups - family, social club, religion, nation and football team - we develop a different conscience related to each of them, although the likelihood is that they all share the same general values.

We even have two slightly different consciences related to our mother and our father. As a child we learn very fast what father likes, what mother expects and how to behave in regard to each of them. For example, a child who takes sweets from the candy jar may feel no qualms in relation to an indulgent father, but desperately guilty in relation to a health-conscious mother.

So conscience guides our daily lives and the remarkable thing is that, as we grow up, we become convinced that this inner code of conduct is our very own, private, independent set of opinions and beliefs. Whatever it is that compels us to behave rightly has been so successfully ingrained in our character that we feel it to be intrinsic to our personality and identity.

Conscience is not carved in stone. Something considered 'good' in one culture may be considered 'bad' in another. In most western societies, if you are given a gift, it is polite to say 'thank you.' However, there are circumstances when, for example, someone living in India may feel offended when thanked for a gift.

Taboo behaviour within one religion may be considered innocuous in another. Christians drink wine and eat after sunset, both of which are simply impossible for a member of the Jain religion. Hindus consider it normal to arrange the marriages for their children when they are still very young, which is a very strange idea for Jewish or Christian people.

To be at variance with the demands of my particular group puts me in deep conflict. The more I want to belong, the more I will conform and the more I will need to make distinctions between my group's values and those of others. This clash of conflicting consciences is the basic cause of all wars and sectarian strife. In recent years, we have seen how fanatic terrorists can do appalling acts in the name of their religion or faith with an absolutely clear conscience.

The stricter our moral values, the greater hold our conscience has on us. So people who are very moralistic usually feel tightly bound by family, religious and cultural values.

Personal Conscience: the Need to Belong

Personal conscience is something we feel as individuals: When I feel guilty, I will usually respond by trying to do whatever I can in order to put things right, so the unpleasant feeling of guilt will go away and I will be reassured that I am still following the rules that permit me to belong to my group. The husband who just flirted with his secretary at the office may feel compelled to buy flowers for his wife on the way home. The child who stole coins from his mother's purse to buy candy may feel he has to confess everything to her in order to be able to sleep that night.

19

This personal conscience has its origins in early childhood. The child wants nothing more than to belong to her mother and, a little later, to her father. She loves her parents unconditionally because her survival depends on it. It is a deep instinct, the most powerful instinctive force in mammals and nature's way of ensuring the child's survival. Without this bond with the mother, the infant will simply wither and die and so she will do anything she can to stay close to the mother.

As we grow up, this need to bond grows wider, including other members of our family and in this way we acquire a family identity. Beyond the family we start encountering other people and gradually acquire a social identity by bonding with a bigger group. This urge to be part of a social collective, from personal cliques of friends to worldwide religious organisations, satisfies our need for a sense of place and position in the world.

Our need to belong is so great that when removed from our homeland, we often exaggerate the rituals that defined our original group. For example, an Indian living as part of the Asian community in Toronto might conform more to the cultural traditions of her country of origin than her sister living in Delhi. She may follow the rites of her religion more strictly and adhere more closely to its rules.

Her group, if it is fearful of being overwhelmed by larger numbers of other religions, might stick together more closely and separate itself from the non-Asians around them. From New York City's Orchard Street to London's Brick Lane, immigrant communities all over the world have banded together to the exclusion of others in order to consolidate their group identity and ensure their survival.

In short, everyone has a need to belong to one group or another. Each group is a 'system' that creates a sense of belonging, governed by our sense of right and wrong. Whatever we do, either going with the dictates of personal conscience or against it, strengthens or weakens our bonding to the system. If we do something that endangers our belonging, we have a bad conscience, feel guilty and expect to be punished. In fact, we often welcome punishment because it absolves us from one of the worst forms of punitive treatment that can be inflicted by any society - exclusion.

Clearly, this sense of belonging and the loyalty we feel towards any individual or group, depends on how important each relationship is for us. And, as I have said, the bonding to our primary relationships, our parents, is going to be the strongest. Our first human contact to mother will be the strongest of all.

The Need for Balance

Personal conscience also responds to a force less powerful than the need to belong, but still very significant. It is something we can call *a sense of balance*. Balance is about reciprocity. It means, for example, that when I give you a gift, you feel you would like to give me something in return. When you have given me something in return, perhaps I will feel like giving you something more.

If the exchange has a playful or loving quality to it, this creates a momentum that deepens our connection with each exchange. Relationships grow and enrich themselves with variations of this form of balancing. It is part and parcel of the joy of relating and one of the essential bonding mechanisms that keep people together.

It is not uncommon, when we have received a gift, to feel a *duty* to give something in return. At the very least, I must thank whoever has gifted me and until the 'thank you' has been made, I am nagged by a sense of incompletion. Equally, if it's me who has given the gift, I will feel entitled to receive a 'thank you' and will feel something is lacking if it is not forthcoming.

Most of the time, we are either in a state of indebtedness to someone who has given to us, or someone else is indebted to us, usually in small ways that demonstrate relatedness, friendliness or intimacy that has been created slowly, over time.

Imagine giving a gift of a thousand dollars to a needy nephew for his college studies and then saying 'no thank you' to the bouquet of flowers he brings around to your house. If you toss his flowers aside, or belittle their significance, you will be denying his need to express gratitude and may seriously offend him. To reject the gift is to jeopardise the relationship. On one level, the nephew wants relief from an uneasy conscience he feels in having received so much money, so he literally 'says it with flowers.' If you are going to maintain the balance of the relationship, your role is to accept the flowers graciously – even if you don't like roses and happen to be allergic to their smell.

Balance also manifests negatively as well as positively. Just as we want to give love and affection when they are shown to us, the urge for reprisal and reparation arises when we feel hurt or wounded. Those of us who have felt seriously wronged can understand the human appetite for 'settling scores,' a primitive and compelling force that can haunt us throughout our lives. Our personal conscience pushes us to make someone 'pay' for any 'injustice' we feel we have received. The need for vengeance is so basic to human law that it crosses the borders of nations, religions or technological differences and resonates with everyone in the common currency of our mythology, our literature and our films.

But, of course, these things are not only present in literature and movies. The cheating, lying and emotional wounding that are the stuff of myth and drama are also part of our real lives.

Social Order and Etiquette

Another situation governed by personal conscience concerns our social relations. What happens when we behave in a community in a way that feels awkward or gauche? At a formal dinner, for example, when you accidentally eat your fish with the pastry knife, or drink wine from a water glass. Or you turn up to the opening night of the opera in your gardening shirt; or appear in an evening gown at what turns out to be an informal disco party. If your dress code does not fit the situation, you feel self-conscious and uncomfortable and so do the people around you.

Social order refers to the collective demand that you acknowledge and obey certain rules governing behaviour and propriety in the social settings of any group to which you may belong. This aspect of the personal conscience is the least binding of our three principles, but even so, it is known to produce some comical situations. In Japan, it is the custom to make a sound when you eat your noodle soup – a kind of homely slurp that shows you're enjoying your food. But in Europe, vocally sloshing food into your mouth is considered bad manners and however hard it is not to slurp your soup, we all struggle to keep such noises to a minimum.

Similarly in some Middle Eastern and Pacific Island countries, a good baritone burp at the end of a meal tells your host you're more than satisfied with his spread. But burp in England and you'll see eyebrows raised in disapproval.

Transgressing conscience that is related to social order usually creates less guilt than the other two principles and it is certainly easier to overcome, but still it can deeply affect us. We can still feel embarrassed by remembering such incidents, even if they happened years ago.

To sum up the effects of personal conscience: it makes me feel guilty when I go against its rules of conduct; it compels me to make amends for something I did wrong, to give something in exchange for what has been received and to make sure I fit into the social order by exhibiting correct behaviour on the right occasion.

Our Collective Conscience

Collective conscience is a much more powerful, hidden and insidious force. It works in an invisible way. It doesn't announce its presence through feelings of guilt if we go against it; we are unaware of where it comes from and it exists without our being able to identify it directly.

Instead of inhabiting the mind of the individual and revealing itself by responding to his personal choices, the collective conscience operates from within the family as a whole and, as I have already indicated, does so without its members knowing about it.

In much the same way that we can identify an electric current only by the effect it has on the light bulb, we can recognise the collective conscience only by the ways in which it affects people's behaviour.

Our work in Family Constellation is to identify this collective conscience. When we understand the laws of this conscience we can bring them into the light of day, understand their implications and intentions, heal the imbalance to the family system and help the client accept what has happened.

We shall now look more deeply at these laws.

In the same way that the personal conscience has three aims, the collective conscience has three principles: *Belonging, Order* and *Balance.*

The Law of Belonging

Everybody who is part of a family has an equal right to be part of that family. Every member of the family, regardless of who they are, when they arrived, or what they did, has an equal claim to his place.

One child may be a gifted musician, another may be sick or handicapped, another may have antisocial behaviour problems - it makes no difference. Even in the extended family, if someone died young or committed suicide, it changes nothing with regard to this basic right to belong. Everyone has to be included and respected equally.

The Law of Hierarchy

Within a family system, family members are ranked according to the time of their arrival. Those who came earlier have a 'higher' rank than those who came later. Older siblings have priority over younger ones; a first wife has to be remembered as being first, a second wife must be remembered as coming before the third wife and so on.

What comes first comes first, what comes later comes later – chronological order has absolute priority. This is not a man-made law in the sense that it has been deliberately created as part of a set of moral beliefs. It is existential; it comes simply with being born into a family system.

This notion of giving precedence to whoever comes first is deeply ingrained in our collective unconscious, something we instinctively feel in a wide range of ordinary, day-to-day situations. For example, when we queue up at a theatre ticket counter, or book seats on an airplane, we automatically assume that those who come first will get better seats; or when unease spreads through a company because a newcomer is promoted above someone who has been there for years and we all think "how unfair!"

It is the same with our families. Deep inside, we are ruled by a sense of hierarchy based on time of arrival and this is triggered when, by behaving in a way unsuited to his position, some family member is not 'in his place' or 'acting above his station.' The English language is full of terms that express this form of thinking: "it was not his position to do that... he was out of order... it was not his place to say such a thing...."

The Law of Balance

Any injustice done to a family member in a previous generation, or committed by a family member in that earlier generation, must be balanced by acts of a later member of the same family.

On a personal level, as I already mentioned, we are aware of the wish to balance something that happened to us, to return a favour or wound we have received.

But there is a far more powerful force in play within a family system. This one compels us to pay not for our own misdeeds, but for something that our forefathers may have done. Whatever negative acts have entered the family system in the past and have not been atoned, will ultimately manifest in later generations – rather like a virus that lies low in the body only to emerge as sickness later on.

So it is not a question of immediate retribution, "an eye for an eye," or "you hit me and I'll hit you back." This is a much broader and deeper phenomenon operating on a trans-generational scale. It echoes the notion from the Bible that tells us "the sins of the fathers shall be visited upon the children." It means that if my grandfather killed his mistress, there's every chance that in some unconscious way I am paying for it.

I need to emphasise that this is not a moral injunction about how we *should* behave. It is not a fabricated code of conduct. It is simply an existential truth. The discovery of

26

these laws happened not through ethical reasoning but through pure observation - through what is known in academic circles as a 'phenomenological' approach to reality.

In other words, in the family system, this is just the way things are and one of the basic laws governing such systems is that if one family member doesn't take responsibility for his acts then someone else in the family will. The collective conscience passes the buck of retribution from generation to generation until it is ultimately addressed, claimed and cancelled out.

Personal conscience makes me want to balance something I did wrong. Collective conscience compels me, without my knowing it, to balance something on behalf of a member of a family who, in all probability, I do not even know.

With the personal, I feel the guilt; with the collective I am driven by an unconscious force. Ultimately, what this shows is that there is a collective layer in our minds that holds us responsible for everything that we do and for the effect our actions have on others. Everyone is responsible, whether they own it or not.

There is another distinction to be made between the personal and the collective that directly relates to our desire for maturity. Individual growth depends on being able to stand alone, in spite of any twinges of personal conscience we may feel regarding our parents and our feelings of obligation and duty towards them. But with the collective conscience we can achieve this 'aloneness' only to a certain degree; in other words we need to be ready to carry a certain destiny that comes with our life and accept the fact that we are part of a particular family and its history. When we accept this, we can begin to rise above it – not before.

The Welfare of the Whole System

Collective conscience treats every member equally, ignores any differences between them and works for the welfare and survival of the whole. This law protects each member's right to belong to the family and also confines people to their place within the system.

In traditional societies, in which continuity between generations is deeply venerated, such laws are the basis for all social interactions. Traditions of hierarchy exist in all primitive tribes and the elders are deeply respected. They have a privileged status above the younger generations and they preside over strict rules of priority, which are observed in a way that no longer exists in our modern world.

In western society, the individual is now sacrosanct and we often see sons and daughters going against the wishes of their fathers. In primitive groups, no one would even consider crossing his elders. The group's interests, represented by the strict hierarchy, come before the individual's interests. Everyone within the group knows about it, adheres to it and accepts responsibility accordingly.

For example, I've heard a true story of a man belonging to a group of nomadic African tribals who seriously injured his leg. When the other tribe members brought him to the hospital, the doctor told the family that if the man's leg wasn't amputated, he would die and that they should decide whether he was to be operated or not.

Rather than respond immediately, the aboriginals went home and sat together amongst themselves to discuss the matter. When they returned, they told the surprised doctor that the operation should not go ahead - the man will have to die.

Something that may appear to be brutal to our western minds shows how the needs of the collective govern every choice within these cultures; it shows how the welfare of the group is sacrosanct. Being nomads, these people were compelled to move continuously, travelling along traditional routes that allowed their livestock to graze on sparsely-available grasses and plants and then moving on as soon as the local grazing was exhausted. A one-legged man would slow them down and this would endanger the group's survival, so they had to let him die.

Everyone, even the man himself, was aware of this and in accordance with the decision.

The Personal Against the Collective

We can see these collective social laws operating in primitive tribes. What is hard, however, is to see the same laws operating within our own modern, twenty-first century families.

The development of personal conscience tends to create different values within a group, based on the belief that some have more right to belong than others. For example, when I do something that is in accordance with the values of my group, I feel I have more right to belong than someone who goes against the norm and does not conform.

This is one of the elements of the famous biblical story of the prodigal son. The 'good' son, who stayed at home and helped his father, feels he has more rights than the son who squandered his inheritance in travelling and extravagant living. The fatted calf should have been killed for him, not for his good-for-nothing brother.

Or, to take a modern example, a member of a company who for years has worked hard and loyally will feel he is more entitled to be part of that company than someone who is always late and who filches the stationery.

However, this personal element can put the individual's interest in opposition to the collective, because the collective does not make these distinctions. As far as the collective is concerned, each son has the same right to belong to the family and each company member has the same right to be part of the company.

What we see in Family Constellation is that the collective conscience is much more powerful than the personal conscience and can even make people do things against their personal conscience in order to fulfil its laws.

To stay with the example of the prodigal son: if I decide to cheat my brother out of his inheritance, because he abandoned his family while I worked hard to support all our relatives, it is justified by my personal conscience saying, "I have more right to the money than he does!"

But later on, I may lose all my money from an unconscious need to punish myself for cheating him. In this way, under the influence of the collective conscience, I will balance out the wrongdoing and put myself back on an equal level with my brother. Or, if I do not create this balance, some later member of our family may have to do it for me.

In traditional societies there was a strong emphasis on what people have in common and individual differences were suppressed for the sake of the overall well-being of the community. This kind of orientation was vital for group survival because life was focused on the fulfilment of very basic needs. To combat hardships like drought, flood, famine, cold, wild animals and tribal enemies, the welfare of the group was paramount.

Nowadays, in affluent western societies, that urgency in relation to group survival is no longer present. Now there is room for variety and individual differences, which is a natural direction for social evolution – more freedom of personal choice.

The downside of this comparatively recent trend is that we have almost totally forgotten our familial connections. But the laws that govern those connections have not forgotten us. They still exist and, like it or not, they still control our actions.

Today's rebellious teenager may believe he is free to do what he likes and on one level he certainly is more free to act and live differently than members of his grandparents' generation. But, on another level, he is deeply bonded to his social group and this collective bond will force him to do things, even against his idea of being free.

I am reminded of the case of a young Australian woman, whom I will call Tracy, who lived in a very wild and free manner and at a young age explored drugs, became a hippie, wandered through India for years and thought that her teenage pregnancy and decision to give away her girl-child for adoption was left far behind her.

But, when new laws allowing adopted children to trace their natural parents came into effect, Tracy, now in her forties, agreed to meet her natural daughter. Shortly afterwards, the daughter committed suicide, leaving her own very young daughter to be raised by its maternal grandmother, Tracy. Some kind of balance had occurred, dictated by the collective conscience of this family. We'll look at more examples of this need for balance as the book progresses.

So, if an individual is going to rise above the entanglements of family bonds, he first needs to understand and fall in tune with his family's collective conscience. When balance has been restored, when old accounts have been settled, when everything and everyone is in rightful order, only then may he consider himself truly free to explore his individual preferences.

This is the purpose of the work we call Family Constellation.

Chapter Three

Exclusion: Who's Been Left Out?

One of the most surprising and powerful insights into family dynamics that has been brought to light by Hellinger's work is to see how a later member of the family, a child, identifies with an earlier family member without having any idea that this is happening. He carries his relative's feelings as his own and acts out that person's life, just as if he were a replica. Mostly, this happens without anybody in the family being aware of it and the person who feels compelled to do it may never have met the one he is representing.

What is the secret behind this surprising phenomenon?

In the case of Max, the Austrian, whom we discussed in chapter one, we learned that when Max's mother was still a very young girl, she lost her father. When a child loses a parent so early, as in this case, the pain is overwhelming. The bonding to the parent is so strong that the child cannot deal directly with such a loss and separation. One way she can deal with it is to try and exclude the impact of his death from her memory.

By forgetting her father and his death Max's mother excludes him from her life and this goes hand in hand with her need to avoid pain. However, the problem is that no pain can ever be entirely avoided and no parent can be forgotten in this way. So Max's mother remains like a stuck record at the point where her father died, unable to really let him go.

In order to complete her relationship with her dead father she would need to fully acknowledge that he died and re-experience the pain of her loss, but this is the very same pain she has been avoiding for so long. She may think that she can just leave it all behind her, but the wound that has been created in her heart and the profound disruption that has occurred in the family system, does not allow it.

Under the influence of the collective conscience, which demands that every member of the family be remembered and acknowledged, a later family member, her son Max, will have to represent his mother's forgotten father within the family system.

Like all children, Max needs his mother's love and attention; he needs to bond with his mother in his own right, which is a natural, healthy and important part of any normal child's relationship with his parents.

But Max senses that his mother is not fully available to him. Without actually understanding what is happening, he can feel that her heart is still secretly tied to her father, who died when she was just a small girl. By identifying with his grandfather and carrying his mother's pain, Max tries to get his mother's love and attention. He starts acting as if he is a parent to his own mother – something we call 'parentification.'

As you can imagine, the demands of the collective conscience are hard on the newly arrived child. Behaving as if he is a parent, Max tries to give love to his mother rather than receiving from her, which is a reversal of the natural direction. Max remains empty, under-nourished as a child in an emotional sense and yet at the same time bonded to his mother. As he grows up, he is unable to separate from her and therefore cannot fully give himself to another woman. At the same time, his own sense of masculinity has been impaired and the reason is clear: Max was not able to receive the male support and attention he needed from his own father, because he was not really acting as his father's son.

In short, the boy cannot really be himself and has no idea why. One basic entanglement, the unsuccessful attempt by his mother to forget her father, creates more and more complexities. Since Max has not been able to fully receive his mother's love and support, he may try to get it from another woman as if he is a child, or from his own children, if he becomes a father. Then his own children will want to give to him, rather than receive and the whole bundle of confused relating patterns continues in a topsy-turvy fashion from one generation to the next.

Max may even develop a life-denying tendency, which could go so far as making him accident prone or suicidal, depending how strong his mother's attachment to her father had been. This is the collective conscience operating. It's the collective conscience wanting to include the forgotten, excluded, or lost relative, so that everybody in the family has his place and is fully remembered. This is what determines that a child has to represent his own forgotten grandfather.

The reason for not remembering someone is usually unlived pain. The younger a person is, the more difficult it is for him to deal with such pain – especially a pain as great as the early loss of a parent. Whenever we love someone deeply and innocently, as children do, the openness of that state creates the possibility of intense pain if we lose the one we love. To be able to fully deal with that pain requires a certain maturity that a child simply does not have.

The earlier the loss, the graver the consequences for the child. According to psychologists who adhere to the "object relations theory" of human ego development, early loss of a parent carries a serious risk of disrupting the healthy formation of the child's identity.

An Excluded Grandmother

Let's look at another example:

Antonella is a 35-year-old Italian woman who has requested a session, focusing on the issue that she had not had a relationship with a man for several years. In a preliminary interview, I learn that her father left the family when she was a teenager and that she did not see him again for another 20 years. She also tells me that her paternal grandfather had sent away his wife, her grandmother, along with two of their children. Her grandfather had then remained alone with their third child, Antonella's own father.

I begin the session by inviting Antonella to select three individuals from a group of 25 people to represent her father, mother and herself and place them in a constellation. She positions her father directly opposite herself, so they are facing each other and she positions her mother to one side. Her own stand-in immediately reports that she is feeling very agitated and cannot look at her mother; her father reports that he is focused on Antonella and the mother says she feels like an outsider.

When we add a representative for the grandmother, Antonella's stand-in feels greatly relieved. Her father also feels better and his attention immediately goes to his mother. Antonella expresses a lot of love towards her grandmother. When we also bring the grandfather into the picture, Antonella reveals that she is angry towards him for having sent her grandmother away.

So, what has been going on in this family?

The grandmother is the one who has been excluded in this family and Antonella is carrying the burden by identifying with her. She carries the anger that the grandmother must have felt toward her husband, even though it was not Antonella who was sent away.

This is a typical example of how a child, out of love – what we call a blind love – unconsciously intervenes in the life-destiny of another family member and then suffers the consequences in her own life. In relating, the young Antonella now expresses her rage not to her grandfather, who is long dead, but towards her own father and towards other men, which is why she has difficulty establishing relationships with men.

We call this a 'double shift.'

1. Antonella is behaving like her grandmother – a shift in the identity of the subject.

2. Antonella is expressing her anger not at her grandfather, but at her father and other men – a shift in the object of her emotions.

In this case, the situation is even more complex. Antonella's father had to stay with his father, her grandfather, while secretly missing his mother and sisters and secretly being angry with him.

Now Antonella's father, as a young child, cannot fully trust his parents, or receive love from them, because one parent is not available and he feels anger toward the remaining one. So in his own life, he will look for his mother, maybe trying to find her in a wife or daughter. At the same time he will identify with his father and feel a strong tendency to repeat what he did - leaving the family - which is precisely what happened.

In setting up this family constellation, when we look at the way Antonella placed herself opposite her father, we can see the repetition of the confrontation between grandfather and grandmother. Her father identifies with his father, carries his burden of guilt, while at the same time searching for his mother. Antonella identifies with her grandmother, is angry and directs her anger towards her father. That her father also left his family only compounds her anger.

What is the solution? First of all, Antonella begins to feel a certain degree of relief when she realises her father was not free. As a child, he was entangled in events beyond his control, even beyond his understanding. This insight helps her to open towards him.

By honouring her grandmother and leaving the original conflict between grandparents to the grandparents themselves, she can now take her place as a child. As a child, she can now acknowledge how much she missed her father, recognising that - considering the circumstances of his own childhood - he did all he could do.

Now that she feels more free from the complex bonding to her father's family, she can begin to look at her own mother. You may remember that, in the original constellation set-up, she was not looking at her mother at all. She now feels able to move towards her, which is a great relief for her. Now, too, she can look at men with fresh eyes, without the anger, suspicion and mistrust that had predominated before.

Here, we were able to expose the origin of the conflict and leave it where it belonged: with the grandparents.

What Exclusion Means

As we have seen in Antonella's case, a forgotten or excluded person is not necessarily someone who died in an untimely way. It is, rather, a relative who has not been acknowledged, who has not been given his or her rightful place in the family system.

So exclusion covers many possibilities. The relative may have been ignored, never talked about, never recognised as being of value; or they may have been turned away by the family because they were handicapped or mentally retarded. Or perhaps they had been absent in hospital for long periods or were sent to boarding school; or, most significantly of all, given for adoption. They may also have been excluded through a deep moral judgment about their behaviour that resulted in banishment from family love.

Myths and stories all over the world contain these neglected souls: excluded people whose memory in some way or another has not been honoured.

In a session, information gathered during the initial interview gives an indication of who the excluded person may be and also indicates who we may need to bring into

38

the family picture. After that, one has to explore within the constellation itself to see if this hypothesis is correct and whether bringing that person into the constellation has any effect.

After hearing Antonella's family history, I concluded that her grandmother might be important, but still I had to test this hypothesis in the actual constellation. The responses of the stand-ins showed that I was on the right track, that I had found the 'missing' person. If it had not been the right person, the stand-ins would not have responded in any significant way when the grandmother was placed in the constellation.

Completing the Past – Including the Excluded

Family Constellation is healing work. It consists of trying to reconfigure family relationships and bring an excluded member back into the family portrait. We are trying to complete something that could not be completed at the time when it actually happened. In fact, all therapy work is completion work; it is an effort to finish an incomplete gestalt so that it doesn't leave a psychological hangover.

Any type of personal growth or individual development work depends on the same basic principle: whatever has been excluded, whatever aspect of one's personality has been rejected, needs to be addressed, accepted and given a place in one's heart. In exactly the same way, within the generations of a family, family members that have been excluded need to be brought back in again; they need to be included, acknowledged and remembered with love.

An essential element of this principle is the understanding that whatever we reject will remain powerful as long as we continue to reject it. This is because the very act of rejecting gives it power over us, gives it energy to pursue us. The ghost that you think is a ghost holds onto the power it needs to haunt you for as long as you're convinced it's a ghost. When you see it's a cobweb in the wind, it ceases to frighten you. Once we say 'yes' and accept whatever we cannot bear to look at, something changes within us. It's not only a matter of accepting; it is a matter of opening to the ghosts we feared and ultimately finding a source of love for them within ourselves.

This principle of opening to our unloved parts provides the foundation for the whole of psychotherapy. Whatever we throw into the basement of the mind, into the unconscious layers of the mind, becomes a hundred times more powerful and returns to punish us.

Pain is a pivotal issue here. The whole problem is created because we want to avoid pain. We may go so far as to say that *all* problems are created around the avoidance of pain. In fact, one of the mind's compulsive functions is to try to save us from experiencing unease of any kind and it does this by distracting us. So the process of healing consists, first of all, in recognising that pain is part of life and that psychological pain is like any other pain. It cannot be avoided.

As far as death is concerned, nature, in itself, has no value judgments. An early death, or death from old age, are simply two different destinies, the one no more significant than the other. It is our own very human but purely arbitrary opinion that an early death is a tragedy and death itself a horror that must be put off for as long as possible, under any circumstances.

Understanding the neutrality of death makes it possible to acknowledge a person who had a difficult destiny, or who may have died young, without feeling sorry for him. This is the work we try to accomplish in Family Constellation, so that healing can happen.

From Blind to Conscious Love

What is apparent in our examples of Max and Antonella is that it is very important to find which family member the child is representing, the one with whom the child is identifying and to bring that person back into the family picture so that everyone can see him. If that person is seen and acknowledged with love, the need to represent him comes to an end and the child is free to be himself - he is freed from identification.

Identification means the child cannot see the other as a separate person. It is an unsuccessful effort by the collective conscience to give the excluded person a place in the family – unsuccessful, because that person still remains excluded, even though a child is representing him.

The moment Max looks into the eyes of his grandfather, the moment Antonella looks at her grandmother with love and respect, the identification ends. The child comes back to his, or her, rightful place. Immediately, the child-parent relationship is healed and nourished. Max can now tell his mother that he respects her father, respects her pain of losing him early in her life and re-establishes the love connection with her. Antonella can say to her father that she remembers his mother and feel the love connection with him restored.

Often this is a great relief for the parent, at other times they may re-live the pain that has been repressed, or notice difficulty in letting go of their own parents – each situation is unique and unfolds in different ways. The significant point is that by re-living the pain, the buried love usually comes to light and it is love that is the real healing.

In his original, blind love, Max identified with his grandfather. Now that he has recognised his grandfather he no longer needs to identify with him. His love has become more conscious and now, in conscious love, he can simply honour the older man. It is this 'honouring love' that makes

41

it impossible for Max to continue to represent his grandfather.

Max also acted out of love for his mother. His need to belong to her drove him to do anything in the hope of relieving her pain and gaining her affection. We call this love 'blind' or 'bonded love.' The child always feels, according to his personal conscience, that he is capable of doing whatever it takes to help his parent endure pain; that he *has a right* to do those things.

It is a kind of magical thinking that children have: "Someone has to suffer, so if I suffer on my parent's behalf, she will suffer less." Of course it is not true; in reality the suffering is simply doubled. Blind love violates the collective conscience that governs the 'sacred order' of things and ultimately nobody benefits. I'll talk about this more in the next chapter.

Who Belongs to the Family System

All members of the family in the primary lineage are subject to the collective conscience. This includes the parents, the children, as well as any children who died young or were stillborn and all the grandparents. Aunts and uncles are also included, but not their children. On occasion, great-grandparents and great-great grandparents may be included. These are the relatives that comprise the extended family for the purpose of Family Constellation.

There are also people who are not relatives, but who have forged a strong connection, binding them to the family because of what happened between them and a family member. These people now belong to the family system and are subject to the laws of the collective conscience. They, too, will need to be represented by a later family member. If there was a former love partner of one of the parents, who had to get out of the way to make room for the present parent, he or she needs to be included.

We also include people, who mistreated or killed a family member and this includes those involved in grave events like ethnic cleansing, such as the Nazis, or people involved in civil war (these issues are dealt with in chapter six). Also, the reverse applies: a person who suffered at the hands of one of the family members – someone murdered, for sure, but also a former business partner who was cheated of his dues. Anyone who was gravely mistreated by one of the family members must be brought into the constellation.

Sample Case Histories

A few examples reveal how an excluded member of a family is represented by a child and the importance of bringing that person into the system:

In a constellation, the woman client positions her first child, a mentally handicapped daughter, opposite the one standing-in for herself. When asked, we learn that the client's elder sister was stillborn and physically handicapped. As soon as she is mentioned, the client's own mentally handicapped child wants to lie down. After bringing the client's stillborn sister into the picture, her handicapped daughter feels great relief. From these two developments we surmise that the handicapped daughter had to represent her stillborn aunt in the family.

A grandfather and some of his children were killed by the Nazis. When the client, a woman, chooses representatives for her grandfather, aunts and uncles — the Nazi victims – she is unable to fully acknowledge her grandfather, or the ones who had died in the concentration camp. The constellation reaches impasse, until I introduce someone to represent the Nazis themselves. Instantly, she feels relief and finds herself drawn to the person

43

representing the Nazis and stands next to him. This shows that, in this family, it is the Nazis who have been excluded and their memory suppressed, so a child had to represent them.

A woman has difficulty with her daughter, who she feels does not respect her. It turns out that her husband had a former wife whom he left ungracefully and the daughter identifies with her. When asked, the daughter says she feels angry with her father and jealous of her mother. The relief comes when I introduce the former partner into the picture and when both parents honour the father's first wife.

To sum up: the work of Family Constellation is to reconcile ourselves with the needs of the collective conscience and acknowledge every member of our family, remembering them in a loving way that will create harmony in our lives.

What we have seen in these examples is that wherever a person who belongs to an extended family has been excluded, the collective conscience demands they be remembered. If they are not remembered, it creates a situation in which a later child identifies with that person in order to bring him back, so that, in a way, he continues to live within the family nexus.

We see how, despite this complex manoeuvre, the original family member still remains excluded, because the child who represents him can only be a distortion of the real person. Awareness of the true situation brings about an existential shift that releases them both.

When we satisfy the collective conscience by bringing the excluded person into his rightful position in the family circle, when he is remembered and acknowledged, there is a sense of peace and relief for everyone. Only then, the one who represents him in the present generation can let go of the burden and be free.

Chapter Four

The Sacred Order

The word 'order' has many meanings: to command someone to do something, to arrange things in a certain pattern, to request a meal or delivery of purchased items and to imply a certain tidiness of character, such as "she keeps her house in good order." I am also reminded of noisy scenes in the British House of Commons, when the elected members are getting out of control and the Speaker has to stand up and shout, "Order! Order!"

In Family Constellation, we use 'order' in a specific sense: as a way of describing a certain sequence and precedence – the chronological line of who came before whom - together with a sense of creating an appropriate arrangement of things. From the blend of these two, we create our use of the word.

Hellinger himself called it 'the order of love,' meaning that whoever comes first, comes first; whoever comes later, comes later and love flows best in a family system when this order is respected. On the surface, our use of the word order is about appearance in time, while at a deeper level it suggests a feeling of comfort and symmetry. Putting it another way: the time of belonging defines one's position within the family and when this order is observed a sense of ease and relaxation arises.

Usually, when there are no hidden imbalances within a family system, a good position for the members of a nuclear family in a constellation is that parents stand first and are then joined by their children, according to their age, in a clockwise arc, with the oldest child standing closest to the parents.

Sometimes, the children stand opposite their parents, facing them, which can also be thought of as a clockwise arrangement, if we think of everyone as part of an imaginary circle. This is the formation in which each family member feels most at ease; each one feeling that he or she is 'in the right place'.

This order has not been created or invented by family psychologists and therapists. It is existential. It was discovered through doing constellations, originally by Hellinger himself and then confirmed by others. It mirrors the fact that we perceive the whole world around us by mentally organising everything – all our sensory input - in terms of time and space and this shows up in the inner pictures we carry about our families. Our minds give meaning to a particular position for each family member.

Unresolved family entanglements usually require changes in the positioning of family members and with each constellation we need to explore and discover this positioning anew, finding out what is the most harmonious arrangement by listening to the feedback from the 'stand ins' or family representatives.

So the time of arriving on the scene, or of being part of a family system, determines the place a person has in the family, which is translated into a position in the constellation. The collective conscience guards over this positioning, which means that everyone in the family has a deep inner knowing about whether they are in their right place. In everyone's mind, whether they are aware of it or not, there is a strict sense of 'family order' which depends on time of arrival.

Let's look at the example of Maureen, an Irish-born client who had seven siblings, four of whom had died very early in life, either immediately after birth or already inside the womb. Maureen complains that she is plagued by confusion and doubt in many aspects of her life and has difficulty focusing on a specific project, or career goal and carrying it through to a satisfactory conclusion.

As an initial step, I put up her family order: the parents first, with all the children standing opposite, according to their age from right to left. In this line-up, I include all of Maureen's dead brothers and sisters and this simple positioning turns out to be a great relief for the client. It is the first time she feels that everyone is present, everyone who is part of the family is here and has taken his or her rightful place in the family line.

To make it more clear, I ask Maureen to come into the constellation as herself, to stand in front of each of her deceased siblings in turn and honour each one's position in the family line, saying simple sentences like, "You are the second one," or "You were here before me, you left a little early and I will leave a little later," or "I am a little older and you are a little younger and you belong to our family and you have your place."

It may seem very simple, but it proves to be a powerful and healing experience for Maureen. For the first time in her life, she is able to meet, acknowledge and address her dead siblings and, even more importantly, to find her rightful place in the family order, thereby ending the confusion she had always felt about her situation.

The right of each child to be part of the family is being respected, which brings a feeling of peace to all those who are representing her family members and especially, of course, to Maureen herself.

So the position a person takes in a constellation can either show 'order' or 'disorder'. When, for example, a daughter is placed next to her father and the mother is placed after her, it signals that the daughter is too important. Due to some imbalance in the family system, she is occupying her mother's place. Accordingly, she will look upon her father as if she is his partner and belittle her own mother.

Everyone in the constellation can immediately feel that something is not right. However, when we place the mother next to the father and when the daughter comes after her, everyone feels that this is more appropriate and all those representing the family members will experience a certain relaxation and relief.

There are more complex systems, such as those that involve a former partner of one of the parents and perhaps his or her children. Then this first partner and children from the relationship need to stand first, followed by the later partner and other children, again in a clockwise positioning and according to each one's time of belonging to the system. Each one has to be given his rightful place and this cannot, and should not, be taken by anyone else. As we shall see in a later chapter, many problems in relationships arise because previous partners are not being remembered.

So the order not only refers to the relationships between parents and children, but in general to the position of a latecomer in relation to those who have preceded him or her.

Now I would like to invite you, the reader, to participate in an exercise of imagination that will help you to understand some of the basic dynamics of what I am talking about.

First gather a few small objects that can be easily handled, such as pens, coins, CD covers, a glasses case, a flower, a wristwatch. The main thing required from each object, or from the design on it, is that it should be able to point in a certain direction, so you can see which way it is facing. Place these objects on a table in front of you; make sure you are sitting comfortably and will be undisturbed for a few minutes while doing this experiment.

When you are ready, close your eyes and begin to recall each member of your original family, including any shadowy figures that no one likes to talk about. Give a little time to each one, recognise how you feel towards each one; note if it is difficult or easy to remember each one. Spend a little extra time on the ones you have a hard time remembering.

Now, among the small objects you have assembled, choose which object represents which family member, then place them on the table in relation to each other and be clear in which direction each 'person' is facing.

Look at the picture in front of you and imagine how each person feels in relation to everyone else. Who is facing who? Who is excluded? Who is not in the right place? Who would like to go away? Might there be a missing person whom you didn't consider until now?

We will not pursue this exercise into a full-blown session, but it is helpful to see the complex dynamics that immediately arise when making a personal constellation of this kind.

Order of Love: Parents and Children

In every family the parents come first – without the parents, there is no child.

In other words, the first and foremost gift that parents make to their child is her, or his, life on earth. One is a parent, simply because one gives birth to a child; that is the essence of being a parent. In this sense, it is a complete package deal; nothing needs to be added or can be taken away from this definition of the parent-child relationship. In this sense, too, all parents are equal and equally good.

After birth, the child receives full-time nurturing from her parents: nourishing food to help her grow, protection against any external threats, loving support to encourage her through the years of learning and so on. This process continues in various ways until she, or he, becomes an independent, self-sufficient adult.

Essentially, a parent gives and a child receives and it's important to understand, from the Family Constellation perspective, that this is a one-way flow in which a parent can give only the whole package and the child can receive only the whole package.

In this sense, the parent-child relationship is greatly imbalanced and a child can never repay directly, in the same way, what has been showered upon her. The act of giving by the parents, which most of us take for granted, is amazing in its abundance and duration. It continues non-stop from birth all the way into adulthood. There are so many gifts that there is no way that the child can ever return them. Only a feeling and expression of gratitude can redress it.

Ultimately, however, the child will repay what was given by returning the gift, not to her parents but to her own children. In this way, nature is constantly taking care of the reproduction of life, working from one generation to another, supporting not just the survival of the individual but also the species.

As we have seen, receiving a gift creates an urge to return something of equal value, but no child can do this. Understanding what the parents have done and not being able to create balance by giving back, may provide a powerful underlying motive why children feel they must do something significant for their parents. If the parents are in pain or suffering this will be difficult for a child to tolerate and she, or he, may try to relieve them of the burden, not realising that it is impossible to carry someone else's burden or fate.

In trying to 'help' her parents, the child feels relieved of guilt. But she goes against the natural order of parenting, according to which children need to receive and parents have to give. Instead, the child becomes the parent to her own parents and thus reduces them into children, which puts the nature of the whole relationship upside down.

We also see children being angry with their parents and this can be seen as another way for them to deal with the feeling of being unable to return what has been received.

Eventually, the imbalance may push a child to leave the parents, using anger as a way to justify his or her departure. But this does not succeed more than superficially, because we can never truly leave a person with whom we are angry. Anger, like love, is a strongly binding relationship.

So we see these two patterns in children: either being angry with parents, or trying to do anything for them. In both ways, the child remains bonded without being able to truly separate.

The natural and mature way to deal with the situation would be to feel and express a deep gratitude towards one's parents for what they have done. On one hand, this connects us to them and gives us strength; on the other, it allows us to separate and leaves us to ourselves.

Respecting Parents

Family Constellation works with the understanding that if family order is not respected, a disharmony appears and creates tension between family members, inevitably resulting in conflict. The moment we show deference to family order, as we do in this work, the way is open for harmony to be restored and this is why we refer to it as the "Sacred Order," not for any religious reasons, but simply to indicate its central importance as a means of restoring balance and harmony in any family system.

If the child can express gratitude and respect toward the parents, there is a shift in gestalt. If she can say, "Thank you for giving me life," or "Without you I would not be here," and embrace their presence in her life, then she can fully receive their contribution and is no longer divided against herself.

The simplified language we use in Family Constellation to acknowledge this sense of order may seem strange at first, because it uses words like 'big' and 'small' which contain all kinds of implications - for one thing, the child may be physically much bigger than her own parents.

However, we use these words because they are recognised by the soul as true and because they point to a deeper existential order of things. When in a session a child says to her father "You are big and I am small," she is acknowledging the Sacred Order. She is not referring to physical size, but to precedence -the parents are larger than the child because they are her source of being.

When we respect our 'smallness' in relation to our parents we are able to receive their energy and gain strength to give in the same manner to our own children. On the other hand, if we try to be 'big' and give to our parents, we will end up trying to receive from our own children, or love partner and everything will be topsy turvy.

There are many ways in which respect for the parents can be expressed, depending on the situation that needs to be acknowledged. For example, a child who was taking sides in a conflict between her parents may need to step back, acknowledging that she is only a child and has no right to get involved. Respecting one's parents may also mean unconditionally agreeing to what a parent has decided for us.

Such gestures may seem inappropriate or unfair to a mature adult mind, especially when we see that our interference or rebellion seems justified, because our parents seem to have behaved in a cruel or stupid manner, but Family Constellation functions in a much more pragmatic and non-judgmental way. It is really only a question of what helps the client to unravel the tangle and the bottom line is that the Sacred Order has to be acknowledged and respected if our family 'ghosts' are to be put to rest.

Hanna, a German-born woman, has never seen her real father. Her mother had an affair with an American soldier, then married a German man and never told Hanna that this second partner was not her real father, but her step-father. Only in later life did Hanna discover the truth.

At my invitation, Hanna sets up the constellation by positioning her mother and her biological father, the American soldier. She does so in a way that allows them to face each other. After a long time, the mother moves towards the man, but when he does not respond, she moves back a step and looks to the side.

When we place a representative for Hanna in the picture, the mother feels shame and anger and tries to stand so that Hanna cannot see her natural father. When I ask the daughter to say to her, "If it helps you, I will not see or look for my father," the mother relaxes and suddenly starts crying, feeling a deep hurt.

Hanna, now standing in as herself, acknowledges her mother's pain but also states that she is leaving it with her and this, for the first time, allows her to look at her true father.

The significant change happened when Hanna agreed to the decision of her mother, who had not told her about her real father. Agreeing to what our parents decided for us brings us again into a right relationship with them, where we are innocent and leave the responsibility to them. The Sacred Order is re-established.

When we complain, or become angry with our parents for their past actions, we are judging them as wrong and therefore taking a superior position. From the perspective of the Sacred Order, we are trying to make our parents "small" and ourselves "big," and this violates the collective conscience. As a result, sooner or later, we will punish ourselves for this as a way of creating balance.

There is a little-understood law operating in human affairs that needs to be recognised here: we always remain bound by what we reject. Whenever we complain about our parents, we are saying 'no' to the way in which they have participated in our lives and cannot receive whatever they have given us. By rejecting them, we think we are making ourselves separate and free, but we cannot genuinely separate from them in such a negative way - rejection is still a binding relationship.

We are our parents. When we say 'yes' to them, we say 'yes' to ourselves. This is not the 'yes' of obedience; it is the 'yes' of acceptance; a 'yes' to what is simply the case. Moreover, we are at the same time saying 'yes' to disowned parts of ourselves, since what I dislike about my father is most probably exactly what I dislike in myself. If I acknowledge my parents wholeheartedly, if I "take my parents in," then I also accept myself wholeheartedly.

As individuals, we rise to our full stature when we accept the flaws of our parents and simply honour them for having brought us into this world. Not that this is easy. It is common to believe that we would be much better off if our parents had been different: more understanding, more supportive, less critical, less strict, even, perhaps, *more* strict. Some of us may even think it would have been better if we had different parents, wanting to swap ours for the idealised mother and father of a friend, or those in a television series.

But with different parents, I would be a different person. By asking for new parents, I am behaving as if I want to be somebody else. How can I be at peace with myself, if all the time I am wishing I were someone else?

From the perspective of the Sacred Order there is only one way to be at peace with myself: to sincerely honour the parents I have. This is a deep gesture of respect, almost a spiritual act, a sacred gesture. When you honour your parents, you don't only honour your mother and father, you also honour your grandparents, your great-grandparents; all the people who came before you. You bow down to where you came from, to who brought you here, to the way life flows through you now.

In deep reverence, you bow down to the origins and source of your life.

Expressing Honour

People who remain angry with their parents and want something different from them live in a state of hope rather than acceptance, with an undercurrent of neediness and expectation. Essentially, they see themselves as victims, which leaves them powerless and thereby denies the possibility of change. They are focusing on the love they failed to get and cannot recognise the love they have already received, nor can they receive the love that may still be available to them. In this way, by constantly hankering for something more from the parents, they remain fixated on them.

Most of us have found ourselves in this painful dilemma at some time in our lives. Whenever we want to change something over which we have no power, we are trapped by the very thing we are trying to change. We think we want to change it because it creates distress and discomfort, but really it is the desire for change and our inability to do it that creates our distress.

So we live in this unhappy double-bind: all our attention is on the thing we dislike and we are unable to enjoy the things that we actually have. The child cannot separate from his parents, nor can he wholeheartedly receive them. On the other hand, the moment he says: "I thank you for what you have given me," and means it, in that moment he can let go of the attachment and move on. Paradoxically, the moment he bows down to the parents and honours them, he introduces the possibility of being free from them.

There are many ways to express this honouring in a Family Constellation session. One way would be for the person who is standing in for the client, or the client himself, to address a parent like this:

"You are my mother and I thank you for giving me my life. I receive it from you as a great gift, with all that comes with it. I thank you for the price you paid and I pay too. I will do something with this life of mine in your honour, so that it was not in vain. You are the right mother for me and I am your right child. You are big and I am small. You give, I receive."

This shows the client's recognition of the place his mother has in the family. This honouring is the only way he can fully separate from his parents. Any other way is bound to be partial. This applies equally to all children, even those who were abused by their parents or who suffer from handicaps of one kind or another.

Returning the Burden with Love

In our earlier examples of Max and Antonella we saw how a child becomes identified with his or her grandparent in order to represent them in the family. For example, Max, identifying with his grandfather, would look on his mother as if she were a child herself, trying to take the load of her pain on his own shoulders.

By bringing the grandfather back into the family picture via the grandchild, the collective conscience seeks to make sure that no-one is excluded. However, in doing so, it goes against the law of Sacred Order, which tells us that a child should be 'small' and a mother should be 'big.'

So now we have a conflict. A child, out of love for his parents, wants to carry some of their psychological baggage for them. Yet when he takes on even a small portion of their problems, he switches roles, becomes larger than them and goes against the Sacred Order.

The scheme of the collective conscience works in opposition to the child's own interests and what is possible for his maturity. So he is locked into the situation and it's hard for him to break out, because he would feel guilty if he did not try to take on his mother's suffering. To him, it would feel as if he was betraying her.

However, nobody can fulfil someone else's destiny. No one can carry someone else's psychological burdens, although every child, driven by a deep and primal survival instinct - the need to belong - wants to do this for a suffering parent. This blind love for the parents, this deep biological bond of attachment the child has for his mother and father, is so powerful that children are sometimes ready to die for their parents.

We call it 'blind love' because the child cannot see the impossibility of his efforts. He doesn't understand and is unable to take into consideration, the fact that each one of us has to deal with the events that happen in our lives, however painful, by ourselves.

This is the difference between being a child and being an adult. Growing up means that we become aware of the fact that we are separate beings, unable to live anyone else's life. But, as we mentioned previously, children live with rich fantasy lives and every child has the magical idea that he can relieve his parents of suffering, thinking that if he suffers, his parent will suffer less.

But the outcome is always the same: rather than reducing the pain to half, the pain is doubled. Now, instead of one person suffering, two people suffer. In adopting the mother's pain, the child denies his mother's right to confront and transcend her own suffering. Not only that, he doesn't realise that the mother also loves him and would not like him to experience the same traumas that she herself suffered. His suffering is not only useless, it even adds to his mother's load.

A client who is married and has a child, sets up a constellation in which his own stand-in feels drawn away from his family and wants to be with his father, who committed suicide when the client was young. Here, we see the familiar pattern of a child trying to adopt some of the father's pain. But the stand-in for his father, realising what is happening, becomes angry. He does not want his son to take on, or interfere with, his personal destiny and keeps pushing the son away from him back towards his own family.

Understanding the uselessness of trying to take on another person's suffering is a major step from blind love to a more conscious form of love. In the context of Family Constellation, the child's unconscious love might say: "Dear mother, you had so much pain in your life and now I want to carry it for you," whereas a conscious love may address the mother like this: "Dear mother, I thank you for my life and for all you did for me. I acknowledge what pain you had in your life and I leave that with you now and I let you carry it by yourself."

This is a more mature approach, but it cannot be done in a cold and distant manner, as if wanting to be rid of the mother and her problems. Only if it is done in a sincere and loving way will the burden move back to the parent, otherwise it will not really leave us.

This profound gesture of returning the burden of suffering is difficult to do, because the child is now faced with a strong sense of guilt, which arises from the longing of a child to belong to its mother, to be close to her. Not helping the mother with her burden, the child will inevitably feel guilty. I will discuss the issue of guilt in more detail in the next chapter.

So, in conducting a Family Constellation session, we try to gauge how much a client is ready to take this step from blind to conscious love and return the burden. It's quite an investment to give up. By carrying something on behalf of our parents, we feel deeply bonded and connected to them and this is something we don't want to lose. Nobody wants to really stand on his own, yet the moment we say to our parents, "I leave all this to you and I thank you for everything," we *are* on our own.

There is no other way to grow up. When we deeply thank our parents and tell them that they have done enough, we are making a declaration that we do not need anything more from them. Yet we resist moving away from the cosy family nest. It is less scary to stay under their wings, however suffocating this may be, than to take flight and discover our rightful place in the world. This is how we remain immature and childish, even as adults.

Ultimately, there is great strength to be found in standing on one's own two feet, but to take this step, to show readiness to be independent from our parents and bring conscious love into our interactions with them, takes courage.

Chapter Five

Family Guilt: the Need for Balance

We have seen how guilt functions in the service of conscience to compel a person to behave according to the values of the social group to which he or she belongs. This feeling of guilt is something we can recognise in ourselves and it affects us when our behaviour goes against those group values.

We have also seen how we experience guilt in relation to the balance of give and take. For example, if I hurt someone, I feel guilty until I have in some way paid for what I have done. Nagging guilty feelings show that I haven't taken responsibility for my actions yet, nor restored a sense of personal balance.

According to the law of balance, the best way to deal with this situation is to acknowledge what we have done, to agree to our 'guilt,' to accept the consequences that result from our actions and do something that restores a sense of equilibrium. This we might call 'taking responsibility.' This can take many forms, from agreeing to stay longer at the office after work in order to balance a mistake due to carelessness, or for a man to take the responsibility as a father, even though he did not choose to have a child with a woman who has become pregnant by him.

If we agree to take responsibility in this way - one might say if we 'carry' our guilt - we do not suffer from guilty feelings; rather, we feel relieved. Basically, it is a realisation that we are essentially alone in facing the outcome of our actions and cannot blame anybody else, not any teacher, not our partner, not our parents. When we try to excuse or justify our actions, or to complain, or blame others, what we are really doing is making an effort to claim innocence and avoid responsibility. We want to rid ourselves of guilty feelings but without paying the price. The readiness to give up this false kind of innocence and become 'guilty' is an essential requirement for a person to grow up psychologically.

However, once again, we need to pause here for a moment and acknowledge an important distinction between the dynamics of constellation laws and any socially accepted system of morality. This distinction needs to be emphasised, otherwise Family Constellation laws can take on the appearance of a moral system and can be used as a weapon in social debates. For example, as an argument against abortion by the "right to life" movement in the United States.

Such an argument might state that, since a woman has become pregnant, she is now a mother and must fulfil her responsibility by giving birth to the child, whom she does not really want, and raising it. Since the man who made her pregnant is now a father, he in turn must support the mother in order to maintain balance.

This is a misunderstanding. In Family Constellation, the focus is on recognising and accepting the plain fact of what has happened, not on what one 'should' be doing. By making a woman pregnant, a man becomes a father. By becoming pregnant, a woman becomes a mother. These are facts. But the question of how people fulfil their responsibility after accepting these facts is something only they can decide, not some external authority, nor any social or religious code of conduct. Seen from this perspective, a woman may accept her responsibility and still decide to have an abortion. I will say more about the abortion issue in the chapter on special topics.

In general, we can say that the need for Family Constellation therapy arises from the deeply ingrained human habit of trying to avoid responsibility for our actions. This creates the burden of imbalance that is carried within a family system, either by the family member who created the imbalance, or by later generations. As we have seen, the function of the Family Constellation therapist is to find the imbalance that is affecting the client within his or her family, see where responsibility lies, acknowledge it and then help the client find an appropriate response. To discover one's true responsibility and act accordingly is both a challenge and a personal achievement.

Family Constellation laws are not moral systems. They have their origin in the biological will to live and, as we have already noted, these laws have their own intelligence, since they developed over thousands of years with the intention of maximising the individual's chances of bonding with a group and maximising the group's chances of survival in a hostile environment.

In this context, that which ensures survival is 'right,' and that which endangers either the individual or the group is 'wrong.' These ancient laws need to be understood and honoured, because whatever has been done 'wrong' will need to be balanced, otherwise people within a family system are going to carry the burden and suffer unnecessarily.

Collective Guilt

The need to regain balance is made more complex by the fact that later family generations cannot ordinarily see what they are carrying from earlier members of the same system. As I explained in chapter two, there is a form of guilt that is more profound, more powerful and more invisible than personal guilt. It is a guilt that we do not consciously feel or recognise, but which is understood by a deeper layer of our minds, a layer that Carl Gustav Jung, one of the pioneers of modern psychology, terms "the collective unconscious."

Some Family Constellation practitioners call it our 'soul,' but this can be confusing, since really it is a deeply hidden layer of the mind. It is better to make a clear distinction between the mind and our innermost consciousness, which, according to the mystics, lies beyond the human mind and all its layers. I will say more about this in part four of the book.

Whatever we call it, this deeper part of the mind is aware of our responsibility to the family system and our compulsion to obey its laws. For example, a woman who has performed numerous abortions without much consideration may develop cancer of the uterus as a way to balance her acts. Or a man, who left his first wife and child without significant reason, may not be able to find a new partner. Or, in general, if we strongly reject our parents, we will find some way to punish ourselves for doing so – no matter how badly they mistreated us as children - and suffer as a form of atonement.

However, we are not only compelled to balance what we have done personally, but also what has been done by someone from an earlier generation of our family. The son of a man, whose sisters had been given to adoption, may open a home for orphans. A woman whose family became rich by exploiting people in the past may keep losing her money. Descendants of a former family member who murdered someone may feel strongly pulled towards committing suicide.

Depending on the severity of an act, the drive to balance can affect generations to come. Many people have observed the ongoing saga of the Kennedy family, the prominent New England dynasty that has spawned one president, three senators and several other politicians and which has suffered more untimely deaths, social scandals and serious tragedies than most small-town inhabitants put together.

Legend has it that this family is jinxed, but to a practitioner of Family Constellation it is obvious that later members of the Kennedy family are atoning for unresolved imbalances caused by earlier generations and it would be a fascinating challenge for any constellation therapist to try and unravel the whole Kennedy story, to see where the real problem lies.

The underlying need to balance acts done within a family system is the third principle of our collective conscience, which we call the 'Law of Balance.'

Balance is a universal principle in which two polarities seek to find equilibrium between themselves. It can be observed in the Taoist symbol of Yin and Yang, where black and white opposites are embedded in each other within a unified circle and in the Hindu law of karma, where acts in past lives are held to determine what happens in one's current life. It can also be seen in Karl Marx and George Hegel's concept of dialectics, whereby thesis and antithesis culminate in synthesis and in the poetry of William Blake, who called this phenomenon, "the contraries without which there would be no progression."

So, when we look at families, we see the force of our collective conscience working to balance out whatever has occurred within the family system. If someone from a former generation did something and did not carry the full consequences of his actions, then without anybody knowing about it, the balancing force will oblige children of later generations to carry those consequences for him.

In Family Constellation, the law of balance does not operate in isolation. Although I have separated the three basic laws of belonging, order and balance, in order to explain each one, in practice they always go together and function in an intermingled way, as the following examples show:

* A client's mother was schizophrenic for most of the client's life. We find that the grandmother has had eleven abortions and in the constellation it shows that the client's mother (the grandmother's daughter) was paying for the

guilt of her mother, becoming ill to balance her mother's deeds. In fact, she was identifying both with the aborted children and with her mother, both with the victims and the perpetrator and in this way became schizophrenic.

* In a Basque family there had been members of the separatist movement called ETA, which has perpetrated many acts of violence in an effort to free the region from Spanish rule. The client's uncle (mother's brother) was shot and killed accidentally by the Spanish police. It turned out that he took on the guilt of his family members, who were part of ETA and in this way got himself killed.

* The brother of a client disappeared and was never found and it was assumed that he had been killed. The client himself suffers from the fear that he may either be killed or commit murder– in the past, he has been closely associated with a mafia-style organisation. The father of both sons killed his own mother and then committed suicide. The underlying dynamic: sons want to pay for the deeds of their parents (law of balance), which is why one brother disappeared and they will also copy the lives of their parents, which is why the surviving brother lives in fear of his own murderous tendency.

* A female client is a direct descendant of the emperor of a country (ten generations earlier). She and her father carry the pride of coming from a royal family. Her father was tortured by a communist regime and she suffers continuously from financial losses. The constellation reveals that both she and her father are paying for the guilt of their imperial ancestor, the emperor. When we put the emperor in the constellation he is unmoved by his people's suffering under his authoritarian rule. Often, later generations pay the price for the exploitation their forefathers inflicted on others

As we can see in these examples, later generations want to atone, or pay the price, for what their ancestors did, even though they were not personally involved. Similarly, if one of their ancestors has been mistreated by others, they will want to take revenge, which is one of the reasons for ongoing conflicts between nations, religions, cultures (we will discuss this more in chapter six).

What is important to understand here is that this happens without anybody's conscious awareness or agreement. Consciously, we will probably attribute certain behaviour to events from our personal life, because we may not even know about the relevant person from an earlier generation. Still, the collective conscience will make us carry his guilt.

Resolving Family Guilt

What we do in a constellation session is try to bring into the open a certain act that we, or a former member of our extended family, has committed and discover with whom the original responsibility lies.

If someone committed a murder, it has to be plainly acknowledged and the killer needs to be called a murderer; if someone left his wife or cheated another person out of his inheritance, it has to be seen and stated. No one can be excused, or be allowed to excuse himself, as everyone is fully responsible for whatsoever he did in his life.

If a mother feels sorry about the life of her brother, who was part of a terrorist group and wants to protect him from punishment - because he is her beloved brother - then most likely her own child will have to pay for what his uncle has done. This is the Law of Balance in operation. Relief for the child will come only when the uncle's responsibility is acknowledged.

Deep in our minds, everyone knows the intrinsic responsibility that comes with each action we take and that no one else can take this away. It may be your brother, or father, whom you love, still you cannot relieve him of the responsibility for whatever he did in his life. The moment a person consciously realises this and accepts it, he has surrendered to the collective laws and something in him feels at peace, just as we feel a certain relaxation when we have taken our appropriate place in the family according to the 'right order.'

Coming back to our examples, this is what showed in these constellations:

* The grandmother with eleven abortions knew about her guilt and wanted to lie down next to her aborted children; she wanted to be dead as well. The difficulty was for her daughter to let her go, letting her carry her own guilt, rather than doing it for her.

* In the Basque family it was easier for a later child to die for the deeds of former family members (and the mother's brother actually got himself killed) than openly acknowledge that there were ETA members in the family. It was easier to keep the secret and carry the guilt than declare it openly and leave the guilt where it belonged.

* The father who had killed his mother did not want his son to pay the price for him. In the constellation, he physically pushed his son away from him several times and wanted him to be with his own son. When his son and grandson wanted to follow him, he was bothered by this and didn't feel honoured.

* The emperor started to soften when confronted with the reality that all his descendants had taken his guilt on their shoulders. It was the first time he could look at the people whom he ruled and not feel aloof; he became human.

The first step for resolution is always to bring to light the reality of what happened: there was an event in the past, within the family system, that caused an imbalance and there was a person responsible for it.

The next step can vary according to the specific situation. It can be that the ancestor accepts his responsibility and does not want the suffering to continue, as in the case of that father who killed his mother and himself. Or, a later descendant may have to confront his forefather with responsibility, as in the case of the emperor, who needed to be reminded that he was an exploiter.

When the father who killed his mother lies next to her on the floor and the love that existed between them is seen, the client-child feels relieved. When the emperor is able to open his heart to the people he exploited, when the grandmother who had eleven abortions can lie down next to them, or when the Basque separatist can start mourning for his victims, resolution begins to occur.

What this means is that, finally, the murderer and his victim, the exploiter and the exploited, the cheater and the cheated, have to face each other and acknowledge what happened in order to come to a state of peace with each other. So, in a constellation, we ask them to face each other and observe the inter-action that happens between them, without allowing the client-child to interfere in the process.

It may take a long time until they can meet and it may not happen within a single constellation, but in most cases a movement begins that leads eventually to reconciliation. Often, reconciliation is a simple acknowledgment that both are now dead and in death they are the same.

To discover whose guilt the client is carrying, we bring members of the former generation into the constellation and observe to whom the client is drawn, to whom he has a strong feeling or affinity. Then the movement towards resolution can begin.

What shows in these cases is that by taking on the transgressions of someone of an earlier generation we disempower them. In a subtle way, we try to interfere in their lives and leave them unable to address their own unfinished business. This is equally true, whether they are alive or dead.

Assuming responsibility for the actions of someone else can actually deprive that person of his or her dignity as a human being. For example, if our grandmother has been mistreated by her husband, or by men in general and she could not, or would not, do anything about it - she didn't show her anger, for whatever reason - then it is arrogant of us to become angry in her place, or want to help her, as if we know better what is 'right' or 'fair' for our grandmother than she does herself. This violates the law of Sacred Order, in which 'bigger' family members cannot be helped by well-intended 'smaller' ones.

As I have said before, what emerges from these constellations is that everybody is fully responsible for his acts; everybody has to live out his life in his own way and bear all the consequences for his actions. No one can do that for him and if someone tries, this person is bound to fail and create more suffering. A perpetrator usually knows, deep inside himself, that no one can take responsibility for what he has done and usually does not want others to get involved.

In the end, a state of peace and resolution can be found only when there is genuine reconciliation between perpetrator and victim, when there are the first stirrings of love between them and all of this may take time – we explore this issue further in the following chapter.

Summary

To summarise the three principles of belonging, order and balance as described in these three chapters:

The Law of Belonging refers to the way in which everyone in a family system has an equal place in that system and has the same right to be there as everyone else. No one in the system can be judged better or worse, no one has more or less right to be part of the family.

The Law of Sacred Order shows that we are all unique. Each person within the family system has his specific position in relation to the others, according the moment he entered the family. No one else can take this place.

The Law of Balance refers to the way in which we are all held fully responsible for what we do. Whatever someone in a system does, has an effect on the whole. We influence and are influenced by, what happens around us. Nevertheless, each individual has to bear the consequences of his acts himself, whatever the outcome.

Chapter Six

Victim and Perpetrator

The topic of victim and perpetrator is closely linked to the preceding chapters on balance and belonging and we shall soon see why. Whenever there is a serious conflict between people, the first thing everyone wants to find out is who is 'right' and who is 'wrong.' If it is a strong conflict in which people are seriously hurt, these kinds of distinctions are built into the law, which then takes action and the question of who is right and wrong is decided by people other than ourselves.

Yet whatever happens on the legal plane, violent acts perpetrated against others have a powerful ripple effect of their own, profoundly affecting the collective psychology of the family in which they occur. The relationship between the one who inflicts injury and the one who receives it is a unique dynamic that demands special attention.

If a murder, or some other major assault, injury, or injustice, has been committed by a member of the family, a bond will be created to this person that is often stronger than bonds between the family members themselves. Because of this bond, the afflicted person, who may not be a relative at all, has to be considered part of the family system. He starts to belong to the family and is subject to the collective conscience, which takes care that every member of the system has to be given his place and needs to be remembered.

What we see in constellations is that the dynamic of bonding goes both ways. If a family member commits the crime, the victim automatically starts to belong to the family and if a family member has been mistreated, then the perpetrator starts to belong.

When a person has been in war, or in a concentration camp, those people who were with him start to belong to his family, especially the oppressors. For example, the Nazis in World War II, or in fact, any kind of life-threatening situation involving violence or injustice is likely to produce a bond of this kind.

On the level of personal conscience and value judgments, family members naturally tend to take sides, form opinions and reach decisions about who is right and who is wrong. We try to create a separation between the 'good' and virtuous person and the one who is 'bad' or evil. We want to reach a conclusion about who is at fault, we accuse or sympathise, identify with some of those involved and exclude others.

However, in the deeper layers of the mind, in the collective unconscious, no such distinctions are made. As we have already learned, the collective conscience wants only to give everyone his place. It wants to take care that each and every individual is remembered without discrimination and it makes no difference whether he is a high-minded hero or a despotic monster. As far as the collective conscience is concerned, every murderer and every victim, every underdog and every tyrant, has an equal right to belong.

On a more superficial level, driven by our conventional, moralistic attitudes, when we judge others within the family as wrong or bad, we tend to exclude them. We ignore them, we cut them out of our lives, we banish them from our hearts and from the family history books. We repress their memory so as not to feel the distress it causes and we try to forget they existed.

The dilemma is, however, that the more insistently family members try to exclude another member from the system - for example, a murderer - the stronger will be the demand by the collective conscience that this person should

74

be represented and someone from a later generation will be forced to do so.

We always see this in a constellation session: no one whose existence goes unacknowledged can be given up totally. He, or she, will be represented in a later generation, whether we like it or not.

As you can imagine, this can be a bitter pill for people to swallow. A Jewish family, which has lost one or more members in the holocaust, may feel that to recognise and acknowledge Nazi death squads as part of its family system would be deeply insulting. A German family whose members suspect that their predecessors were involved in gruesome medical experiments on prisoners in concentration camps may simply want to deny that anything like that happened.

As we saw in an example in chapter three, a woman was unable to acknowledge her own grandfather, who was killed by the Nazis, until someone was introduced into the constellation to represent the Nazis themselves, bringing them into the family system. The client immediately felt relief and was drawn to the person standing in for the Nazis, showing that the client herself had been representing the perpetrators – and therefore rejecting the victim, her grandfather - because they had been excluded and their memory suppressed.

Here is another example:

Anne, from Sweden, comes with the issue that her father is violent with her and in the constellation she places herself standing opposite him, illustrating her conflict with this parent.

Asking about her family history, we find that her grandfather (her father's father) was murdered. When we include the grandfather (victim) and someone to represent the man who killed him (perpetrator), we find that the client's father carries the energy of the perpetrator and the client herself identifies with the grandfather, the victim.

Both sides are represented and the violence that happened to the grandfather is being replayed by later generations. The father identifies with the perpetrator and becomes violent, acting out the aggression on his daughter, who identifies with the victim. In this way, a conflict between victim and perpetrator is replayed as a conflict between daughter and father; it is a double shift.

Why does this happen? According to constellation dynamics, a victim becomes focused on his murderer and vice versa, creating a strong bond between them. In Anne's family system, the grandfather focuses on his murderer, causing his son to attempt to get his attention by identifying with the perpetrator. Then, because the son is focused on his father, his daughter identifies with the victim (her own grandfather) in order to get her father's attention. So the violence between father and daughter has its roots in the child's effort to get her parents attention.

However we explain it, the solution remains the same: we discover the original conflict and let perpetrator and victim face each other without anyone else interfering. Anne needs to withdraw herself from her grandfather and respect his destiny. By acknowledging her father's love for his father, she is able to give up the desire for more attention, which helps her to withdraw herself from the conflict with him. She finds a safe place with her mother.

What we see in these constellations is the extraordinary strength of the bond between victim and perpetrator and, to make this fully visible, we need to place both of them in the constellation. This bond is often stronger than the connection to their own families and later members must, in some way, respect this dynamic, which is often difficult for them.

Later members of a family may want to take revenge on behalf of the victim, or pay the price for the perpetrator, but as we repeatedly see, by taking such burdens upon themselves they only create more suffering. In fact, they have no right to interfere in these affairs. To abstain from interfering is a difficult step to take and people are often reluctant to keep their hands off a situation where they feel so inherently involved. They think they are being disloyal to the relative concerned, as if abandoning him or letting him down.

Giving Up the Role of Judge

Finding relief by leaving behind the complications of past entanglements may be something we think we want, yet in practice it is often problematic, because it requires us to go beyond both the personal and the collective conscience.

Such a step demands that we give up the position of judge. We don't take sides. We relinquish the desire to accuse the perpetrator, or take pity on the victim. Rather, we honour the victims and withdraw from the perpetrators. Relinquishing the judge requires us to move beyond notions of good and evil, divisions of right and wrong. We leave the guilt in the hands of the perpetrator and recognise that the outcome for the victim is something that only he, or she, can deal with.

It is also a question of being able to give up feeling close to one's own family, which takes courage and may even make the client feel guilty, because if we are too identified with our family, too bonded, we will not be able to see the bigger picture.

We also need to be careful how we describe the perpetrator. If a man murders another man then he is called a murderer. But being called a murderer need not be a condemnation of his essence as a man. He is called a murderer because of his act of killing another human being and, of course, he deserves to bear the consequences for it.

However, a more accurate distinction – a distinction without condemnation – would be to call him a "man who killed someone," rather than using a term which implies a continuous and habitual state of murderous intent. In this way, we don't stand in judgment over him as a human being, but only acknowledge the act of killing and this will make it easier for us to include him within the family system, in the context of belonging and balance.

In a converse way, the same is true for the victim. If a man gets killed, or has suffered in an exceptional way, he still deserves to be seen as a whole human being, rather than as some hopeless, tragic figure, whom we now must pity.

A woman disabled from an accident and now living her life in a wheelchair may be seen only as a cripple. But being handicapped in this way is only part of her life. In fact, she is a woman like any other woman – a woman who happens to occupy a wheelchair - and if her being in the wheelchair is the result of someone's reckless driving, we do not have the right to seek compensation; only she has that right. If we make it our own project, as people do who want to take revenge in the name of someone else, we are taking away some of her dignity as a human being.

This is certainly a difficult position for us to take and demands considerable insight and maturity. We need to see, understand and support the fundamental principles of family dynamics, which do not follow our personal notions of justice and fairness, however much we want them to.

Addressing this Dynamic in a Session

In Family Constellation what we generally do is find out who has been excluded and who is now identifying with the victim or perpetrator. It becomes visible from the position in which the client places them in a constellation and is also indicated through physical responses and feelings reported by the stand-ins, or representatives.

Usually, we place a client opposite the family member with whom he identifies. This brings to light the love the client feels for this person. Alternatively, we may place the client next to this person, where he tends to feel more relaxed and at ease. Bringing this love to light is itself a deep shift for the client, because he starts seeing the motivation that has been making him do certain things. It was out of love for a former family member.

This, already, is a lot to absorb for the client. Sometimes, after seeing the real motive for his actions, life takes a different turn and the client may be able to step back from interfering with the fate of someone who was killed, or may leave the guilt to the one who was the killer. Even if the client cannot completely leave the situation, he is nevertheless likely to regain some of his innocence and part of the burden caused by identification is removed.

What is Identification?

Identification is a deeply unconscious and largely unrecognised process. When I am identified with someone, I cannot see that person with clarity, because I have become one with him, or her. It is rather like having your nose pressed up against a television screen; you are too close, so you cannot actually make out any of the images playing there.

However, when I consciously step back and look into the eyes of a person with whom I have been identified, everything changes. Direct eye contact with the person forces me to see that I am different; it brings me into the present moment, into reality. Such a gaze will bring me out of my identification and make me recognise myself as separate from the other.

Then, and only then, does it become possible to acknowledge what has happened to that person, to honour his destiny or guilt, depending on whether I have been identifying with a victim or a perpetrator. It means I can now give wholehearted credence to his right to carry his own destiny without my interference, including my acknowledgement of the pain he had to go through, because of what happened in his life.

In an ideal situation, the deepest relief for the client is to witness reconciliation between victim and perpetrator, so in a constellation we often include both and make them face each other, insisting that they should look at each other and then observe what happens between them.

There maybe many deep feelings involved, such as pain, hatred, fear, aggression, despair, guilt and shame, all of which can come up in the representatives of either victim or perpetrator, depending on the specific situation and how far the movement towards reconciliation has gone.

In a final stage they may lie down together, indicating that they are dead, or, if the perpetrator is still alive, indicating that he deserves to die as well; or they meet in an embrace. Of course, we do not always reach the point where this kind of positive and healing outcome occurs in a constellation.

The movement towards reconciliation can take place only between the original perpetrator and the original victim. A later family member, such as the client, who has been identifying with one of them, has to step back and leave it to them, otherwise the reconciliatory movement is hindered.

The moment victim and perpetrator face each other a process of healing begins and once it has begun it does not really matter how long it takes to complete. In the end, the two opposing forces will be pulled towards each other – there is always an inner movement towards reconciliation, towards making peace, reflecting the universal principle that the more two energies oppose each other, the more they also attract one another.

In a constellation, this shows in the relief that perpetrator and victim feel when they lie down next to each other on the floor, their reconciliation having happened in death. It is a process that doesn't need to be completed in this or further constellation sessions. It has to complete itself in the realm of the dead, in its own time.

In a constellation, we simply help these two antagonists face each other honestly and sincerely. This will change the situation for the client, the later child, who identified with one of them and, by asking the child not to take sides and looking at a greater force beyond them both, we also help both victim and perpetrator come to terms with what happened. It works both ways.

National and Cultural Conflicts

There are many examples of two opposing forces within a family system and, as much as there is opposition, there is also a strong collective drive for them to meet. Identification with one side of the family by a later member is a blind and unsuccessful effort to represent the excluded party and, rather than helping reconciliation, prevents true reconciliation between those with whom the conflict started.

Identification with one side against the other is a dynamic that also lies at the root of conflicts between nations and between opposing political factions within a single nation. For example, whenever I come across clients from countries where there has been a civil war, I have noticed that the fight continues within the client's family, often over many generations.

Sebastian is from Barcelona and both his parents are Spanish. His father's father was on the side of the

Republicans in the civil war and spent seven years in a concentration camp after the conflict ended. His mother's side of the family was on the side of the Nationalists and General Franco, who, after defeating the Republicans, ruled Spain as dictator for many years.

When we put up the constellation, we see mother and father stand separately and the children are divided on either side, with the client standing closer to his mother than his father. The mother can't look at her husband; he is like an enemy. The picture gives the impression of two factions at war with each other; the two parties of the civil war are represented by parents and children, the front-line goes right through this particular family system.

Sebastian, the client, is standing close to the mother but at the same time looking at the grandfather who was in the concentration camp and identifying with him. The constellation shows that the mother is not allowing her only son to come close to his father, because she is identifying with the Nationalists and her husband's family was Republican.

When we place all the dead people from either side of the civil war and lie them down in the centre next to each other and when everyone looks at them, something relaxes in the mother and she can start looking at the father. This turns out to be a great relief for the client.

Finally, towards the end of the constellation, he is able to give a space in his heart to both sides of the civil war, for both parties, without judgment – and of course for his grandfather.

Often, reconciliation can be found once the opposing factions have taken a good look at the casualties of their fighting. When they have both looked long and hard, not just at their own dead, but at all of those who were killed – the total death toll – they can mourn together and this often brings them closer, ending the conflict.

Banu is a pretty Turkish woman, in her early thirties, who reports that she has an ongoing issue with abandonment. Whenever she forms a love relationship with a man, she always thinks he's going to leave her. In addition, she has a brother who has been diagnosed as psychologically 'borderline.'

In the constellation, her father is drawn away from the family, with her brother standing in his way. Upon inquiry, we learn that her grandparents, on her father's side, were Turks who had to leave Greece at the fall of the Ottoman Empire. There was a mass exchange of populations at that time, when national borders were created and re-drawn: Turks were driven out of Greece to the newly-created state of Turkey and Greeks were forced out of their old Ottoman regions back to Greece. Many people died on both sides.

When we add representatives for Greece and Turkey, then also for Christianity and Islam, the centuries-old conflict between two nations and two religions comes to light and we see how it is carried on in this family.

Banu's father carries for his family the grief of missing his homeland, Greece, which is made deeper by the fact that the family had to leave most of its wealth behind and he also carries anger against Christians. His son, Banu's brother, identifies with the Greek Christians, who are the excluded and hated ones in the family, but also with being a Turkish Muslim, who are the victims in this saga. This split seems to be the cause of his psychological illness. Banu, our client, identifies more with being Turkish and carries anger against Christians on behalf of her father and his family.

The solution for the client is to honour the Christians, who also suffered and were killed during the upheaval and in this way step out of being involved in the conflict, while at the same time acknowledging the suffering of her father's family. In this way, we discover that her obsession with being abandoned is a feeling she has been carrying for her grandparents, who had to abandon their home in Greece and with whom she identified in order to get her father's attention.

On a deeper level, the work here would continue by letting representatives for Islam and Christianity look at each other and at the victims of the wars between them.

I have worked with many similar examples, including Taiwanese clients whose families were split in the war between Nationalists and Communists, French-Vietnamese clients whose families still carry the conflict between French colonialists and Vietnamese Nationalists and clients from Northern Ireland who carry the conflict between Catholics and Protestants.

Whenever there is a polarity, like the ones we have described, there needs to be an understanding that we carry both parts in the family system to a greater or lesser extent, depending on the degree to which one part has been excluded. Real peace and unity can be found only if we allow both sides to become one in our hearts.

This can be supported by a small meditation that was suggested by Bert Hellinger and I will introduce it here in a modified form:

Sit comfortably with your eyes closed and imagine a strong conflict that happened in your family between its members. It may have occurred several generations back.

Identify the two people who were fighting, or the two opposing parties and look at them in your imagination, first at one side, then at the other.

Notice if there is any judgment or a feeling of taking sides. Slowly, allow your heart to open to both sides, especially making room for the person - or the national or religious group - whom it seems difficult for you to embrace, or with whom you had a negative judgment.

Now, imagine as if both sides are meeting inside your own heart and becoming one.

Hellinger discovered that in cases of schizophrenia there is mostly a hidden murder somewhere in the family and the schizophrenic person has to simultaneously represent both the murderer and his victim, flipping from one identification to the other, creating the dual personalities the schizophrenic will often inhabit. The healing would be to bring this murder to light, helping the client out of the identification and letting the two opposing sides meet.

Working With These Dynamics as a Facilitator

The challenge for a Family Constellation facilitator who works with the issue of victim and perpetrator is to forego any tendency to make value judgments. He needs to avoid choosing between one side and the other, expanding sufficiently to include two seemingly diametrically opposing sides. This means that facilitators need to have worked with their own family dynamics and reached a point where he, or she, can remain non-judgmental or non-moralistic. This is an absolute requirement.

At the same time, the facilitator must be prepared for resistance from clients who find such inclusion unacceptable. One can see how difficult this is when one considers, for example, modern Germany's attitude towards the Third Reich. It is hard, even now, for Germans to give the Nazis their place in the annals of German history and to accept that these people were also Germans like themselves. The tendency is to drive them out of personal memory and pretend they never existed. Or rather, in the case of the Third Reich, it is not that Germans nowadays pretend that the Nazis never existed, but they have been educated to say: "We must always remember, so this will never happen again," which is a different way of not letting something be over.

For this reason, Hellinger himself is a controversial figure in his native Germany, because he describes the nature of the collective conscience and its demand for belonging without reference to 'good' and 'bad,' without trying to decide who has been behaving in an unacceptable way and without covering these basic constellation dynamics with socially acceptable cosmetics.

Indeed, for most people his neutral position would be hard to defend and understand, were it not for the fact that this is just the way things are. In constellation sessions, we often see that the greatest healing force for a family system comes from the perpetrators, not the victims, as these are most often the excluded ones. The more we continue judging them, or denying their existence, the more we will re-create them again and again. The collective conscience won't allow them to be forgotten and we can see this in the rise of Neo-Nazi movements in modern Germany.

Taking offence, or denial, is not the way to put to rest the conflicts and wars our forefathers were involved in.

Chapter Seven

The Dead and the Living

Most of us tend to look upon life and death as if they are in opposition to each other, as if death is a calamity that has to be postponed as long as possible. Either we tend to live as if there is no death, distracting ourselves from its inevitable arrival, or we live in constant fear of it. Accordingly, we tend to create a strict separation between those members of our family who are dead and those who are alive, without realising that for the collective conscience there is a continuity, even though the dead and the living obviously belong to different spheres.

If we set aside our unwillingness to face the subject of death, it is evident that those who have lived before us play an important part in every ongoing family system and affect the lives of the generations that follow them.

Perhaps this is one reason why it is a central practice in all primitive cultures to emphasise the worship and veneration of ancestors, because they know intuitively that in many ways the dead still rule our behaviour. They understand that the dead are not really dead; what occurred in their lives is part of our life now; what happened to them in their time is affecting and influencing us all.

When we observe in a constellation how our grandparents are part of our life, we begin to see how their influence can go in two opposite directions with different outcomes. It can be either a positive influence or a negative one, depending on how we relate to these ancestors through the generations.

Let us say you had an uncle who died very young. A positive outcome would be one in which this uncle has been fully recognised and appreciated by your father, both as his brother and as the one who has died and then given a heartfelt farewell. On the other hand, if your uncle was in some way ignored by your father, or forgotten by the rest of the family, he may have a negative influence on you – negative in the sense that the demand by the collective conscience for recognition might compel you to identify with him and thus represent him within your family system.

One example of how the dead influence the living occurred when Harold, a client from England, came with the issue that he feels alienated from his father, who never seemed to pay him much attention during his life.

Setting up Harold's family constellation, we learn that his grandfather (his father's father) spent several years as a front-line soldier in the First World War, witnessing horrendous casualties and inhuman conditions. In the constellation, he is pulled away from his family to the dead ones - the ones who were with him in the war and who died at the front.

Only after the client's representative had honoured all the dead from that war and acknowledged his grandfather's suffering, could his grandfather turn and look at his son and grandson for the first time. Then also the father was able to see his son, our client. Before, he had followed his father's pull towards the dead and could not look at his own offspring.

This is an example how war victims, even when they are not relatives, have a strong influence on a family. In this case, there was such a strong connection between the grandfather and his fellow soldiers that the dead became the excluded 'family members' who demanded recognition.

In the same way that psychotherapy involves addressing rejected parts of ourselves, in Family Constellation we address the forgotten people of the past, allowing those who belong to our family system to become present to us now. We need to recognise them in this, the present moment and give them a dignified place in our heart.

The people from our family's past who tend to be forgotten are those whose lives have diverged from the norm. They are the ones who, in one way or another, suffered through unusual circumstances – those who died young, who committed suicide, who performed acts of exceptional violence, who were subjected to violence. Sometimes they are the black sheep, the playboys, or runaways, the ones you'd "rather not talk about."

But it is precisely the people we would rather not talk about who, above all, need to be recalled. When we do, we almost always find that there are no hard feelings, no residual resentments and they will usually give us their blessings, which is an important gesture of reconciliation and healing within the family system.

Blessings from the Dead

The following case study shows how a dead person can give a blessing:

Rosella is an Italian client. Her aunt, who was the older sister of her mother and the first child of her grandmother, died at birth. She is not remembered in the family.

In the beginning of the constellation session, Rosella positions the representatives standing in for herself, her mother and grandmother in a way that leaves them all facing in one direction, not seeing one another and this indicates a missing person in the family system.

We assume that the aunt is missing, so her representative is introduced and placed in front of the three women. Rosella's stand-in immediately feels better, happy to see her aunt and when we lie the aunt down on the floor – indicating her death – Rosella lies down next to her, an indication that she feels closely connected to her aunt.

I ask Rosella's representative to stand up and go to her mother and the grandmother then moves closer to her dead daughter. The grandmother starts feeling pain and, crying, goes to her knees and holds Rosella's aunt in her arms. Everyone in the constellation feels touched and relieved.

Creating a solution picture, I place the women in order: first the grandmother, then the aunt, then Rosella's mother, then Rosella herself (her representative now leaves the constellation). Then I invite the grandmother to introduce her first child, the aunt, to her second child, Rosella's mother, using the statements: "This is your older sister. She left very early, she is first, you are second."

The aunt and Rosella's mother, the two sisters, look upon each other with love. The mother says, "I am happy to see you and have you as my older sister. You always have a place in my heart." Pointing to Rosella, she adds, "And this is my daughter, please look at her in a friendly way."

Now Rosella bows to her grandmother, then to her aunt, saying, "Dear aunt, I am your niece, please bless me."

The aunt smiles at her with affection.

Then Rosella looks at her mother and says, "Dear mother, your sister has a place in my heart. I feel how much you missed her. Thank you for staying with me."

Rosella and her mother hug each other and the session comes to an end.

As we can see, a dead family member who is not remembered rightly has a strong influence on the whole family. The grandmother had not completed her mourning for her first child; maybe she couldn't cope with the pain of losing her and unconsciously she wanted to follow her into death. In these situations, often a later child will say, 'I do it in your place' as we can see in Rosella's case. One of the consequences may be that Rosella may behave in life as if she is dead, not allowing herself to live fully.

When the dead aunt is included in the picture and mourned for, something is completed and she gives a blessing to Rosella, who is then more free to live her own life without any hangover. The sentences used in the constellation show the solution by acknowledging the missing person and respecting the right order. The unresolved love connection from the grandmother to her first child is at the root of the whole entanglement.

Blessings from the dead emerge as a positive and empowering influence. If we receive their recognition, after remembering them sincerely and open-heartedly, we are likely to feel relieved, sustained and supported. If we are unable to remember them, nor to acknowledge their significance in our life, we won't receive the strength they have to pass on to us, nor will we be free of them. Under the influence of the collective conscience we will remain identified with their fate and unable to fully pursue our own life goals

Clinging to the Dead

Forgetting a person whose departure has caused us heartfelt suffering is one of the most common ways to try and avoid pain. But there is another way, too and that is to swing to the opposite extreme and cling to the memory of the person who died. This seems to be a common pattern of human behaviour: when we don't have a problem remembering what has been painful, we are usually unable to forget it – another way of not allowing an experience to come to a final closure.

This clinging can manifest as a decision to remain in an endless state of mourning, such as the famous historical case of Queen Victoria of England, who, after the death of her beloved husband, Prince Albert, wore black for the rest of her life and for a long time forced her children to do the same. Or, perhaps, we find ourselves talking non-stop about the departed, or we put them on pedestals and write eulogies about them.

When later generations in a family system do this, it becomes a kind of disrespect, because it violates the collective conscience. The person we have lost was here before us and what happened to him is part of his own private destiny. Just because we have lost him does not mean that we own him. His life's outcome is exclusively his; it belongs only to him and later members of the family have no right to get involved.

Those of us who cannot forget the dead may recognise their significance and their place within the family system, but still cannot leave them in peace. There are many ways we require their attention: we feel we haven't loved them enough and so must now exaggerate our love in their absence; we feel they owe us something for having left us behind; we are angry with them, as if their death were deliberately designed to wound us.

However, what often shows in this kind of constellation is that the dead are perfectly in accord with their destiny and also wish us well. From their side, there is no problem. Only we, their descendants, are not in accord with how life goes on.

The Delusion of Self-Importance

A frequent variation in the way in which we are trapped by past events is the feeling of responsibility. It is common to feel personally responsible when a loved one dies, as if we ourselves are directly involved in the reason for their passing. A mother whose baby dies of pneumonia, for example, is likely to feel that she didn't do enough to protect her child from sickness. She feels guilty. She wonders if, had she arranged her life differently, events might have turned out less tragically.

When we feel responsible, or guilty, we live under the impression that it was in our hands to have created a different outcome. Rather than accept the existential reality of what has occurred, we torture ourselves with self-accusations. Rather than remembering her child with love and gratitude, then moving on, the mother remains attached to her dead baby, fixated on her own suffering and self-reproach.

If this continues, there may be other children, but she will not be available to them. If she stays in this state, her preoccupation will be with the child that died, rather than with the ones who are alive and playing at her feet right now.

There is another dimension to this scenario, which is perhaps less evident: when a mother blames herself for the loss of her child and remains fixated, she interferes not only in her own, but in her baby's destiny, too. She doesn't credit her baby with an independent existence, a personal fate of its own. She sees her baby as an extension of herself, its fate intricately wound up with hers.

In the case of a baby, it is perhaps understandable for a woman to experience this level of identification; the child, after all, has only just emerged from her womb. But imagine if it was a sister who had died, or a husband. She may feel an equal amount of guilt, yet wouldn't they also deserve an independent destiny?

An example of this came to light in a recent session where a woman's younger sister had been killed in a concentration camp and, all her life, she had felt guilty and responsible that her sister died, while she herself survived.

Now what does this mean? It means, first of all, she thinks it could have been different. Maybe if she had done something different, her sister would not have died. This, of course, is not the case; she could not have done anything.

Second, by feeling responsible she saves herself from fully feeling the pain of losing her sister.

Third, she interferes in her sister's fate. Her sister's fate was to die, while her own fate was to survive. Not to allow herself to live fully, out of guilt, means she is neither respecting her sister's destiny nor her own.

Fourth, it means that she will not be fully available as a mother to her own children.

It is, of course, a very traumatic experience to have seen your own sister being killed and almost no one will be able to live a normal life after such a traumatic event. It is painful; it is difficult to continue; it is easy to feel guilty, or to feel that events could have been different.

But the fact is, we each must go our own unique way, in our own time and we need to do it without the emotional entanglement of holding on to loved ones who have died. To become aware of the processes behind our attachments can be the first step to becoming free of them.

Dying in Childbirth

One of the strongest issues in a constellation is when a mother dies in childbirth. This can affect children over many generations. What happens is that the death of the mother is considered almost like a murder by the collective conscience, as if the man who made her pregnant had murdered her. In a sense, this is true: by making love to her, by making her pregnant, he brought about her death. Of course, it was not intentional, but nevertheless it was the result.

We can speculate that one reason for this being considered such a 'crime' by the collective conscience was the immense importance of women in primitive cultures as the bringers of new members into the tribal system and the threat to the survival of the clan that is represented by the death of a young, fertile woman.

In order to fulfil the demand for inclusion and balance by the collective conscience, a later child in the same family system may carry a sense of guilt – even though no crime was committed - perhaps by refusing to have children, or by rejecting men.

The solution is to bring to light the real facts, so what actually happened can be consciously understood. In a constellation addressing this issue, the mother who died giving birth has to be honoured by being given a central place and everyone needs to bow to her. Including her and recognising her in this way means that we honour the risk that she took in giving birth, especially in former generations, when childbirth could be a question of life and death - and that she wanted to do it. This gives her dignity.

Often this is not enough, as her husband remains excluded, since the collective conscience holds him responsible. When we bring him into the picture, it is often the case that later family members do not want to face him, or honour him; they feel him as a threat. This is a misunderstanding of what really happened. It shows that the collective conscience is powerful, but unfair and blind as well.

The solution is to let the man and the woman who died face each other, bringing out the love between them. It is touching to see this. They acknowledge their loss to each other: she lost her life and he lost his wife and sometimes the child died as well. There was love, there was risk and the fact is that the mother died. This has to be brought into the open. It gives strength to later members of the family, especially when they feel this love as the force that also created them.

Nowadays, a mother dying in childbirth is a relatively rare event, but mothers can still die young and this is usually a disaster for the child who is left behind. Losing your mother in childhood is one of the most traumatic events of an entire lifetime – all the more so, perhaps, because the trauma goes into the unconscious layers of the mind and is 'forgotten' by the conscious mind. We will deal with this in the following chapter.

Real People and Real Events

When we refer to the dead in a constellation session, are we talking about the actual people from the client's past who died, or are we addressing the part of his psyche that their memories are now occupying? This question also applies to the client's living family, in the sense that, in flesh and blood, none of these people are actually present in the room. So, are they really here, or not?

In fact, the collective conscience doesn't make any distinction between the dead and the living. When we set up a constellation, we operate from the understanding that the stand-ins not only represent those who belong to this family system, alive or dead, but actually, according to the operations of the collective field, they somehow 'become' them.

Of course, they do not start to look like them, or take on any ghoulish looks of dead people, but in some mysterious way they act as transmitters for these beings. They carry their pain; they sense the truth of their histories; they have the power to free the bonds between generations once those who have been ignored or excluded feel they have been remembered and honoured. In this sense the representatives are the actual people.

This understanding is not based on theory or speculation. It is an empirical observation based on the experiments of Hellinger and others. So in family constellation we are always working with actual people. These people may be 'in our psyches' but they are a memory, not a fabrication. We are not dealing with dreams and fantasies of the unconscious mind. We work with the real person, knowing that real people are affecting our minds and we work with real events, knowing that they too are making their mark on our psyches.

We are not concerned with the stories that we create about those events. We do not bother what the client thinks about what happened, or the 'how' and 'why' of what our parents did to us, or whether they were right or wrong.

What we are dealing with are the events themselves. Real events, as they occurred in space and time, are the meat and gravy of this work. What factually happened is what matters. Facts influence the dynamic of the constellation, not how we interpret or judge them.

Feelings that arise during a constellation session are the result of these events, so one question for a facilitator, regarding feelings, would be: is the client dealing with the event, recognising and accepting it, in which case emotional expression can help the person pass through the experience and heal it; or is the feeling just a way to avoid dealing with some painful issue? This is a distinction between a primary emotion, which leaves a person stronger afterwards and a secondary emotion, which drains a person's energy. We will address this issue further in chapter twenty-one.

Mostly, people who talk continuously about their feelings in a session are more interested in being listened to and in being able to talk, than in actually changing anything. Often, they already have their own interpretation about a particular situation and don't want their theories and beliefs to be disturbed. The real importance of what happened is lost amid lengthy analysis.

For example, I conducted a session with somebody whose grandfather was killed in a concentration camp during World War II. When I talked to this person, addressing the fact of his grandfather's death brought him in contact with a deep pain, but he also had a strong tendency to talk about what happened between him and his father and his complaints about him.

He kept on wanting to talk about something else, obviously wishing to avoid the fact of what happened to his grandfather and in this way to avoid feeling the pain that he also carried for his own father. Staying with the simple reality of his grandfather's death would have brought him not only in contact with pain, but also in contact with a deep love for his father. So rather than going in a big circle - focusing on his anger for his father, analysing it, expressing it and so on - I suggested that he should remain focused on the fact of what happened to his grandfather and skip the other stories.

Mostly, the function of a story is to avoid or confuse the therapist – in other words, to avoid being guided towards discomfort or pain. So in Family Constellation we ask people to stay connected to important happenings in the family and feel the impact of them, without giving any other comments.

When the Dead Learn from the Living

What we see from these case histories is how much the living have to learn from the dead. Before the lesson is fully internalised and healing can occur, we must pay our debt to the one who has died. When we have done this, through the interchanges in a Family Constellation session, we become free to move forward in our own lives with less burden from the past.

In a constellation, these interchanges occur when we place a stand-in for the one who has died and we invite the living person look at her, sometimes bowing down to her, as described earlier and remembering her with love. A gesture of this sort is usually enough. The one who has died will feel recognised and acknowledged; she will return the gaze with warmth and affection and she will feel satisfied by a sense of completion. Sometimes she will even give the one who is alive a blessing and if she does so, then the living person receives something from the one who is dead.

On occasion there is also a message, such as, "I am at peace now," or "I am proud of you," or "I want you to carry on with your own life," or even, "I don't want you to get involved in what I have experienced, it is none of your business." In this way, the living person learns something new from the one who has died. He finds something shifting inside himself, followed by a sense of peaceful relaxation.

In some instances, this dynamic works in reverse: the dead have to learn something from the living, for example, in the case of a sudden, or accidental death. What we may see in this situation is that the one who has died has not fully realised that he is dead. He behaves as if he was still alive and becomes like a ghost. He attaches himself to a living person in such a way that the living one feels the presence of the dead soul clinging to him.

One man, Paul, lost his brother as a boy in a boating collision and even now, as an adult, still feels the presence of his brother hanging around him. When we place the brother in the constellation, he doesn't feel that he has died and wants to interact with his brother as if he is alive and it emerges that he is very attached to his brother.

In this case, we remind the dead brother that he is actually dead. In the constellation, I invite Paul to say to his dead brother, "You are my brother and you were drowned in an accident. You are dead and I am alive."

As soon as he says this, the dead brother looks as if he is waking up from a dream, as if until now he had not fully realised that his brother Paul had survived and he had not and that they were no longer together.

In this unusual case, the one who died needs to recognise that he belongs to the world of the dead, not the living. When he does recognise this, there is a certain 'let-go' experience for both brothers, a relaxation that comes with the acknowledgement of a factual reality and the relinquishing of a dream.

The dead and the living are both subject to the collective conscience, even though they belong to different spheres, or realms. Sometimes the living forget about the dead and need to consciously remember them, without ignoring the fact that they are in two different worlds. And sometimes, more rarely, the dead need to be reminded that they no longer belong to the sphere of the living. So a dead person has to be allowed to be dead and a living person should take his life fully in his hands and live it as totally as possible.

Chapter Eight

The Interrupted Movement to the Mother

In his work with family dynamics, Bert Hellinger describes two main reasons for suffering. One is because of entanglement in the family system, the origin of which is usually in a previous generation and this is what we have been examining in earlier chapters. The other is an interrupted 'reaching-out' movement, which originates in an individual's personal life story.

For entanglements, a constellation session is recommended, while for the second type of problem Hellinger suggests a different kind of intervention, which we will be describing in this chapter. This type of intervention is similar to 'Holding Therapy,' which was originally developed by Dr. Jirina Prekop, a pioneering psychologist well known in Germany for her work with children.

Every child has a natural, built-in instinct to reach out towards his mother; a movement that we can describe as 'primary love.' This love is very powerful and unconditional and, as we discussed earlier in the book, it is how nature ensures the survival of the child. In the same way, a mother has a built-in instinct to care for her child and, as a result of these two instinctive drives, the mother and her child develop a deep bond with each other.

An interrupted 'reaching-out' movement is a child's emotional withdrawal from his mother, or sometimes from his father. The cause lies in a traumatic event in the child's personal life and is not the result of the entanglement problems we have been discussing up to now.

This event usually occurs very early in life, during a mother's pregnancy, for example, or during birth, or soon afterwards and is very painful for the child. Perhaps the

101

most damaging trauma is an early separation between mother and baby, such as when the mother dies soon after giving birth, or for some reason she cannot take care of her child for a long period, perhaps when a baby is born prematurely and has to be kept in an incubator, or when the mother has fallen ill.

It may also occur when birth is a life threatening experience for either mother or child, or where there are external life-threatening situations during pregnancy, like war. Any form of early separation from the mother or life-threatening experience - inside the womb, during birth, or soon after - can cause an interruption in the natural movement of the child towards the mother. When this movement is stopped or interrupted it remains fragmented and does not lead towards completion and fulfilment.

In order to grasp the full significance of this event one has to imagine the situation of a newborn baby who is totally dependent on the mother for his survival. He is not merely dependent, he is in a symbiotic union with her; he has not yet developed boundaries of his own and is unable to distinguish between himself and his mother.

In the normal course of growing up, he would slowly move from this total oneness with the mother to a sense of himself as more and more separate, a process of maturing that we call individuation. The baby matures and grows into a child and as he grows, bit by bit he gathers his own identity and boundary structure. The child slowly transforms from being one with the mother to being one with himself. This is the basic model of child development.

To be a child, by definition, is to be in the process of separating oneself from one's parents. A child may be gradually becoming an individual, but he is not yet an integrated personality and much has to happen to him before he can stand on his own two feet. As long as he is still young, his parents will continue to have an essential life-sustaining function for him.

So, when a child loses one of his parents at an early age, it is bound to happen while he is still going through this maturation process and while he is still dependent on them. To lose either parent in this transitional stage, or to be separated from them for a long period, is a deeply disturbing experience. The earlier this happens, the more traumatic it is for the child and when it happens before the age of eighteen months it leads to the situation we describe in this chapter. As the mother is the most important figure for any child, the interrupted contact with her is usually the most traumatic.

A child is too vulnerable, too immature, to be able to digest the pain of such a separation in the way an adult can. There is no way he can absorb the full impact of the experience, so he goes into shock. His psyche responds with barriers and compensations of all kinds. However it manifests, something in his psyche remains in limbo, hanging like a record stuck in a groove.

What becomes of a neglected baby is well known from research on child development: At first he cries in anger and despair; he cries and cries until a moment arrives where he becomes silent. This is not the silence of a contented and peaceful baby; it is the silence of an infant who has given up, who has abandoned the attempt to get his mother's attention and who has contracted and retreated into himself.

The contracted child has now learned not to ask for what he needs. He will stop reaching out towards his mother and will become incapable of following his own life-sustaining impulses to receive what he needs from her, even if the mother returns later and is again available to him. So the period of separation is crucial to determine whether the child will develop a mistrustful and withdrawn personality and whether, even after becoming an adult, he is likely to develop a pattern of not coming close to other people. Typically, a person like this will – as an adult - approach until a certain boundary line is reached and then move in a circle rather than going towards someone to receive love in a straightforward way.

We sometimes experience a similar pattern in our own lives, when we expect to get hurt and try to protect ourselves. We may want love or affection from someone, but rather than going towards them to get it we become afraid, stop and move backwards or take a circuitous route and remain at a kind of distance, wanting something badly while at the same time avoiding any possibility of getting the thing for which we are longing.

What we are doing here, of course, is avoiding being rejected. An adult person who is intensely caught up in such a pattern - beyond the lessons of her actual experience of being rejected - is nearly always being unconsciously manipulated by her past, trying to avoid repeating a painful experience of rejection in childhood.

This is the source of many neurotic types of behaviour. Rather than going in a straight line towards a target in order to receive, we move sideways or backwards, or in some roundabout way that doesn't lead to fulfilment and brings us back to the initial point, where nothing is gained or achieved.

Restoring the Bond

Once we understand the original early-childhood scenario the solution in a therapy session becomes clear. The therapist can try to restore the interrupted movement, the bond, the flow of love between parent and child. He can help the client to complete the reaching out movement - to complete what could not be completed at the proper time.

He himself can play the role of the mother and help to re-establish the bond by creating a safe situation in which the client can re-experience, in small doses, some of the pain that occurred in childhood when the mother was not there. This time, however, he is not left by himself, but the therapist, representing the mother, is holding him while he goes through these painful emotions. This is a healing process that allows what happened in childhood can become integrated into the client's adult life.

Rather than setting up a constellation, Hellinger suggests that the therapist should sit opposite the client and, after creating an atmosphere of trust and safety, invite the client to put his arms around him, so he can be held by the therapist. In addition, the therapist may encourage the client to breathe deeply and within a short time the client will get in touch with every child's basic need for the mother's love, as well as the pain that comes when the love connection is cut by separation.

The main thing the therapist has to do, while this is going on, is to hold the client the way a mother holds her baby – it is a simple technique and yet it has a profound effect.

To a certain degree, the client re-lives his experience of being separated from the mother, of almost dying, feeling old pain that he may not have allowed himself to acknowledge since the original traumatic experience. As a survival measure, he cut himself off from the pain and remained numb, or frozen, but can now safely re-experience what happened while lying in the therapists' arms.

Thus, the negative experience of being separated is overlaid by the positive experience of now being held and supported. This is a well-known Neuro-Linguistic Programming (NLP) technique, where one erases a negative experience by overlaying it with a positive one. The positive experience is 'anchored' in the body, because now the therapist, who functions as a substitute mother, is holding the client.

This process may be the only thing the therapist needs to do in a single session. It demands from the therapist the capacity to be patient, supportive and to go on holding the client, even if – at some point in re-living the original abandonment - the person may be trying to push the therapist away, which sometimes can appear like a physical struggle.

The therapist has to keep holding the client while he goes through all the different stages of the experience and remain until the person comes to a point of completion, which will be indicated by taking slower, deeper in-breaths and becoming calm and peaceful. The client will eventually be ready to come out of the embrace and look at the therapist, who is standing-in for the mother and who may suggest some sentences to say to the mother in order to complete the healing process. For example, the client may be asked to consciously thank his mother for giving birth to him and in this way indicate his readiness to receive from the parent.

Of course, this work of restoring the interrupted movement may not be completed within a single session and may take slightly different forms according to each individual. Also, there may be issues relating to the family system arising at the same time for the client and it is up to the therapist to pick the most important issue to work with, leaving other issues for a different time. It is not advisable to mix both approaches within one session.

Whether a client's issue is related to an interrupted reaching out movement, or is more related to a family entanglement, is something to be decided according to information gathered from a pre-session interview. For example, if there are certain facts that indicate an early separation from the mother, or a traumatic event.

As I mentioned before, an interrupted reaching out movement can also be related to the father if, for example, he died when the child was very young,. in which case it would be helpful to invite the mother be a link in connecting the child with the father. For all children, the mother is the most important figure and she may need to

lead the client-child to the father and introduce him –
sometimes, too the mother and father hold the child
together.

It is important to note that an interrupted movement in
early childhood is the only instance where the movement of
reconciliation has to come from the parents. The child
cannot move on his own; it is the mother who must make
the move towards him. The original trauma took place at a
time when, as a very small baby, the client could do
nothing for himself, so the therapist standing in for the
mother replicates what the actual mother did not, or could
not do, which is holding the child and taking care.

In most other cases, the movement of reconciliation has
to come from the child/client; it is the child who has to
move towards the mother if he is to receive something and
not vice versa. Normally, in a constellation session, the
child goes to the parents, bows down and makes himself
available to receive from them. During the course of this
action, the parent has the role of giver and functions as an
abundant presence.

Chapter Nine

Family Dynamics Behind Illnesses:
Basic Patterns of Entanglement

Up to now we have seen different patterns of how a person can be 'entangled' in the life of an earlier member of an extended family system. These patterns not only influence the psychology and behaviour of the individual concerned, but can also be the cause of certain illnesses, such as cancer, depression, heart disease or multiple sclerosis. In other words, illnesses that are not caused by a virus or bacteria.

Entanglement occurs when a person identifies with an excluded member of the family system and takes on his, or her, feelings and attitudes. It is as if one 'becomes' the other person, identifying with him in an unconscious effort to maintain the memory of a forgotten family member through repeating that person's suffering.

Hellinger has described a typical case: a family in which the first-born child died early and the later children grew up using cups with their names written on them. One child in this family was given a cup with the name of the deceased elder brother, indicating his identification with the sibling who died. A child in a situation like this may grow up thinking that he is living his own life, with his own attitudes and feelings, while all the time acting as if he is his brother.

We have explained how this process of entanglement is no one's decision, but is the result of an unconscious collective force - the collective conscience - and we have also shown how difficult it is for an individual family member to free himself from this force. The client may not even know the earlier family member with whom he is identifying, may have no idea what happened to this person and the situation may be further complicated by a family secret that no one wishes to reveal.

The effects of identification will vary according to the specific situation that caused imbalance in the family, but can include emotional disorder, psychosomatic illness and even psychosis. Inevitably, it affects a person's ability to relate with others, as he is not really being himself; in fact, he is a stranger to himself.

The solution for this identification is to find the excluded person and help the client see him as a separate being, acknowledging his existence and destiny as separate. To facilitate this process, we use solution sentences that will help to resolve the entanglement that occurred and these sentences sometimes need to be repeated several times until the client can clearly recognise the other as separate.

Then he can step back. Often, this healing gesture of stepping back requires the client to move closer to another family member, usually one of the parents, as a kind of protection, for example, when the client has been identifying with someone from his mother's family, he may need to come closer to the sphere of influence of his father, or vice versa.

Hellinger describes three basic patterns of family entanglement, which can lead to sickness or suffering. He calls them 'following', 'taking over' and 'atonement for guilt.' We will look at each of them in turn.

Following

If there was an untimely death in a person's immediate family, such as a parent dying as a result of accident, sickness, war or crime, there will be a tendency for one of the children in the family to say, "I want to follow you," and this child will tend to become accident prone, suicidal or develop a sickness, as if symbolically turning his back on life and saying to the parent, "If you are dead, I don't want to live. I want to follow you into death."

Again, we see here the blind love of the child. If the child was able to consciously look at his parent and consider what his parent would want for him, he most probably would not even consider following, since in the vast majority of cases the parent would want his son or daughter to live.

Examples of a child unconsciously wanting to follow a deceased family member have been given in earlier chapters. For example, in chapter one, Max, a client, wants to follow his grandfather, who died early; in chapter seven, a woman wants to follow her sister, who was killed in a concentration camp; also in chapter seven, Rosella wants to follow her aunt into death.

Take Over

Rosella also says to her grandmother, "I do it for you," which is the second scenario that causes suffering - wanting to take over another person's burden. A "take over" scenario might begin with a parent who wants to follow someone from his earlier family into death and continue with one of his, or her, children, realising this tendency in the parent and saying, "Rather I die than you, dear mother/father." In other words, wanting to take over the parent's tendency, wanting to save the parent, out of blind loyalty. The 'rather me than you' dynamic may cause a child to become sick for her sick mother, or in some other way try to take over for a suffering family member.

Hellinger has described the case of a very poor family, where the mother was pregnant and both she and her husband were worried about lack of money and living space. One of her young children became aware of these problems, triggered by the fact that a new family member was shortly going to arrive and so became sick and eventually died, in this way trying to make space for the new child.

We have described how children often function from the magical belief that one person can relieve the suffering or burden of another person; that if somebody who came earlier in the family is sick, then someone else can take this on himself and in this way save the other person. Of course, this child-like belief, while deeply touching, is not in accordance with reality. In reality, now two people will fall sick.

Again, if the child could be fully aware of all the implications, including how a mother would feel - seeing her child unnecessarily trying to take her own suffering upon himself – then, of course, the child would not be so easily misguided. But in blind love one only sees oneself, while in conscious or knowing love one can see all the implications and understand the motives of other people involved.

This crucial transition from blind to conscious love is what happens in a Family Constellation session, when the client faces his parents and other family members, receiving direct feedback about how they feel and what they want, understanding how he has been unconsciously carrying a childlike attitude into his adult life.

It is not always an easy task to leave behind the burden and the bond. True separation takes courage, a readiness to be alone and a willingness to tolerate a sense of guilt - a recognition that even though we want to help there is nothing we can do. The practice of 'honouring' that we use in Family Constellation takes us to this critical point, where we can bow down in respect and let go of a burden that we unconsciously took on. When we then stand up and leave the person's fate to himself, we are truly separate and on our own.

For example, in chapter three, Antonella is taking over her grandmother's anger against the grandfather and expresses it against her father; in chapter five, a client takes over the murderous impulse of his father, who had killed his own mother; in chapter six there are many examples of taking over for victims and perpetrators.

Atonement for Guilt

Another reason for sickness arises from what Hellinger calls 'atonement for guilt.' This can relate to personal guilt. For example, a woman who has had many abortions in a casual way without understanding the deeper implications of her behaviour, may develop uterine cancer as a way of atonement. Or a woman who rejects her mother may get breast cancer as a kind of self-punishment, because the collective conscience does not allow a deep rejection of a parent.

It can also relate to the guilt of another family member, that the client has 'taken over,' as we described in chapter five. For example, if a murderer did not get punished for his act, a child may take on himself the guilt of what his forefather did and be ready to commit suicide or become sick.

Other examples from chapter five: a mother became schizophrenic through taking over the guilt of her mother, who had eleven abortions; a family member got himself killed to atone for the guilt of his family's former terrorist members.

These are the main patterns of entanglement that are discovered in constellations and can be the psychological causes of diseases triggered by imbalanced family systems.

Dealing with Sickness

Often, we think of illness as an enemy, as something to get rid of, whereas, in fact, it is a message from the body that we need to decode. Sometimes, the body wants to heal an old psychological issue or emotional wound through sickness and we may be able to discover and understand its message. Sometimes, too, an illness remains inexplicable in spite of our best efforts to understand it and this needs to be received and appreciated as something beyond our grasp, beyond our control.

In both cases, one has to learn to break the ingrained social habit of seeing sickness as an enemy that has to be fought against. This combative attitude is, unfortunately, quite prevalent in our high-tech medical world, where we tend to think in terms of 'conquering' the disease - take, for example, the book title: 'How to Conquer Cancer' and you will immediately see the point. The temptation is to think we are in control and capable of defeating the disease, simply by acquiring more and more scientific data and by introducing more and more complicated and expensive medical equipment.

What we come to see in constellations is that often an illness is forcing us to look at an excluded person and the effort to get rid of the disease is similar to the way one wants to 'get rid of' or exclude a person from the family system. In this sense, an illness is a healing effort of the collective conscience. Taking the illness into our heart, accepting it in this way, reflects the way we can take that person into our heart. Then, sometimes, the need to be ill is no more relevant. When the collective is healed, the person may also be healed.

A client with a Jewish background had a strong headache for most his life that seemed to occur on Saturdays, which is the Jewish holiday. He didn't consider himself very religious or even think much about having Jewish forefathers. In the work, we found that his grandmother had escaped from Poland and lost most of her family in the holocaust. After he had deeply honoured these forefathers and told them "I am also Jewish," his headache disappeared and never returned. As a side effect, his chronic short-sightedness improved drastically.

In this case, the client's physical symptoms reminded him about his origin, which he had forgotten, but the collective doesn't allow events of such magnitude to be simply ignored. When he consciously remembered and acknowledged what had happened and where he came from, the headache was no longer needed.

In short, when we are ready in some way to embrace the illness and understand its origins, we may both heal the disease and become aware of the excluded person.

One should, however, have an attitude of humbleness in the face of these mysteries, rather than thinking that a certain therapy, whether medical or psychological, will solve all problems. Some things can be revealed to us by life in this way and we can understand them, but many events remain hidden from our minds. Dealing with sickness also requires us to acknowledge the mystery of life and the limitations of human understanding.

We may also see in constellations that a sick person is in a secret agreement with his illness. For example, having dealt with many of these cases, one can often see a hidden smile in a person's face when he talks about his sickness. It mirrors the secret agreement he may have with being identified with an excluded person in his family system.

If a client has a question about a physical problem, or sickness, one approach to the issue is to place a representative for the client and another for the disease in a constellation. Watching the interaction of the two, it may become apparent that the representative of the illness is actually a family member from the person's original family, perhaps somebody who has been excluded or rejected.

As I said before, when the client includes the missing person consciously in his heart, the need for sickness may no longer be there. However, our work with constellations is not primarily aimed at healing the client, but at revealing a certain truth that was hidden. It is not about getting rid of a problem, or changing reality, but about creating understanding - an opening to something, or someone. Disease is part of life and may not disappear through a new understanding of one's family dynamics. The whole art of good therapy is to have no goal and to investigate the issue without jumping to conclusions, or forming prejudices.

A Tumour in the Uterus

A client, a middle-aged American woman called Nora, wants to understand the underlying dynamic behind her sickness, a tumour in her uterus. We set up a representative for Nora and one for the tumour, facing each other at a little distance. The tumour immediately looks down on the floor, indicating that it is looking at a dead person and is unable to look at Nora's stand-in.

So I ask Nora herself, "Who do you feel the tumour is representing?" After watching closely for a while the client says, "I think it is my father." Then I ask her, "Who has died?" The client answers, "My mother, when I was five months old."

We introduce a representative for the mother and ask her to lie on the floor between Nora's representative and the tumour, in the place at which the tumour has been staring. Now I ask the tumour to represent the father of the client. Representatives for both the mother and the client are very moved and after a while the father can look at the client. Now I ask the mother to stand up and look at her child. The client cannot come close to her mother, because as we

116

saw in chapter eight, separation happened so early that the child cannot move on her own to the mother. They look at each other for a while, then I ask the mother to move close to the client and hold her, which she does and soon the client's representative is sobbing.

At this point, I bring in Nora herself to replace her representative and to experience this hug for herself. She does and, crying, softens visibly. I invite Nora to look at her mother and say, "thank you." Then she looks into her mother's eyes and says to her, "In me, you are still present. Now I will stay," meaning that now she has the will to live and the intention to survive her illness. She also looks at her father and tells him the same thing: "Now I will stay with you. Please look on me as your child."

The father is asked to say to his child, "I will take care of you and look on you as my child." Further, "You remind me of your mother and you remind me of how much I loved your mother." Nora is visibly moved, goes spontaneously to her father and hugs him. She repeats, "Now I stay with you as your child."

The phrase 'as your child' is important, as well as the acknowledgment of the mother, to prevent the daughter having to replace her mother. Also, it is important that she goes to her father, not vice versa. She could not move to the mother, because she was too small, when she lost her, but now she can move to the father.

In this example, the illness may have been a way for the child to unconsciously say to her mother, "I want to follow you into death."

When she consciously takes her mother into her heart, the need to follow her may no longer be there. But it needs to be emphasised that the work of the therapist is to bring this dynamic to light, not to try to heal the sickness. Healing may be a secondary effect; it cannot be the main concern. In fact, to even inquire afterwards about the effect of the work on the client - if the illness has improved - is a subtle interference in the client's life outcome.

Multiple Sclerosis

An English woman called Jennifer wants to understand the cause for her illness, multiple sclerosis, which has been developing rapidly for the past year. When I place representatives for her and the illness in a constellation, it is soon revealed that she is carrying a lot of aggression, indicated by the fact that she is clenching her hands into fists; in fact, it looks as if she is carrying a murderous energy.

After some time, I interrupt the constellation and ask her about her original family. She tells me that on her father's side, the first wife of the grandfather died giving birth to a child - both mother and baby died.

As we discussed earlier, when a woman dies in childbirth it is often perceived by the family system as if the woman has been murdered. This would explain the client's aggressiveness.

We now arrange a new constellation, placing representatives for the grandfather, his first wife and the child who died. The child lies down on the floor and I allow the grandfather and wife to move on their own. The grandfather is in a deep inner struggle, at first trying to turn away from both the child and his wife - he must have felt guilty about his wife's death - and then coming back and slowly moving nearer to his wife. They stand close, she leans her head on his shoulder, then she lies down next to the child, while the grandfather is very moved and starts crying. Then he lies down with them. The client and client's father are watching and are very moved. They come closer to each other and hug deeply.

In general, diseases like multiple sclerosis, epilepsy and also panic attacks are often the result of a repressed murderous impulse, which according to Hellinger indicates that there was a murder in the family, or, as in this case, a perceived murder. The client identifies with the excluded perpetrator, taking his energy upon herself and the sickness can be seen as a manifestation of her effort to hold back this aggressive impulse. In this example, the healing lies in bringing to light the actual love that existed between the grandfather and his first wife, understanding that no one was murdered, or responsible for her death and then honouring her and her child.

In the case of schizophrenia, there has often been a murder in the family and the person who is schizophrenic is identifying with both victim and perpetrator at the same time, because both have been excluded from the family. This double identification is one of the reasons for the creation of a dual personality that is typical of schizophrenia and also of manic depression.

The relationship between Family Constellation work and different diseases has been well documented in other books, so it is unnecessary to give further examples here. Hellinger himself has done a lot of research work with sick people, including those suffering from cancer and schizophrenia. As a result, he has discovered certain dynamics behind these diseases, which have been briefly mentioned here and which can be used as a working hypothesis in constellation sessions.

Naturally, it is important to confirm whether any of the dynamics relating to illness fit the facts of a particular constellation session and the therapist must be ready to adjust theoretical concepts to reflect reality. This is what Hellinger calls the "phenomenological approach." One watches phenomena and concludes from these observations, without any fixed idea or prejudice.

Part Two

Understanding Current Relationships

Chapter Ten

The Man - Woman Relationship

There exist two basic types of relationships in the family system: one between a superior and an inferior, such as the relationship between parents and their children and one between equals, such as a man and a woman who become husband and wife, or who agree to live together.

In this chapter we try to understand the characteristics of a relationship between equals, between a man and a woman and to see how it is different and also affected by the dynamics of earlier parent-child relationships.

When we look at the difference between a child and an adult, what is immediately evident is that a child is relatively helpless and therefore does not have much responsibility, whereas an adult is more responsible for what he does.

In order to grow up, we need to be ready to give up the child-like feeling of having no responsibility and being taken care of by others. Even though this sounds obvious, the truth is we often find ourselves relating to an adult partner as if he or she should provide for us and we behave like a disappointed child if it doesn't happen. In some way or other, we are resisting the natural process of taking care of ourselves and still want someone else to look after us.

The Balance of Giving and Taking

When we examine what goes on between a parent and child, we immediately see an imbalance: the child is dependent on the adult, the mother or father gives more and the child takes more. When we look at the relationship between couples, we see a balance, a reciprocation of giving and taking in which both partners play the roles of giver and receiver in roughly equal amounts.

In essence, a man is receiving from the woman what he is missing and giving to the woman what she is missing; a woman is receiving from the man what she is missing and giving to him what he is missing. Both must be ready to exchange in a balanced way. They must be ready to show that they need something from the other.

This exchange of giving and receiving happens at all levels - material, sexual, emotional, mental, spiritual - and is the sustaining force that maintains the relationship, deepening the commitment of both partners. The more they give and receive from each other, the stronger the bond will be between them.

In the parent-child relationship, bonding is already a built-in factor; a child is biologically bonded to his parents, whether he likes it or not. In the relationship between man and woman there is a choice to come together, but as soon as they create a bond through their exchange, separating becomes difficult. This is one reason why people often feel afraid to give or receive too much, because they fear they will lose their freedom to do what they want.

In the parent-child relationship the sentences we use to express the intrinsic dynamics are, 'You are big and I am small, you give, I receive.' In a man-woman relationship it is more appropriate to say to each other, "I have something that you need and I'm ready to give it to you; also, you have something that I need and I am ready to receive it from you."

Where Problems Start

Partners bring into the relationship whatever burdens they carry from their family of origin, so it is clear that the parent-child relationship will have a strong impact on the man-woman relationship. If a person wants to 'give' to his parents, a situation which, as we have seen, is an entanglement that goes against the natural hierarchy and order of a family system, then he may want to compensate by receiving from his partner, as if the partner is his parent. In this way, everything is turned upside down.

What would need to happen to remedy the situation and restore balance is that he would have to "shrink" and become "smaller" in relation to his parents - becoming a child rather than playing parent - and in relation to his partner he would need to grow 'bigger," learning to take responsibility and giving more.

In the process of giving and receiving, a normal relationship between a man and a woman will swing between moments of imbalance and a desire to restore balance and any tension between partners is usually contained in this dynamic.

But there are many situations where the problem runs deeper. For example, we may find a woman behaving towards her partner the way a child would in relation to its parents. She might make herself helpless and dependent; letting the man know that she has nothing of value to offer him and that she needs much more than she can ever give. As a result, she becomes needy in adult situations; she expects unlimited support and manipulates things in such a way that she is always being taken care of.

For example, in one constellation session, a woman who all her life took care of her sick mother behaves towards her husband like a needy child. She stands in the constellation of her present family next to her two children, as if she was another child, not like a mother. She is receiving more in the relationship and it is she who eventually leaves the marriage, also leaving the children with her husband, for him to take care of them - it is usually the one who receives more that leaves the relationship.

But, in this case, the husband is also responsible for losing his wife. In the constellation, it is revealed that he systematically acts like a parent to the woman, supplying everything without waiting to be asked and behaving as if he needs nothing for himself. He lets his woman know that he is ready to give whatever she wants and there is no need for her to give anything back because, basically, he doesn't need much. She has no chance to restore balance, to get even with him and to learn to take her responsibility as a mother and wife.

In another example, a man in a relationship is treated like a prince, all his wishes are fulfilled and it is he who finally leaves his partner. This is a typical response in a situation where the imbalance gets too unbearable. It usually is harder to receive than to give, one feels the pressure to give back and when there is no chance, one leaves. When, in his next relationship, this man's partner was more demanding towards him, it worked better, as he became aware of his own needs and qualities as a man.

When one partner unconsciously asks the other to be a parent, or adopts a parental role, the balance between two equals is disturbed, upsetting the equilibrium of the relationship. What is required of a man and woman who come together in a partnership is that they ask something from the other and are at the same time aware of what they owe to the other. The challenge is to take a position in the relationship where both partners give only as much as the other is willing or able to give back, or receive only as much as the other is ready to receive in return.

This kind of penetrating insight into relationship dynamics requires a deep understanding. Usually, imbalances happen without either partner being aware of what is going on; their abundant giving, or their compulsive taking, are built into their behaviour patterns by early family conditioning and often include a tendency to pull out of the relationship when the imbalance becomes too big.

Take, for example, a young couple who came to see me recently. The wife had walked out on her husband, leaving him to take care of their two children. She was under the impression that he had created the problem between them by having a brief love affair and it was she who insisted they go for therapy.

What emerged during the session was that the problem in fact lay with the wife, in her tendency to leave men at the slightest opportunity. She had done this several times before, always citing minor infractions in the relationship as an excuse and always blaming the man. It appeared that her husband was putting more into the relationship than she was and demanding too little in return. His tendency, which colluded with his wife's, was to feel himself incapable and unworthy and put all the blame onto himself.

In this case, I was able to help the wife to take responsibility for her anger against men, something she had taken over from her mother, who had left her father. I was also able to help the husband take no more of the blame than was actually his. This couple did not continue the relationship, but were able to separate from each other peacefully.

In any relationship between a man and woman as love partners, it is generally a healthy response for couples to make demands on each other, just as long as it is balanced by good-natured attempts at exchange and maintaining balance. Problems start arising if one partner is not ready to show his needs and be a receiver, or doesn't feel capable or willing to give. Similarly, there will be problems if one of the partners continuously behaves either like a parent, or like a child. In both these situations, there will be a problem of imbalance within the relationship and if such problems are allowed to continue over a period of time divorce frequently follows.

Lars, a married man from Finland, is overly worried about his eight-month old daughter and takes too much responsibility from his wife in caring for their child. This tendency shows a lack of strength, a lack of confidence in his own "maleness," and we learn that Lars' father lost his own father at an early age. After creating a line of men in his family system, with his father and grandfather behind him and receiving their strength, Lars discovers that he can begin to relax about his own family. At the end, he says, laughing, "Now I feel less important." It showed that he carried the pain for his father and felt responsible for him, so he, in turn, lacked strength as a husband and father.

If we are going to truly maintain balance, we have to be a child to those who have given us life, an adult with those whom we have chosen to partner in a relationship and a parent to our own children. Instead of complaining that we didn't get enough love from our parents, we take responsibility for our grown-up place in the world and for the role we play as a parent. As far as family dynamics are concerned, what matters in life is what we do and how we act. A man who is a father is responsible to his children because he chose to be a father, not for any other reason and in this respect it is irrelevant how he feels about it.

Family Constellation's model of the social personality can be summed up in this simple statement: in relation to our parents: *we* are small and *they* are big; in relation to our children, *we* are big and *they* are small; and in relation to our life partners, we are both equals.

Just to emphasise the point: if we feel 'small' in an adult relationship, or treat our partner like a child, then the relationship has become unbalanced, due to something unresolved from the original family, or a previous partner. This imbalance can be related to one partner and not the other, or to both of them.

There are many occasions when unresolved problems in both create a functional harmony between them; where both partners are acting out roles that match each other's needs so well that the dysfunction never comes to light.

For example, a masochist needs a sadist, a dominating person needs someone who is in need of being dominated and if such people can find each other, they will sometimes create a perfect fit. A man who wants a mother may find a woman who searches for a son. A man, who doesn't respect women, may find a woman who doesn't believe she deserves respect from men.

Positive and Negative Exchange

Built into the balance between giving and taking is the subtle movement of a swinging pendulum. It means that if I do something for you, there is a momentum in this gesture that will ultimately lead to a need from your side to do something for me in return. This is not a conscious, contractual business exchange so much as a natural in-built dynamic of relating, created by our personal conscience.

It is obvious to see how this operates in a relationship when it is working positively: we connect with each other through a harmonious to-and-fro of giving and receiving. My love for you creates the urge in me to give you something and when you have received something beautiful from me, this in turn creates a desire in you to give something back and so it goes on, deepening the relationship with each swing of the pendulum. This is what we call a positive exchange.

However, the swing of the pendulum is just as valid when operating negatively, when in a relationship we do difficult, painful, or obstructive things to each other. That is to say, if I treat you badly - if on a material or emotional level I take something away from you - you will probably feel the desire to take something away from me in return.

Take the example of a woman who has cheated on her partner. She has gone with another man and this has bruised the relationship. On the surface of it, we may think that if the husband can be understanding and forgive his wife, this is the most mature and civilised response.

But not according to the laws of family dynamics; the Law of Balance requires a true sacrifice to be made on the part of the woman in order to keep equilibrium in the relationship. The husband would need to ask something from his wife that is difficult for her to give; she needs to give up something that she values in order to give him something that he values. For example, it could be that she cancels an important job appointment to go with him on a weekend trip to the mountains. This sacrifice needs to be a subjective experience – it has to be felt by the offending partner as a real loss - not just an empty gesture.

Forgiveness is a cherished ideal in most Christian-based societies, but in terms of family systems it often implies a humiliation of the other, because in forgiving you are bound to put yourself above your partner in a morally superior position - "holier than thou." One has no right to forgive, or ask for forgiveness, because this destroys the balance of the relationship. Moreover, in asking to be forgiven one wants something from the other, rather than showing one's readiness to deal with any consequences of what happened. There is a difference between saying, "I am sorry" and "Please forgive me." Most likely, the 'forgiving' partner will keep bringing up the issue again and again on later occasions, indicating that equality in the relationship has been lost.

Other examples: a wife is not so available to her husband, because of being entangled in destinies of her original family, so the man 'balances' by having an affair. A woman, who had a child with a married man, who never left his wife to be with her and help to raise the child, takes revenge and doesn't allow the father to see his child.

This is the oscillation of give and take in its negative mode. If, at each swing of the pendulum, each partner asks a little less than what the other has done, the relationship is not damaged and balance is restored. If on the other hand, the act which is intended to redress balance is greater than the original offence, there is danger of a vicious cycle, a deepening negative exchange. In this case, the other gives back more negativity and does a greater injury than was done to him and in this way we enter the realm of revenge.

If a wronged husband were to give back disproportionately more of the negative, for example by cutting off from his partner and having a series of affairs with other women, then the love between the couple would soon be damaged. If it continues this way, then this vengeful form of redressing balance will destroy the relationship. In healthy relating, however, the couple will return the negative but to a lesser degree and this, in turn, enables them to return to a positive exchange.

So in the positive exchange, we give a little more and in the negative a little less; in both cases, because we love each other.

The day-to-day basis of measuring and balancing the good or bad things we do to each other is a difficult matter and seems to require a lot of careful consideration. Yet most of us will know, deep in our hearts, whether we are giving more than we are receiving, whether we are getting more than we give. Somewhere, deep down, however little we may want to accept it, we normally know whether we resent all the giving we do, or are too demanding in what we want to receive from the other.

These ideas may not be in the forefront of our conscious mind and we may not want to openly admit them, but on a deeper level we usually understand whether or not there is balance in a relationship and, as a result, the truth emerges during the course of a constellation session. And, if at first it is not clear, it is likely to be obvious to a third person - usually the therapist or facilitator who is working with a couple.

An Italian man fell in love with a woman from abroad and invited her to give up her job in her home country in order to move to Italy and live with him. She eventually agreed, left her job and went to Milan to be with him. However, she immediately noticed, even while being greeted by her partner-to-be at the airport, that he was not too pleased to see her standing there with her suitcase, in effect saying, "Here I am to be with you".

Rather than going into the 'victim role' and blaming him, she tactfully raised the issue, brought him to the point where he could admit his true feelings and then asked him to pay her air ticket back home, which he did. His gift of a plane ticket helped her overcome any personal resentment and feeling of being victimised; it also helped the man - by redressing the promise he didn't keep - to overcome his guilty feelings.

This is a simple example of how we need to ask for what we deserve and how we need to give what we owe. The concept of balance helps us become aware of this need. If the "innocent" one does not make her demand, then, according to the Law of Balance, she will be turning herself into the "virtuous" one in the relationship and putting herself in a superior position to her partner, who then has to take the role of "sinner".

In many cases, it is the arrogance of the innocent that breaks up a relationship. The people who feel their trust has been betrayed, who feel righteously indignant, or holier than thou, are often more responsible for destroying the balance in relationship than the "sinning" partner, who does some mischief, but who at least usually knows it - sinners are more humble and less arrogant than saints.

The notion of turning the other cheek is an important pillar of recommended Christian practice, but this well-known biblical injunction has clouded the natural need for friends and lovers to create balance between each other.

The Law of Balance makes it clear that at times we have a right to ask for something from our partner and at times the other has a right to ask something from us. In order to maintain a relationship, we must listen to what the other is demanding from us.

Asking for something from the other is an intimate matter. It tests the relationship and makes us explore its boundaries. We have to find our own limits and true capacities, without pretension. These are things everyone in a relationship has to work out for themselves; it can be a delicate and elusive art, but it is part of one's inner maturing. It makes it clear that with all our frailties and shortcomings we are simply human and however understanding we may be, we are not able to love unconditionally.

Bonding in Relationship

The moment a man and a woman come together in the sexual act, a bond is created. This is a biological connection, an instinctual drive of nature that wants parents to bond with each other in order to care for the child that, without modern contraception, would normally result from the sexual union of a man and a woman. It is really nature's way of guaranteeing the survival of the species and is often mistaken for love, because it binds two people together and makes it difficult for them to separate.

Bonding may be accompanied by some form of love or affection, but equally, may not. Naturally, whenever love is combined with sex, the bond is stronger and often people have a very strong bond with their first lover. From then on, the strength of the bond tends to diminish with each new partner.

Most of us have experienced more pain in separating from earlier partners than from later ones and perhaps the most pain of all when separating from our first love. The pain experienced in separation indicates the strength of the bond that existed between two partners. By the time we come to separate from our fifth or sixth partner, we tend to feel much less pain and we "get over it" sooner.

The quality of love that is present in a later partnership may be deeper than earlier love experiences, while the biological bond may be quite small and when seen from this perspective it is easy for us to understand how love and bonding are two distinct things.

In assessing the strength of a particular bond, we need to examine each case on its own merits. For example, a one-night stand will not necessarily elicit a strong bond, but we cannot ignore the fact that such a bond may have been created. In the case of a rape, the bond may be greater than that of a one-night stand because of the violence involved; when a woman is forced to submit against her will, the pain and anger involved in this act often create a stronger bond than love.

Sometimes, we may have sex with a casual partner without giving much thought to it afterwards, but in fact, the moment you have sex with anyone, something of significance has occurred and it needs to be given its due. In terms of understanding the unconscious forces at work in family dynamics, every sexual relationship, however short-lived, needs to be acknowledged and considered.

It is not so easy to dissolve a bond once it has been created. We can truly leave a former partner only if we are grateful to that person and acknowledge his, or her, significance in our life. If we don't do this, we are not really separated and the bond continues, making it difficult or impossible for a new partner to come close to us. Moreover, the new partner is bound to feel a certain sympathy with the previous partner. For example, if a man leaves a woman casually, without feeling any pain or loss, his new woman may be concerned that she will be the next one to be treated in the same fashion, so how can she really open up and trust this man?

A couple comes for a session, because they feel they cannot reach the depth of intimacy that both desire. The woman had a former husband and gave birth to a daughter with him. When we bring both men into the constellation picture, the attention of the woman's representative goes to the previous husband and the present boyfriend stands aside.

Asking the client what she sees in this picture, she says, "Marrying this man was a mistake." In other words, she has remained in the attitude of blaming the ex-husband, who seems to have been violent with her and she cannot bring herself to acknowledge him. In this way, she has been unable to let go of her former husband; her anger creates a strong bond and she is not really available for the new relationship.

The impact of a first relationship is bound to be strong, which doesn't mean that one relationship is intrinsically better or worse than any other. It means that we need to understand that whatever we do in life has an effect and leads to consequences. This is especially true of something as intimate and biologically fundamental as sex.

The degree of bonding also affects how much desire there is for two people to keep together, regardless of the ups and downs they go through. Without bonding, a couple will tend to separate as soon as there is some difficulty. If the bonding is strong, they will be able to tolerate difficult periods and stay together.

Bonding has other aspects, too. Whenever there is love between partners, bonding is strengthened and whenever there is an active and healthy exchange of giving and receiving, bonding will be further strengthened.

Having said all that, it does appear from our work in Family Constellation as if human beings have a limited capacity for deep bonding. As I already mentioned, the energy for it is stronger when we are younger and tends to diminish with each new relationship, making us less likely to have strong bonding after having had many relationships.

It is neither good nor bad to have one or many partners, but each choice has certain consequences that are different from others and we cannot pretend that, having made a certain choice, all our options still remain open. Our life takes a certain shape according to what earlier choices we made and this means that we have to face up to what we do, or did, in our lives.

Even if you were not deeply in love, any sexual relationship will have a greater or lesser influence on your life, for no other reason than that you were together and this phenomenon needs to be acknowledged. For example, if a client in a constellation wants to complete an old relationship in which she is somehow still entangled, we may invite her to say to her former partner: "Thank you for the time we had together. It gave me a lot and what you gave me will stay with me. What I gave you, I gave with love and you can keep it."

When she does this, she acknowledges that this man was in her life and, having done this, she can make her peace with him. When honouring has taken place in this heartfelt manner, one has completed an old relationship and one's energy is now free and available to connect with a new partner.

What we started in love can only be completed in love. The more we loved a person, the more we will feel pain in separation and to feel this pain is both necessary and healing - a way of acknowledging the effect of the other person on our lives. If we don't do it, a deep layer of mind and heart still feels the bond and doesn't allow us to move on. Once we acknowledge it, we are enriched and empowered, free to approach with love and totality whatever new encounters are coming our way.

Order in Relationship

As we already discussed, according to the Law of Sacred Order the parents come first and the children second. In the case of couples in a present family, however, there is no first or second. The man and the woman start their relationship at the same time and, in terms of timing, there is no precedence between the man and woman.

However, on a practical level, through observing family dynamics in many Family Constellation sessions, we find that family members often feel more at ease if the man stands in the first position in a constellation picture. The reason for this is not hard to comprehend: traditionally, the man is the primary breadwinner and foremost protector of the family. In the system, he represents the family's outer welfare and is usually responsible for its external security, while the woman is closer to the children and constitutes the main person "inside" the family. This is the reason why the man usually stands in first place in a constellation picture, if he is the one who takes care of the family externally.

The positioning of the man first, however, is not an absolute rule and the facilitator has to decide for each client what position is most appropriate. This can be a controversial issue, especially in today's climate of hotly-debated gender politics and social sensitivity to any implied female inferiority.

Nowadays, sometimes the woman is responsible for the outer security of the family, so she may need to be standing in first place. There are also quite specific occasions when it is essential that the woman stands first, for example, whenever there is a difficult history in the woman's family, an unusually painful event, such as a mother who died in childbirth. In a case like this, in order to acknowledge the pains of the past, it is often better for the woman to take first position. So the function of the man or woman within the family, the role he or she plays, or the weight of tragic events in the past, will help decide who stands first in the family order. By order, I am referring to how we arrange the family stand-ins in a clockwise circle, looking for a place where they feel most at ease with each other.

To better understand male precedence, let's take another look at tribal cultures, because family constellation dynamics have their roots deep in our ancestral heritage, at a time when external dangers to the family were very real and often life-threatening. In this kind of primitive culture, no one questions the man's responsibility for the security of his wife and children and, indeed, for the security of the entire clan. His position in this role demands that in times of danger the whole family follows him, because unless they do so he cannot protect them.

In cases like these, the man is undeniably in charge; there are no discussions or votes taken. His authority is absolute and to question it would endanger everyone. Therefore, as far as the order in a constellation is concerned, the one who is responsible for the security of the whole takes precedence in the positioning of the family and this is normally the man.

However, it is the woman and specifically the mother who is the main figure in a family, because she is the one who gives life and takes care of the children. So whatever the man does has to be in the service of what we may call "the feminine." By feminine, we do not mean that he should serve the woman herself - a man serving his woman is in danger of treating her as his mother - but serve the feminine principle, the protection of his woman, the nurturing needs of the children and the welfare of the tribe as a whole. The man works on behalf of the family and his

138

authority has to operate in the service of his woman, his children and future generations.

It was Bert Hellinger who said, *"The woman follows the man, the man serves the feminine,"* a statement that, predictably, has been greeted with a fair degree of controversy. It has been misunderstood as supporting the domination of women by men and the supremacy of the male principle. But rather than taking it literally, consider it metaphorically: Hellinger's point is that only if the man is acting in service of the feminine - not caught up in displays of male chauvinism - is it right for the woman to follow him, so long as he is in the position of providing material and financial welfare for the family.

Again, it needs to be stressed that we are not talking about any idealistic, philosophical, modern-minded social principles here. We are looking at the basic rules of family dynamics and trying to understand them in an effort to disentangle ourselves from unnecessary burdens carried from the past. In Family Constellation sessions, the therapist needs to see how these laws apply to each particular case in order to bring relief, peace and freedom to the client.

Take a couple where the woman comes from one country and the man from another. What we observe is that when the woman follows the man to his country and they settle there, they usually have more chance of a successful relationship than if the man follows the woman.

Traditionally, this is how it has been in most cultures: the young wife goes to the husband's household, or his place of origin and sets up her home there. Rarely, will the man go to the woman's place of origin and when he does, things often do not work out well. This does not mean that it is impossible, but there are more likely to be obstacles that create problems.

On the other hand, as long as one can recognise these patterns in a constellation session, there is more chance that difficulties will be understood, balance recreated and problems put right.

Nowadays, in Europe, the United States and the developed world, things are often very different and we need to take into account shifts in the way society changes - specifically, the radical differences in roles played by the sexes. Men and women no longer have clearly defined social roles. This is part of an ongoing process of homogenisation and in itself is neither good nor bad. In fact, there has long been a blurring around the edges of gender role-playing. Sexual moral codes, class and gender divisions that, up to eighty years ago, used to bind most societies together, have all but vanished in technologically-advanced countries.

So in Family Constellation we take families and relationships as we find them and we examine things freshly without any ideological prejudice. If we want to find the best solutions in any given relationship, or in a given family, we must be prepared to ignore both traditional habits and modern attitudes and treat each case objectively, observing what happens and deciding each case on its own merits.

The marked increase in recent years in gender confusion has created insecurity in both sexes. In this, Family Constellation can be of great help. By examining the roles between family members and couples in particular, Family Constellation helps people to focus their energies around their natural strengths as men and women and find their rightful place within the family matrix.

Chapter Eleven

Growing in Relationship

The natural practice of all animals is to find a mate and human beings are no exception. The sexual attraction between men and women not only brings them together but keeps them together and, with the arrival of children, transforms them into families. Clearly, there would be no species without children, but the primary force that starts the ball rolling is the attraction of the polarities we call male and female. In animals it is known as mating. We humans call it love, sex or marriage.

When we look at the sexual dimension, we can see a man and a woman as positive and negative poles of a magnet, drawn to each other by an attraction which is usually beyond their control and which operates in spite of them. The more strongly the man is rooted in his male energy and the woman in her female energy, the greater the polarity between them and the stronger the attraction.

The man and woman want to be close, they long to melt into each other and become one and, in order to do this, must dissolve their differences. This is one of the deep longings of a love relationship: the urge to banish differences and become one with the beloved. Yet, as soon as the force that attracts them towards each other has brought them together, the polarity is lost and the need arises to move apart to find it again. You can observe in many relationships that there is a primary movement that brings lovers together and a secondary movement that pushes them apart, so there is constant movement towards and away from each other.

Sexual polarity implies a deep difference between two partners, a division that can be neatly summed up by the expression, "men are from Mars and women are from

141

Venus." So, parallel to a strong attraction, a man and woman experience differences that may get in the way of harmony and make it difficult for them to come close and this tends to create a certain dilemma in their relating.

The Martian and the Venusian observe the same world through different eyes and each longs for the other to share that vision. The man wants his woman to see things his way and the woman wants her man to feel as she does. For example, she may wonder why he is so cool, stubborn and can't understand her moods and he wonders why she can't be more rational about things and less emotionally volatile.

In other words, men and women expect the other to see things the way they themselves see them, to feel things as they feel them, to know the world through their own values, sensitivities and expectations.

Respecting the Opposite

One of the basic lessons of relationship is to respect the other as different and equal. Having acknowledged the difference between the sexes, one can enjoy it rather than trying to manipulate or destroy it. For a man, a woman can remain a mystery, an intriguing puzzle that is never solved - nor needs to be - and for a woman a man can be inexplicable; there is no need to understand the other completely.

When one includes the polar opposite as equal, one becomes whole, like the well-known Chinese symbol of yin and yang and in this way two apparent opposites become complementaries and each partner becomes more than merely half.

For example, Martin and Stephanie are a German couple who have been together for more than 10 years. Stephanie has a quick mind that jumps from one thing to another and she manages to do many things at the same time and yet stay very relaxed - something Martin is never able to do.

When Martin does something, if he is going to stay relaxed, he wants to do just one thing at a time and complete it and doesn't want any distraction. If Martin tried to work in the same way as Stephanie, doing five things at once, he would soon get tense and everything would go wrong.

Conflict arises when Stephanie starts a job with a chaotic approach and Martin's inclination is to stop her and encourage her to go in the same methodical direction that he would go, assuming that she, like him, is bound to get lost and confused and that this will slow things down.

If Martin can drop the idea that Stephanie should be doing things his way and instead let her continue without interfering, he allows an expansion of the relationship. When Martin can say, "Aha! So this is how she does things... and, hey, it works for her and is just as valid as the way I do things," then he has deepened his understanding of the feminine principle, which is less systematic and goal-oriented and broadened his grasp of the world around him. Martin may even have discovered a new way of doing things, opening to an unexplored potential inside himself.

This is one of the first challenges of a man-woman relationship. To fall in love and want to live together is one thing, but to stay involved in such a way that you are ready to learn and grow with your love partner, is a far more challenging step to take.

Same Sex: Weaker Polarities

So far, we have talked about heterosexual relationships. When it comes to homosexual relationships, we are dealing with a different situation. What tends to be missing in a homosexual relationship is the polarity between two opposing energies, the magnetic pull between the contrasting forces of male and female.

It is true that, in many long-term homosexual relationships, one partner adopts the "female" role, while the other adopts the "male" role, but generally speaking they do not include such extreme polar opposites as heterosexual partners. So, for homosexual couples it is easier to be relaxed and in harmony with each other, but the downside is that there is less dynamic tension, less mystery, less possibility of personal growth and transformation.

Generally speaking, homosexuals are bound to learn less from their intimacy with each other than heterosexuals in a deepening relationship.

Receiving Family Differences

When we appreciate how difficult it is to allow differences within a heterosexual love relationship, imagine how much harder it is when one of us remains closely bonded to his or her original family.

Our original family is responsible for most of our belief systems, our values and our world view. In addition, it is from our family that we have acquired our impression of the opposite sex, specifically our mother's impression of men and our father's impression of women.

Therefore, the second major lesson to be learned in relationship is to be able to see your partner not just as a member of the opposite sex, but also as a person who comes from a family with beliefs and values that are likely to be different from your own - sometimes even someone from an entirely different culture.

When you fall in love, it is not just one man or woman that you receive into your life; he, or she, comes with a whole family background as part of the package. This means you must not only learn to love an individual who is diametrically opposed to yourself in terms of sexual polarity, but you also need to love and respect your partner's parents and a family that is different from your own. This may be even more difficult.

For example, imagine you are a Catholic man who has fallen in love with a Protestant woman. If you are loyal to your family and to your Catholic childhood and she is loyal to her Protestant family, then, even within the single Christian religion there will be differences of practice and belief systems which may make it hard for the pair to find common ground. This, in turn, will interfere with your chances of getting truly close to her.

Now, if you have children, there will be more difficulties. Your wife may want your child to follow her family's way; you, as the father, may want the child to see things the way your family sees things. If this happens, there will be constant conflict about how to educate your child.

To be able to come close to a partner and respect her, you will need to recognise and appreciate her background and belief-systems and perhaps come to value them as much as your own and, in order to do this, you will have to take distance from your own family. Both of you, to some extent, need to be able to step out of your family of origin and leave it behind.

Of course, this is a difficult step to take, because it means having to move away from your deep identification with your own family's values and your partner needs to take similar distance from her family. In this case, you, the Catholic man, would need to acknowledge that your partner's Protestant background is neither better nor worse than your own.

This is not as easy. Think telling your Catholic family that their values are neither better nor worse than those of a Protestant. It is likely to make you feel very guilty, because it will seem as if you are abandoning your own family and being disloyal to them.

Lorena, a Spanish woman, has two children with her Cuban ex-partner. Her intention in this session is to make peace with him in her heart - he left her and moved to the United States. At first, the session proceeds slowly, but when we put one person in the constellation to represent Spain and one for Cuba, things started to move. The representative for Cuba makes fists at Spain and, in response, Spain moves back. It becomes clear that Lorena's ex-partner identifies with Cuba; he carries the national resentment of all Cubans against Spanish colonial attitudes and history of conquest in the Caribbean. He left her because he could not stay with a Spanish partner - it would have made him feel too guilty towards his ancestors. Lorena now understands the dynamics of the situation and can deeply bow to Cuba, to all Cubans and can finally make peace with her ex-partner and honour him as the father of her children.

Recently, during a counselling session, I talked with a young Israeli woman who had a German boyfriend and was proposing to marry him. However, when her Jewish mother heard of her daughter's proposed marriage she cut off all contact and refused to either see or talk with her. Moreover, the young woman's Israeli friends sided with the mother and admonished her, saying, "What are you doing to your poor mother?"

Now, whichever way this young woman moves, she will be in difficulty - stuck between a rock and a hard place. Either she will marry and feel guilty towards her mother, or she will not marry and feel guilty towards her lover.

To be able to accept the separation from her mother and tolerate a degree of guilt will be a sign of great maturity. It is this quality of inner strength that is needed for any form of personal growth. By giving up the closeness to one's original family, one becomes more alone and centred in one's own being.

One inevitable conclusion from such situations is that, in order to be able to respect and be with your partner, you must be able to bear, or tolerate, a sense of guilt that comes as a result of moving away from your own family. The ability of each partner to leave the closeness of their original family effectively defines what is possible in terms of achieving closeness in their own relationship. This is usually clear from the very beginning, when they meet.

Negative Bonding is Stronger

In addition to positive attachment to the values we grew up with, there is also the possibility of a negative reaction to one's own family. Many people break away in pain and anger, openly opposing their family's values and even saying that those of other families are better. But, in terms of family dynamics, as we have described in an earlier chapter, a negative reaction towards one's parents usually indicates an even stronger bonding and, as a result, we may be unconsciously following our family's values more closely than those who did not break away. It's a law of paradox: what we oppose and do not want to become, we are most likely to become, because we are bound by what we reject. Anger is love upside down.

Respecting a Partner's Entanglement

Everyone, in one way or another, carries unresolved business from the family of origin. We all carry pains for our family members to a greater or lesser degree, or we identify with someone from our extended family, even without knowing about it. So when a man and a woman come together, they not only have to acknowledge the other person's family, they also have to acknowledge what the other person is carrying from that family, that he or she is probably entangled in some way.

This creates a limitation within the relationship, which will last as long as the original entanglement has not been dissolved. So each relationship has its possibilities and its boundaries, depending on how much we are tied to our family.

Whenever partners want to help each other overcome their entanglements, for example, by unconsciously offering themselves as a substitute for a missing parent, they in some way disrespect these boundaries. In an indirect way, they are disrespecting the partner and his love for his family of origin. Instead, we need to acknowledge what the other carries and what we carry and keep them separate.

Often, this is one of the basic difficulties in relationship: a man tries to solve with his woman something that has been left unsolved with his mother, while a woman may try to solve something with her male partner that can only be resolved with her father. The deeper reason for wanting to relieve a partner from pain is that we cannot tolerate it ourselves. When people comfort another, it is often not so much out of love, but because it reminds us of our own pain, which we ourselves do not wish to acknowledge.

We naturally want to be as close to our partner as possible, but a husband who is tied up with his mother cannot come very close to his wife, while a wife who is entangled with her father cannot come very close to her husband. Rather than trying to make a husband give up his ties to his mother, all a wife can really say is, "I respect your love for your mother". If he, in turn, projects his mother on her, she has the right to say, "I am not your mother," but she has no right to change him, or help him overcome this hangover.

In terms of family dynamics, we are not able to pull anyone else out of his or her entanglements, nor do we have the right to do so. The more we try, the more likely it is that the relationship will be destroyed. For example, the more Lorena tried to hang on her Cuban partner, the more angry he became, until finally he left. If she had simply acknowledged his love for his Cuban ancestors, without trying to involve herself, there would have been a much greater chance of him staying.

These kinds of complications come in many forms. On several occasions, I have talked with men who have been sent for counselling sessions by their wives. However, the wives are unaware that there is a built-in tendency in such situations for a man to sabotage such well-intended efforts by a wife to "straighten him out." Really, the wife is acting like a mother and therefore interfering in the man's relationship with his mother. So a man owes it to himself and his dignity to destroy this effort, thereby proving that his wife is not his mother.

Maturity in a relationship means being able to say to the other, "I see what you bring from your original family and I respect that. I won't attempt to change you or save you, or in any way try to make it different for you." In the same vein, one needs to be able to say to the other, about oneself: "This is what I bring with me from my family and what I need to do out of love for my mother and father. Please allow me to carry it without interference."

To accept one's own helplessness in the face of another's distress is often a difficult experience and many relationships run into difficulty in this area. But if we can accept each others boundaries, we can also feel how each love relationship is a great opportunity for personal growth. Much depends on how deeply we can see beneath the surface behaviour of our relationships and understand the family dynamics involved.

When partners find themselves in miserable relationships but are unable to separate, it is mostly because they project a parental figure onto the other. When we feel that we cannot live without the other, we are feeling like a helpless, needy child relating to a parent and we cannot see the love partner as an ordinary human being. Rather, this partner is seen almost as a demon, or a god, with total power over us, something quite inappropriate for a relationship of equals. In an ordinary relationship, without such projections, it may seem to be difficult to live without the other, but not impossible and in fact - when separation actually happens - it frequently comes as a surprise how easily we can move into being alone.

In a constellation session, it is sometimes helpful to remind a person about the ordinary nature of an adult relationship and to help them to come out of childhood projections by saying to the other partner, "I can live without you and you can live without me."

The Deepening Relationship

We have established the need to separate from one's original family in order to have a deepening relationship. By *deepening,* I mean a relationship where both partners develop and mature as a result of their mutual experiences and in order to understand how this works we need to look at the origins of the child-parent relationship and how the child develops into an adult.

In most tribal cultures, the growth of a young boy from childhood into manhood is marked by significant rituals and particularly at the time of puberty when authority over him is transferred from the mother to the father. After such ceremonies, the boy is no longer allowed to sleep in the same area as his female relatives; he has given up his intimacy with his mother and has been formally initiated into manhood and is not allowed to go back.

150

He is now a man and he has to enter the sphere of men. His initiation ceremony has made his father's male strength available to him and now he receives this paternal energy and takes it into himself as his own. This makes him a mature adult. Only as a mature adult is he ready to enter into a relationship with a woman.

In our modern Western society, rites of passage are less obvious, but they still exist. A boy may imitate a father who chops wood, tinkers with the mechanics of a motorbike or car and prepares fishing tackle to go to the local lake. These are superficial activities that mirror inner change and a way for a boy to take the father's strength and energy into himself.

For a girl, the process is different. The girl child also starts life close to her mother, but at a certain age, when she begins to mature, she moves towards the father whom she idealises and reveres. He becomes the focus of attention as the growing girl explores her awakening sexuality through her relationship with him - there is no actual sexual connection between them, but he is the first man in her life and it is natural that through him she will learn about male-female attraction. She even starts seducing the father, playing with male energy as embodied in him.

Yet despite this attraction, at a certain age she needs to give up closeness to her father and move back towards her mother. It is a kind of surrender to the mother, a recognition that her mother is her father's wife and that she must give up her childish love affair with him, if she is to claim her own potential as a woman.

She again honours the mother as the most important parent - this time, in a new way. Through her mother, she becomes grounded in her own feminine strength, receives female energy from her and embodies the essence of womanhood in her urge to seek a mate and become a mother herself.

So, for the boy, it is a single movement, away from the mother towards the father. For the girl, it's a double movement: away from the mother to the father and then back again to the mother.

Demonstrating Closeness in a Session

It is easy to demonstrate in a constellation how closeness to a mother or a father can disturb the relationship between two love partners. For example, a man and woman can be placed opposite each other to represent a couple and then the man's mother can be placed next to him, on one side, while the woman's father can be placed next to her. When we watch the representatives of the couple, it is usually easy to see their discomfort; to see how the man's energy is preoccupied with his mother and he is not really available to the woman, while, similarly, the woman's concern is with her father and she is not really interested in her man.

When, however, I place the man's father behind or next to him and the woman's mother behind or next to her, both immediately feel stronger and more interested in the love partner. They see each other more as man and woman and have more respect and attraction to one another. As an experiment, a whole line of men can be placed behind the man and a whole line of women behind the woman and the effect is a remarkable strengthening of the respective male and female energies.

This simple demonstration shows what is required for men and women to be strong enough to create a lasting relationship. A man needs to give up the closeness to his mother and move closer to his father and a woman needs to give up her father and come closer to her mother.

So, giving up the opposite-sex parent is one of the basic requirements for a deepening love affair. When they do this, the man becomes more connected to his maleness and

152

the woman becomes more grounded in her feminine qualities. Both of them learn from the same-sex parent what it is to fully embody their sexual identity.

Whenever I work with a client on this issue, it quickly becomes evident from the behaviour of the representatives where the problem lies and whether a person has been able to separate from his opposite sex parent, or has remained a 'mother's boy' or 'daddy's girl' - whether he, or she, has been able to honour the same sex parent or not.

If a woman cannot face a strong man, it indicates that she may need to turn to her mother and receive her energy before getting deeper into the relationship with her partner. This may take time and indicates to what degree one is prepared for a mature meeting between man and woman.

Coming close to a partner, one may begin to see how a certain strength is missing and then start to explore what needs to be received from the parents, especially in terms of coming closer to the same-sex parent, or taking more distance from the opposite-sex parent. In this way, one also sees how to move closer to a love partner and understands one's appropriate place within the relationship.

Exercise

This is an exercise of imagination to help the reader understand the effects of conscience and family guilt and the conflicts that arise as a result.

Make sure that you are sitting comfortably, in a quiet place and will not be disturbed for about 15 minutes. Close your eyes.

Imagine you are from a strict Catholic family, where your parents go to church every Sunday. Because you are now at university and are developing ideas of your own, your parents have reluctantly come to terms with the fact that you live a different kind of lifestyle from them.

Recently, you have fallen in love with a fellow student, someone you feel may become your ideal love partner. After meeting a few times, you discover that he or she is from a Jewish family, but it doesn't matter much to you.

Scenario 1:

After several weeks of being together, you want to introduce your new love partner to your parents and soon they invite you both to dinner one evening at their home. The day of the appointment arrives and you know that your mother or father will want to ask your lover some questions about himself or herself and his or her religion.

How does this feel?
Imagine yourself sitting at the dinner table.
How do you feel when you look at your parents?
How do you feel when you look at your lover?

Scenario 2:

You avoid talking about your parents and never want your lover to come near your parents' house.

As your relationship develops, ask yourself: how you feel when you visit your parents' home and they ask about your partner? How do you explain yourself?

Also, ask yourself: how you feel towards your lover, in relation to your future together? How do you see it working? How will you balance these two worlds you are trying to keep separate?

This exercise will help you gain an understanding of how conscience works and how our conscience towards our original family is frequently in conflict with our conscience towards our partner.

Chapter Twelve

Evolution of a Relationship

In general, a love relationship between a man and a woman widens over time from a narrow, laser-like focus to a broad expansiveness. In the beginning, the lovers are focused on one another and tend to forget the rest of the world. Each looks only at the beloved, feeling certain that this is the one person on earth who can bring him, or her, all that was ever wanted or needed

In this honeymoon state, drowned in the intensity of their feelings for each other, lovers regard other people as unwelcome intruders into their private world. They may lose interest in the details of daily life and become blind to any obstacles that lie in the path ahead of them. Lovers are so caught up with the other person that they feel what the other feels, wrestle with the other's problems and get involved in everything the other wants to be engaged in. They experience joy when the other is feeling joyful, distress when the other is distressed; they want to be with the beloved all the time, cannot get enough of them and often feel lost without them.

Ellyn Bader and Peter Pearson in their book *In Quest of the Mythical Mate* call this enmeshed stage of love relationship the "symbiotic stage" - the stage of union and identification with the beloved. If two people are going to form a bond and understand what it is to merge with the other, it is essential for them to move through this honeymoon phase of relating.

In this stage, we overlook differences and magnify similarities. We don't see the other as he or she really is, rather, we live in a dream. There are hidden bio-chemical reasons for this: while we are experiencing "true love" the body is busy releasing hormones that activate parts of the

155

brain responsible for gratification and de-activate those parts responsible for logical decision-making. In other words, romantic love is spurred on by a biological process; it is nature's way of keeping couples together long enough for childbirth and early nurturing, so as to insure the survival of the species.

We call it "falling in love," and in a sense it really is a kind of fall, because we tend to lose all sense of proportion, get lost in dreams, succumb to our biological drive and surrender to the forces of nature. This fall into love compels us to behave impulsively, often pushing us to make changes in our lives that no other force could have persuaded us to do, such as giving up a steady job, packing up all our things, saying goodbye to our family and moving to another country, just to be with the beloved.

However, even though we are driven by our biology, this does not mean that romantic love is without significance. After all, it may well be our first experience of dissolving as a separate "I." Falling in harmony with the lover is likely to be our first taste of giving up our ego boundaries, our psychological defences, our protective armour and merging into something larger than ourselves.

Love-making in this state can offer a mystical and ecstatic experience, bordering on the insights of Tantra, the Indian spiritual path which teaches that through deep sexual union both partners can obtain a glimpse of the eternal. In orgasm, we may enter an inner space of meditation which can be an encouragement to pursue individual spiritual growth long after the romantic phase of this particular relationship is over.

When the Honeymoon Ends

Waking up from the honeymoon stage of a love relationship can be an abrupt and disillusioning experience, especially when hormone balance is restored in the brain and the rational, decision-making process reasserts itself. Instead of looking through rose tinted spectacles, which see only the beautiful aspects of the beloved, we gradually become aware of each other's faults and defects. It can be tough to suddenly see that the one you loved so passionately is as full of human flaws as you are.

Sometimes the contrast is so drastic that you may be convinced that the other has changed, or perhaps deceived you in some way, or even betrayed you. This is the moment when people who are habituated to move from partner to partner usually bring the romance to an end, so they can have the opportunity at some future time to fall in love again and re-activate the experience that hormonal change generates.

On the other hand, this is also the moment when something more real and lasting can begin. It is only now that you actually start learning to love in a mature way. During the honeymoon stage, everything is easy because little is required of you; the body's biology is doing most of the work for you.

But now, you start meeting each other all over again, as if for the first time - acknowledging good sides and bad sides, beautiful and ugly aspects. Now you are exploring being together, growing more intimate with this stranger.

As a relationship moves beyond the honeymoon, partners start re-establishing their boundaries and noticing ways in which they are not alike. Bader & Pearson call this stage "differentiation." These authors liken the stages of a love relationship to the development of an infant who moves from a symbiotic attachment with the mother towards a sense of separate self, gradually taking more distance from the mother and voicing his own desires and preferences, which may be different from those of the nurturing parent.

Similarly, a healthy relationship needs to be able to develop to a point where it can contain a wide variety of conflict and differences. Partners have to learn to love each other's peculiarities and accept what they at first disliked. Hellinger has coined the expression 'love at second sight', which neatly defines this phase of relating. Love at second sight is not biologically motivated, therefore it is less passionate, less driven, less out of control. It may start with disappointment, but it is a personal achievement for both partners to get over this obstacle and take a conscious step towards a new level of harmony.

After "falling in love," we may call this stage "rising in love." We rise above our dreams, our disillusionment and differences, expanding our capacities to include in our hearts someone very different from ourselves. Now, you look at your partner freshly. You see him not as you would like him to be, but as he really is and this may also mean acknowledging the limits of what he can offer in terms of fulfilling your expectations. You become aware that some aspects of your life can be easily shared, but in others your partner is very different from you and togetherness in those areas may not be possible.

For many people this is too difficult a step to take, too big a challenge. They cannot bear to go through this discord and they deal with it by separating, or else turning the relationship into what Bader & Pearson call the "hostile-dependant couple," in which both partners dislike each other, blame each other for their unhappiness, but, not wishing to face life alone, compromise and agree to go on living together.

Expanding in Love

In order to continue, a love relationship has to grow in the direction of being more inclusive, not exclusive. It has to expand and embrace more people. One can see that when a relationship has matured, other people are no longer experienced as a threat to intimacy, but instead are invited to participate in it. After all, a relationship is designed by nature to provide the nurturing atmosphere for a child to grow and nothing is more "intrusive" than a new-born baby. When this new being enters the world of its parents, the seclusion and privacy they enjoyed as a couple is lost forever. Now the partners have brought someone else into their lives and the relationship has expanded.

This is why the arrival of a child usually helps a relationship to develop - the couple has found a new reason for being together. It has given them a common cause for their love and creativity, enabling them to move deeper into knowing each other. Partners without children often have a more difficult time to sustain this phase of a relationship. In order to keep growing and evolving, they may find it necessary to create a common project together, such as a joint business venture.

When a client places two representatives in a constellation to indicate the dynamics of a love relationship, each picture will indicate a specific situation. For example, if both are placed in a way that they are looking somewhere else, this may mean they are not so interested in each other, but are concerned about a third person, who may have to be brought into the picture - maybe a previous partner, or someone from the original family.

Typically, however, lovers will be placed looking at each other, standing opposite, because, as described earlier, their chief interest is themselves and they don't see anybody else. But this absorption with the other cannot last forever and if partners who have been together a long time are placed facing each other by a client, this may indicate that he, or she, is experiencing serious conflict within the relationship.

On the other hand, if they have become literally "partners" in the sense of joining together in a common project or goal, perhaps in parenting a child, or running a business, they will usually be placed next to each other, looking together in the same direction at someone, or something. In this way, they support each other and their focus is not the other any more, but something beyond them both.

When a couple's children are placed in a constellation, they are usually most happy and satisfied when they see their parents standing next to each other and they like to be close to them. If they see their parents standing opposite and facing each other, they often feel safer when they stand back and create some distance from their parents.

For example, in one constellation, the client placed his parents standing opposite each other and in serious conflict. The two children were placed quite close to the parents, almost in the middle between them and were clearly tense and unhappy in this position. The therapist led the children a few steps back from the parents and here they could breathe more deeply, look at each other and smile, experiencing a strong sense of relief. With the children out of the way, the parents were forced to look at each other and deal with something that, until this moment, they were able to avoid with the help of their children.

Acknowledging Limitations

One can describe the development of a relationship as moving from an initial state of fantasy towards a more down-to-earth attitude, meaning the relationship gradually becomes more rooted in reality. As previously mentioned, this can be a painful process, but it can also bring a welcome experience of relaxation, as both partners can now drop their efforts to make something work which is essentially an illusion – and after all, sustaining a high level of excitement can be a very tiring phenomenon.

Robert, a man in his mid-30s who is with a love partner,

160

comes for counselling because he finds that his woman is not as available as he had imagined she would be when they first met. He is reluctant to give up the high degree of expectation he felt during their honeymoon phase and now feels resentful towards her. During the course of the session, however, he notices that to deal with his frustration on his own, without constantly demanding the presence of the other, is bringing him an unexpected inner strength. He begins to understand that he has been projecting his mother onto his woman and as this projection dissolves he realises that she needs to lead her own life and this gives him the freedom to lead his life as well.

In this kind of situation, each person in a relationship has to discover afresh what he, or she, really wants and where there is common ground for togetherness. Where a couple has been talking of "we" before, they now start using "I" more frequently. In fact, there should be a certain balance between "we" and "I". There are things which a couple has in common, represented by "we" and there are things which belong to the individual alone, hence the need for "I". If couples talk only about "we" they are usually enmeshed with each other and entangled in issues from their original families and if they talk only about "I" they may be trying to keep each other at a safe distance, because both are afraid to lose their identities.

Both "we" and "I" need to be present in a healthy relationship, indicating the ability to merge and lose oneself and simultaneously the capacity to maintain one's own boundaries and an appropriate sense of separate identity. In an ideal situation, one could say that two integrated individuals who have found satisfaction in their own lives, have developed a bond that is equally nourishing as it is inspiring.

Of course, not every relationship develops in this way. If a man is still bonded to his mother, he may not have the strength to tolerate the fact that his wife does not seem to be fulfilling all his needs. Or, if a woman is still in love with her father, she may get disturbed if her man is not behaving like Prince Charming most of the time. In these kinds of situations, lovers often find partners that fit with each other: "Daddy's Little Princess" will meet "Mummy's Little Prince" and neither of them will be fully available to the partner.

On the other hand, if one of them starts becoming more mature within the relationship - let's say daddy's "little girl" starts to grow up and becomes more of a woman - then the other partner will also need to grow up if the relationship is to continue. It takes two to tango, as the old saying goes and each of us is 50% responsible for what happens within any love relationship.

Love as a dance is a beautiful metaphor. When one partner steps forward, the other must step backward; when one indicates a movement to his right, the other must move to her left in order to stay in harmony with him. So, between couples there is a constant interchange between self-assertion and surrender, advance and retreat, drawing a personal boundary and yielding to the other. This back-and-forth dance of energy needs to be a constant two-way motion if the relationship is to survive.

Whenever couples get together in relationship they will experience that their love has limitations. Once they accept these limitations, the relationship can function in a realistic and ongoing way. In addition, as each person resolves issues related to his, or her, original family, their mutual capacity to relate freely within the relationship will grow and their love can mature.

Claudia, a South American woman in her early thirties, is worried that her children are carrying her problems. In the constellation, she places her husband and herself next to each other and her two children just in front of them, but turned away from them, so they all stand like a group, looking in the same direction. Father and mother both feel uncomfortable.

After asking for more information, we learn that Claudia's mother was suffering from schizophrenia for 20 years. We place her mother in the constellation and Claudia immediately cries deeply and hugs her.

We put the children at the side of the couple, standing together, where they feel better. Now the parents face each other and Claudia's mother stands next to her. The husband feels confused and we learn that in his family his father had a schizophrenic brother. When we put his father next to him, he feels better, but cannot go very close to his wife.

When they both acknowledge what they carry for their parents, seeing that this entanglement does not allow them to come very close to each other, there is a new sense of balance and relaxation between them. They both agree to a certain distance, respecting the other and understanding what each does for his parent.

In another step, we invite Claudia to acknowledge her mother's suffering, to thank her and then take distance from her, in this way experiencing that she can let go of the feeling that she needs to help her mother. Claudia says to her mother, "What you did for me was enough and I thank you for it. I manage very well. I have two sons and I am very proud of them." Then she looks with pride at her sons, with a smile and without the previous worry that she is passing her problems to them.

Lopsided Love

In a relationship where both partners are living in dreams, there may, or may not be, a problem. But if one is dreaming and the other is becoming more alert and conscious, there will certainly be trouble. If they remain together, there are now two possibilities: Either the less mature partner will become inspired by the changes in the other and will want to develop himself, or the more mature one will start back-pedalling and compromising - the second option is more likely to happen if fear of separation is too great. True maturity, however, would mean that one becomes less afraid of separation, more ready to stand on one's own.

For a contemporary love relationship to work and be healthy it is clear that, after the honeymoon, the relationship itself should not be the primary concern in life for either partner, because this will place the other on too high a pedestal, which means you will expect a great deal from this person and also feel that you need to give a lot in return. Consequently, you will find yourself and your partner falling short of your expectations, creating a sense of continuous frustration that will destroy the relationship.

Putting it another way: the more you put a love partner above you, the more you are seeing him, or her, as your parent. Consequently, a relationship between two "extraordinary" people, who elevate each other, seeing themselves as Romeo and Juliet, or Prince Charming and Cinderella, probably won't last long, but two ordinary people with ordinary defects have a good chance to develop together.

If a client comes for counselling with the issue of separating from his love partner, the decision about what to do usually focuses on what is important for their growth. Is it better for them to stay together and pass through whatever difficulties they are currently experiencing? Should they try to develop skills to deal with conflict, gathering strength to stand alone, while staying within the marriage? Or should they acknowledge that each relationship is bound to end, sooner or later and accept the fact that their paths now lead in different directions - that they have outgrown each other?

Changing partners as soon as an obstacle arises is as

childish as clinging to each other when love has gone and both situations show an attachment to one of the parents. In many cases we see the man is clinging to his mother, or the woman to her father.

By its very nature, love is a changing phenomenon and the love between a man and a woman changes more than any other kind. The love between parents and children is biological and therefore more stable. It is not our choice; it is given by birth, so we are not free to change it. But the relationship between a man and a woman arises out of free choice. We have chosen it for ourselves and this is why it is so fragile, because the same mystery that brought us together can pull us apart at any moment. This fragility is one of the main reasons why love creates so much anxiety - something so fragile is easily broken.

The bottom-line for any love relationship must be: when we cannot grow in a relationship any more, this is the time for separation.

Acknowledging Former Partners

It is a great art to separate at the end of the love relationship without becoming angry or indulging in ugly behaviour. It means you are aware that things have changed, you both acknowledge and accept the new situation and agree to go your separate ways.

At this delicate time, it is important to see where your own responsibility lies for the break-up and to carry responsibility for exactly that amount, no more and no less. To carry less means to behave as a child and to blame the other for what has happened; to carry more means to take an unfair amount of responsibility and give the partner none, treating him like a child.

It is worth remembering that no future relationship will ever really work if you carry a hangover from the past. In the same way that you may cling to your parents in a negative way, blaming an ex-beloved is just a way to hold onto some kind of illusion - "if only he, or she, had behaved differently, we would still be together."

Lin Shu, a woman from Taiwan, has two children, a boy of 21 and a girl of 17, from her first husband and she now lives with them in second marriage, while still carrying resentment towards her first husband. In a pre-session interview, we learn that her mother committed suicide when she was ten.

When we set up the constellation, the first husband is out of the picture and therefore excluded, while the second man stands in the position as if he was the father of her children. The representative for the client stands like a child, next to her children and both her children and the man feel very uncomfortable.

When we bring the first husband into the constellation and place him in front of the whole group, everyone feels relief. In the work that follows, we help Lin Shu to acknowledge her first husband, whom she has been excluding and to take responsibility for not being available to him, due to the fact that she unconsciously wanted to follow her mother into death. This new understanding helps both the client and her first husband to open up to each other again and remove any residual blame for the way their relationship ended.

The next step is to help Lin Shu take responsibility as a mother, which is exactly what her own mother could not do - hence her suicide - and here we see how behaviour patterns tend to repeat from generation to generation. The daughter is, in effect, following the mother, in the same way that her mother followed some earlier member of her family.

In order to give strength to Lin Shu, we need to help her emerge from her anger against her mother and let her go with love and this becomes possible when she fully acknowledges her mother's own entanglement in her previous family. In the course of this process, we check regularly with the children to see if they are feeling any relief and whether they can start to trust their mother. The reaction of the children gives us a clear indication whether or not their mother is really able to be responsible and take care of them.

This constellation shows how a relationship can break up because of what one carries from the original family. Also, it makes it clear that the healing has to happen now, in the present and relief comes through acknowledging each partner's entanglement with the past.

Renée is a 42-year-old American woman who has been married and is now separated from her husband. Her daughter is 13 years old and stayed with her father after the separation. The husband already had three sons from a former marriage before coming together with the client. Renée was given for adoption by her own mother within four months of being born.

The placement of representatives shows that Renée's daughter is much too 'big' in this constellation and is angry with both her parents. She behaves towards her father like an angry lover, identifying with her father's first wife and also feels anger towards Renée, our client, for leaving her - thereby replicating Renée's feelings towards her own mother.

As the session progresses, we include the father's first wife, which relaxes the daughter, especially after the father acknowledges his love for this woman. Then the mother, our client, also honours this woman, acknowledging her as her husband's first wife: "I honour you as the first. Please look friendly at my daughter."

In another step, we help Renée to become reconciled with her birth mother by thanking her for giving her life and then taking distance from her by agreeing to her decision to give away her child. Then she can move towards the woman who is her adoptive mother. Looking at her own daughter, Renée says, "I kept you," and "I was also angry with my mother, at first." This gives her strength and helps the daughter to come out of her resentment towards Renée.

In the end, our client is able to look at her child with pride. Her daughter is now enjoying the feeling of standing close to her mother and it becomes clear that it would be better for the daughter to now live with her mother.

This case shows the importance of honouring a former partner and illustrates how both partners had an unfinished business that didn't allow the relationship to continue. We also see how a child in a family – Renee's daughter - identifies with a former partner of one of the parents. The former partner suffered a loss and the collective conscience tries to balance this, so a child of a later marriage feels drawn to represent the former partner and tends to behave like an angry or disappointed lover towards her parent.

Here, we see two reasons why Renee's relationship didn't continue:

1) Renee, as the second wife, feels loyalty to her husband's former partner and, as a result, doesn't allow herself to take him fully - this often happens when there are children from the first marriage.

2) She chose a man who is not fully available, mirroring the fact that she herself is not fully available, because she remained attached to her own birth mother, who gave her away. This also seems to be the reason why she didn't keep her daughter after the separation, because she was missing motherly strength.

The main work here for our client is to thank her birth mother and let her go. The other steps then become relatively easy: asking the first wife to be friendly towards her daughter, thanking the man for having a child from him, acknowledging the fact that both of them were not fully available and finally becoming ready to support her child as a mother.

Separating Peacefully

In order to separate peacefully and with love from a former partner, a client needs to find a way to feel grateful towards this person. This becomes possible if the client can acknowledge what happened in the relationship in a truthful and realistic way and is ready to take responsibility for his, or her, share of it. If truth is expressed, if facts are seen as they are, this will be a relief for both partners, as we saw in the above examples.

In other cases, I may ask a client to say to a former partner, "I am grateful for the time we spent together and I thank you for what you gave me - it will stay with me. And whatever I gave you, I gave with love and it's yours to keep. I leave your responsibility for what went wrong between us with you and I carry my own responsibility with me. Now I let you go and you, please, let me go, too."

At other times, I may ask the person to say, "I honour what guides you and I honour what guides me," referring to a larger force that moves our life in a certain direction, or perhaps referring to entanglements within the original family.

Sometimes, I invite the client stand in front of his former partner and spontaneously feel what needs to be expressed in order to honour the love that once existed between them. The response from the stand-in for the former partner gives us an indication as to whether the client is being sincere. If a former partner feels recognised, he is usually ready to let go of any attachment and move out of the picture.

This is a loving way to separate. These experiences show us that a loving attitude can continue between former lovers even after they have gone their own ways - love has nothing to do with being together or apart. Being in a relationship and being in love are not synonymous, and this shows itself in a relationship between separated parents: they have had children, so they will always be strongly bonded, even though they are no more in a relationship. Experience from many sessions shows that it is possible to fully separate only when love has been acknowledged. In other words, real love gives freedom.

Chapter Thirteen

Having Children

The evolving relationship between a man and a woman is pushed by their natural instincts towards having children. Nature's most basic impulse is towards sustaining life and ensuring the survival of the species, so it wants men and women to meet and bond in order to create new life... in other words, to have babies.

It is the bonding between man and woman that ensures the welfare of the child, which is why such a powerful, cohesive force is related to sex, not to love. The bonding ensures that both mother and father will stay together long enough to provide for the new child, who cannot survive on his own, who depends on the nurturing atmosphere provided by the parents.

It is not just the child who grows in this environment. The child also helps his parents to grow, in the sense that they are required - simply by the arrival of a new member in their family - to include another person in their relationship, to expand and go beyond themselves; beyond what they personally want, like or dislike. Their decision to have a child, or several children, will shape their whole lives. They let themselves become a vehicle of a bigger life force, and by agreeing to all the consequences of this decision they can grow beyond personal boundaries and gain strength.

Love partners who decide not to have children do not experience the same biological push to expand, but they can attain to a similar expansion and strength in other ways, such as devoting themselves to a major project, or to a spiritual path. The key motivation is that they are ready to devote themselves to something beyond their personal desires – maybe something they feel deep in their hearts –

and let themselves be guided by this. Then they also expand.

When we looked at the parent-child relationship in previous chapters, it was from the child's standpoint. Now we look at the same phenomenon from the parent's point of view. In a way, it is the same perspective: a child has to be a child, a parent has to be a parent, so the same Family Constellation laws apply. But the challenge in being a parent is very different. A parent is required to stand in his or her own strength and take responsibility for being a father or a mother, which means giving unconditionally to the child. When this happens, a child is at ease and does not need to carry anything for his parents; he can simply receive what his parents give him. In this way, over time, he will become full and then, as an adult himself, he will be able to pass on to his children whatever has been given to him. This is the natural cycle of sustaining life from generation to generation and nature's way of safeguarding the species.

On the other hand, if parents have children mainly for other reasons, such as, for example, a desire on the part of a woman to catch a particular man through becoming pregnant by him, as a way of binding him to her, or if one or both partners want to have children as a way of avoiding a sense of meaninglessness in life, then the chances are that they themselves are missing something from their parents. As a result, they will want to receive from their own children what they have missed when they themselves were children.

As we have seen, children are very sensitive to the needs of their parents and, out of a deep and powerful instinct to belong, are ready to do anything for them. So they will try to give to their own parents, which means they will not be in their rightful place as children, according to family order. In this way, they remain empty and then, as grown ups, they will want to receive from their own children and so on.... In this way, the burdens of the past are passed on from generation to generation.

When parents accept their responsibilities and are able to experience their own strength as givers, they will feel comfortable in their roles as mother and father and their parental duties will come easily to them. They will not worry much about being a good mother or father, they will find fulfilment in giving to their child and, as a result, the child will usually be content and undisturbed. When, however, parents continuously worry about being good enough, then the child is bound to sense this and will also feel insecure and uncomfortable.

Another significant point to remember is that a child essentially receives half his gifts from his father and half from his mother. In this sense, the child embodies both parents. This means that, when a parent loves a child fully, he must at the same time love the other partner, because the partner is present in the child whom he loves. One cannot hate one's partner and truly love a child who is the outcome of a sexual meeting with this partner.

When, in a previous case study, a woman says, 'marrying this man was a mistake', one consequence of her attitude is that she also expresses dislike for her own child. This is one of the implications of a relationship in which love has not been acknowledged and it has to be made evident to clients who come to Family Constellation sessions with these kinds of problems. We have examined in the last chapter how children represent former partners of the parents and this is because some acknowledgment of love is still missing.

The reason why every child wants his parents to be together is that he feels whole; he doesn't need to divide his loyalties. Of course, this does not mean parents should never separate, but it certainly means that, if they truly love their child, they will keep feeling a sense of love and gratitude to their ex-partner. Then a child is at ease, even if his parents do not continue in their love relationship - we saw examples of this in the last chapter.

Another important point is that by having a child, a man and woman say the final good-bye to their own parents, because they themselves are now taking on this role. If they do not take this step, they are not really available as parents to their children and consequently the children may get pulled into taking over destinies of their parents' original family.

Patricia, a client from Sydney, Australia, is a mother of two daughters. When we put up her present family in the constellation, her daughters are looking at something, or someone. One looks down, one looks up and both look away from the mother, who is looking at them.

Asked what happened in her original family, Patricia tells us that her mother and father both lost two sisters early. When we bring in these dead aunts and lie them on the floor, both of Patricia's daughters feel very much drawn to them.

As the session progresses, we find that the client's mother wanted to follow her two sisters into death. But her child, Patricia, is saying, "I do it in your place," and the client's daughters are now saying to her, "We do it in your place".

At this point, Patricia is not ready to leave her mother with the pain she suffered at the loss of her two sisters; the client remains determined to try and help her mother, even when the consequence is clear that her two daughters are being drawn towards the dead and are unable to fully live their own lives.

After seeing this dynamic and the client's inability to go further, we interrupt the constellation.

At a later time, we are able to continue the work and can complete the movement that has been started. Patricia is now ready to bow to her mother, honour her and let her go to her dead sisters, saying, "I let you go to your sisters and I will stay with my children." Now she finds strength to face her children, telling them, "I am your mother and I stay with you." She is able to resist her tendency to collapse into crying, which has been her pattern throughout the two sessions and is now happy to embrace her daughters.

We see here the conflict of a mother, torn between her own mother and her children. Finally, it is the love for her children that helps her say good-bye to her mother and remain with them, as a mother in her own right. So, being a parent can help people become mature and leave behind an entanglement with a member of the original family, becoming an integrated person.

In this way, having a child can be a challenge. It can make you face unresolved issues in your family system, coming to terms with reality and help you find your own resources for parenting, caring and nurturing. It can be an invitation for you to take distance from attachments to childish ways and help you become mature. It all depends on the individual and whether or not he, or she, can rise to the challenge.

One significant implication of these family system laws is that parents need to take responsibility for making certain decisions and act on behalf of their children without feeling the need to consult with them. These days, we often see examples of parents who are unable to decide, because they lack a certain strength and integrity, so they ask the children what they want, thinking that this is helpful for the child, when in fact they are simply indicating a lack of parental strength and responsibility.

This is a delicate point. We are not advocating any authoritarian education system here, nor a return to the days when "children should be seen and not heard," but social trends swing from one extreme to the other, from pro-authoritarian to anti-authoritarian and back again. When parents take a decision, it should be truly in favour of the child and one of the things that becomes obvious in a constellation is whether the parents see only themselves and their own problems – being entangled in the past - or whether they can actually see the child and act responsibly.

Children are usually too young and immature to make life-affecting choices and, if they are consulted, everything depends on whether they are really capable of understanding the issue and making a genuine choice. For example, if the parents are separating, a child should generally not be asked to take a decision as to which parent he wants to live with. It is like asking a child: "Whom do you love more?" putting him in an impossible situation.

If the parents decide with whom the child should live, he can remain innocent and can continue to love both his parents equally. To ask your daughter whether she prefers to go with you, or with her father, is a very disturbing situation for a child of any age. Parents usually resort to this strategy when they cannot come to an amicable agreement between themselves. Yet how can a child be expected to decide something so momentous? Intrinsically, a child loves both her parents. If she is forced to follow one of them outwardly, then inwardly she will follow the other.

An extreme example of this would be a situation in which a boy's father is a criminal and the mother prevents him from seeing his father to make sure that he will not become like him. In this case, the boy may seem to follow his mother by not having contact with his father, but may develop delinquent behaviour at school as a way of expressing his love for his excluded father.

Separating with Children

We have talked about the problems of couples separating. If there is a child, the bond between partners is going to be a strong one and separation will be more difficult. Yet we all know that many couples reach a point where they need to go their separate ways, however hard and painful it is and it is their right and freedom to do so.

For the welfare of the child, the biggest hazard is that parents often separate with feelings of acrimony, bitterness and blame, sometimes cutting all ties with each other and in this way laying a heavy burden of anguish on a child, whose loyalties to his mother and father are now hopelessly divided.

In this traumatic situation, the obvious is overlooked: each child is the product of both parents. However bitter the split, however much distance the man and woman put between each other, each child will remind the parents of their former partner. A child, in essence, is the outcome of the love between a man and woman and will remain so even when all love has died between them.

What many couples deny and are unable to accept, is that their mutual love continues in the child. When a father looks at his little boy, or girl, on some level he also sees his former wife. He cannot say, as many divorced fathers do, "I love my child, but I hate my ex-wife." As far as family system therapy is concerned, if you hate your ex, you cannot fully love your child. This is why it is essential, for the maximum well-being of the child, that parents separate with love.

Law courts decide custody cases using different criteria, but in Family Constellation we tend to say that the child, as a general rule, should stay with the parent *who is most able to love the former partner* - the one who can look at this child and through him wholeheartedly receive the presence of the other parent, feeling some residue of love and gratitude for what has been shared in the relationship.

It is often, but not always, the woman who is most angry after separation. From this standpoint, in a custody case where the mother is still angry with her former husband, a child is likely to be safer and more content with the father than with the mother. However, each case has to be examined on its merits, taking into account the specific nature of each entanglement with the family of origin and its effect on each of the parents. As a general rule, children are safer with the less burdened parent and this is true whether the parents are separated or not.

A Spanish woman is divorced from her husband and there are two sons from their union. During the constellation session, we discover that her mother's father was shot by a firing squad in the civil war and that she identifies with the person who shot her grandfather. After seeing and understanding her entanglement, she is then able to honour her ex-husband and say, "I am sorry, I could not stay with you". In this case the children are safer with their father.

A man, whose father and grandfather were part of the Mafia is married with two children. It shows in the constellation that his children identify with the victims of the mafia. The safer place for them is with their mother.

The age of a child is also an important factor to be taken into account. Obviously, a small baby has to remain with its mother.

A child is less burdened whenever the father can say, "When I look at you, I remember how much I loved your mother;" or when the mother can say, "If you become like your father, it is perfectly okay with me." As long as these things can be felt and expressed with equanimity, the child will feel relaxed and relatively happy.

Who is the Client?

When we work with these issues in a constellation, we need to be clear from the start with whom we are working - are we working with a client who has an issue of entanglement with his parents, or is the client a parent and has a question about his, or her, child?

In the first case, we have to take the responsibility away from the child and give it to the parent, allowing the child to be unburdened and innocent. But if, for example, a mother comes as client and has a question about her children, then we have to help her acknowledge and accept her own strength as an adult woman, taking responsibility for herself and not burdening her child.

So it is important to know who is the client, because the session will manifest differently depending from which side we are approaching the constellation. During the course of a session we have observed that usually the reconciliatory movement between parents and children has to start from the child. The child has to go to his parent. If it is the parent who wants to move towards his child, it usually means that he wants something and this means he is in danger of burdening his child.

A man goes to his son with tears and crying; they hug each other. From the man's behaviour, it is clear that he himself is behaving like a child, not like a grown up. When we put his father behind him, he immediately stops crying and feels stronger. His son relaxes.

Sibling Rivalry

It is common to find clients coming for a session to sort out problems with a brother or sister. What we see many times in constellations is that conflict between siblings actually belongs to their parents, or to some other relative.

179

A conflict between earlier family members is being played out by the children who have identified with someone from the extended family; they are not in their 'rightful' place; they are entangled.

We can sometimes ease a conflict of this sort by helping siblings find their place in the hierarchy - the family order. But if the conflict persists, it usually means that the identification runs deeper. For example, a conflict between sisters can sometimes be eased if their mother is brought into the picture. If this doesn't help, it means one of these sisters cannot honour the mother, instead, she takes the mother's place and her siblings are not comfortable with that and are resisting it. If the original conflict can be resolved in a constellation session, then the sister can return to her rightful place in the family order and harmony will be restored.

A healing sentence for one sister to say to the other may be, "Even though I am a little older/younger than you, I am only your sister. We are both children." In this way, they remind each other that, as children of the same parents, they are actually in the same boat.

It also happens that a child wants to follow a brother or sister who died early; or feels she must replace a dead sibling in the family nexus. The solution may be to bring the forgotten child into the picture and invite the client to acknowledge and honour him. Sometimes it is healing for the living sibling to say to the one who died, "You are my dear brother/sister and you left a little early, but I remember you with love. Please be friendly if I stay on a little longer. I will join you when my time has come."

Chapter Fourteen

Dimensions of Love

We have talked about love and relationship as an exchange of giving and taking between partners. However, love has many dimensions and operates on different levels and in this chapter we look at the various ways love manifests in our lives.

Sex

The first and most basic dimension of love is sex. Sex is an animal energy and the foundation of life. Sexual desire is connected with the survival of the species and naturally plays a significant role in the man-woman relationship. It is a strongly felt biological urge of the body, just like eating and sleeping. A sexual encounter creates a bond between couples and, as we said before, if sex is accompanied by love, this bond is stronger.

Sex without love is an exchange of energy, a give-and-take situation, but does not require any gratitude or respect for the other partner and this sometimes reveals itself in constellation sessions as a form of mutual exploitation – the other person is used to fulfil the biological need of the body. If this is the truth of the situation, it needs to be acknowledged, rather than pretending to be in love or creating any kind of illusion in the other partner. Usually, in their hearts, both partners know what is happening, may secretly agree to it and if this is openly admitted they will start to relax.

Sometimes, people carry a blaming attitude for a sexual encounter, claiming that the other partner only wanted sex and are unwilling to accept their share of responsibility for what happened between them. In a situation like this, the facilitator may invite one partner in a constellation to say to the other, "I used you," making it clear that he was only interested in his sexual pleasure, while the other answers, "and I allowed you to use me." This can bring clarity, helping one partner to come out of the victim role and the other to come out of shame and guilt. Both partners wanted their sexual pleasure fulfilled, which is perfectly satisfactory so long as it is acknowledged for what it is, without condemnation or expectations of anything more.

Acknowledgment of the facts, seeing things as they are, creates a sense of balance and mutual responsibility between two partners. In this way they express a certain respect for each other, which, by the way, also means that their relating gains an extra dimension and is now more than purely sexual – respect being a form of love.

In terms of family dynamics, denial and blame are not helpful outcomes of any sexual event and even a brief or shallow affair needs to be seen and honoured for what it is.

Love

When we go beyond the biological level, love is a psychological need and an experience of the qualities of the human heart, including care, sensitivity and gratitude towards the other. Without love, we would feel alone and isolated in the world. On this level, love is a give-and-take relationship, an exchange between two people that is carried out with respect and gratitude. With love, we do not relate to the other as an object, but as a whole human being.

If two people involved in a sexual relationship are also in love with each other, they are bound to feel gratitude towards the other. They not only become aware of their own needs, but also those of the partner. They give to the other what he needs and receive from him what they need. So the readiness to show one's need to the other is important at this level of love. This is not the need of a child, who needs from a parent, but that of an adult, who is aware of his incompleteness as a man or woman.

Love, like sex, is a mutual exchange of energy, but with the added dimension of the heart, including qualities like intimacy, trust and respect. I am grateful to my partner for receiving my gifts and I am grateful to him for sharing his gifts with me, giving us both a sense of closeness, harmony and a sense of being at home in the world.

In therapy, we deal mostly with this level of love - how love is expressed in relationships. The Family Constellation notion that 'love has to follow order' takes into account the different nature of relationships between parents and children and between partners. But relationship is not an end in itself; it is a means to learn about love; a life-lesson in loving and being loved. When our relating is combined with understanding and awareness, it has the potential to teach us about love so completely that we may learn about a state of love-without-object, that of a loving friendliness. When love is unaddressed and is open to everyone, it has become compassion.

Compassion

Mystics talk about a higher dimension of love, which can best be described as compassion. Compassion is not a give and take relationship; it is all giving and there is no expectation of getting anything in return. In fact, it is not really a relationship at all. Compassion is a state of being, an overflow of love and the purest form of sharing.

In ordinary love, we feel grateful that the other partner is giving to us, while in compassion a person is grateful when the other receives. In this way, compassion is a form of unconditional love. It requires nothing and is therefore not bound by any urge to balance out mutual needs; there is no contract, no fixed arrangement, no expectations; it transcends gender differences and has nothing to do with being a man or woman, nor with two people falling in love. Compassion is love in its purest form, unattached to blood lines or gender.

This means that compassion is really beyond any relationships that we are examining in family system therapy, but still, it is worth noting here, because it is recognised as the highest form of love and is significant precisely because it goes beyond family dynamics.

Compassion is not something unknown to ordinary people. Even in our daily lives, most of us have experienced moments of unconditional love, instances of giving where there is no expectation of receiving anything in return, giving from an abundant overflow for no other reason than the joy of sharing.

I mention these three states – sex, love, compassion - to make it clear that love has many dimensions and cannot be completely defined by theories and concepts. Our capacity to create theories about life comes from the logical, rational aspect of the human mind, which, by its very nature, seeks to explain everything in practical terms and is intimidated by things which it cannot reduce to a formula. Seen from this perspective, our ideas and theories about relationships, including Family Constellation, cannot explain everything there is to know about love; the containers they offer for comprehension are just too small.

Relationship dynamics provide important insights, but love itself is and will always remain, a mystery, so when we discuss relationship in constellation sessions we need to be aware of this. Many times, as an outsider, we can only stand back and look on with amazement at the immensity of the love that moves people. It is impossible to define it, or make sense of it. But fortunately we don't even need to try; it is enough that it should manifest and express itself in our lives.

Learning about Ourselves

Another problem with relationship theory is that it tends to ignore other dimensions of personal growth. For example, I find myself having to contradict some of Bert Hellinger's statements, in which he says that, in order for a relationship to work, a man has to be a man and not develop his female qualities and a woman has to be a woman and not develop her male qualities.

This is true only within a certain frame. It can apply to an ordinary relationship, which is held together by mutual needs and where the bonding between a man and a woman is desirable. But this leaves aside any further development of these two partners and the desire they may have to explore deeper layers of themselves.

C. G. Jung was the first Western thinker to discover that each person has a male and female psychological aspect. A man usually identifies more with his male side, while his female side remains hidden in the unconscious part of his mind, but this hidden element is mirrored back to him by the women who come into his life. In fact, in many ways, the imprint of his inner woman dictates the choices of the kinds of women to whom he is attracted. Similarly, a woman usually identifies more with her female side, while her male side remains unconscious and is mirrored back to her through her male partners.

Jung's theory is now widely understood and there are many types of courses, including those dealing with Tantra, which help a man discover and explore his "inner woman," and a woman to become acquainted with her "inner man." The primary aim of such Tantric explorations is to widen the experience of love-making for both partners, giving them a taste of what the other is naturally experiencing as a member of the opposite sex. It also makes it easier for people in relationships to understand their partners - how they think, what they want, what they experience.

I don't want to discuss the whole psychology of male and female polarity here, but I feel it is necessary to show that there are models of human dynamics that depict different aspects of self-understanding and also different dimensions of the man-woman relationship. Through Family Constellation, we come to understand a certain aspect of relationship, which is perfectly valid, but it is not the whole story.

In all relationship work, we are really learning about ourselves through being related to others. The need for the other reflects a need to get in touch with disowned aspects of our individuality, to become whole in ourselves. So, through the other we are really relating to ourselves, learning to love and own all that has been suppressed, hidden and unexplored.

Once we have been able to become fully integrated individuals, our dependence on other people becomes less, or perhaps even disappears. Then love has a different quality; it is no more a need, or an attachment. So, two things are necessary for our development: acknowledging our need for the other and enjoying the challenge of an intimate relationship, while and at the same time growing in understanding and love to a point where it is no more a relationship in the usual sense.

Chapter Fifteen

Special Topics:
Incest, Abortion, Adoption, Homosexuality, Love Triangles

Some readers may be disturbed by this chapter because it offers controversial insights into events that may occur in the original or present family, including incest, abortion, adoption, homosexuality and love triangles.

One of the problems in dealing with such issues, which are difficult enough for people to experience by themselves, is that they are surrounded by moral attitudes, opinions and perspectives that cloud and confuse events that have always been part of human life. People who take a moral position have fixed ideas about how things ought to be and are incapable of seeing events clearly because their preconceived attitudes get in the way. In fact, rather than helping, moralists are usually the very people who make it impossible for people to find genuine solutions to life's difficulties and this in turn contributes to further alienation, unhappiness and more unresolved problems.

In Family Constellation therapy, if we want to understand these situations and be of assistance to clients, we need to leave behind all moral attitudes, ideologies and belief systems and abandon any notions about what is good and bad. When we say that some act or event has certain consequences, we are referring to consequences we can observe in a constellations session: we see the problem, we see what it leads to and we see what steps result in relief and resolution for the client. In other words, this is an entirely pragmatic approach, aimed at benefiting the client. It is not meant to be a final word on how any individual, or society in general, should deal with these issues.

This chapter will give only a brief summary of the family dynamics behind each topic, as a way of introducing these issues. It is not possible to cover each area in detail here – whole books have been written on these subjects – and there is no fixed solution covering all possible situations.

Incest and Sexual Abuse

There are many variations of abuse, depending on the degree of the abuse and who did it. In general, we can say that whenever a female client comes to a constellation session with a personal history of sexual abuse or incest in the immediate family, the therapist can usually observe two things going on: there is the obvious perpetrator, the father; and behind the scenes there is the hidden perpetrator, the mother. Acknowledgment of a mutual, unspoken agreement between the father and mother may provoke objections from those who feel that to implicate the mother and make her partially responsible will excuse the father's behaviour and allow him to escape from the full weight of his responsibility.

This reaction is understandable, but if it results in a decision to ignore the mother's role then it is not going to be helpful in bringing a client to a state of resolution and healing. What we see in constellation sessions dealing with this issue is that the mother either has a tendency to leave her present family, or is not sexually available to her husband, or both. It is often the case that the mother is carrying something from her original family that pulls her away from her husband, so there is an imbalance in the relationship - the woman cannot, or is not willing, to give herself equally in the relationship and, as a result, she may reject her partner sexually. In order to balance this tendency, she unconsciously offers her daughter instead.

Natasha is from a Russian family, living in London and has been sexually abused as a child by her father. In the constellation, the mother looks away, not seeing her husband or child. The father looks at his daughter, but not as if she is a child, rather, he feels a sexual attraction towards her. The dynamic indicates that because the mother is not available as a partner, the daughter has to step in, which creates the incestuous relationship between the client and her father.

From the interview, we get an idea why the mother is being pulled away. Her grandparents and previous family were Jews who had to escape from Russia during the pogroms at the end of the 19th century. The mother seems to carry a deep longing for Russia, for her family and also a continuing resentment about what happened there.

When we place the grandparents and a person representing Russia in front of the mother, she feels better and eventually is ready to turn around and look at her child, our client. This comes as a great relief for Natasha, as now she no longer needs to take her mother's place.

The solution sentences reflect the original dynamic that led to incest. She says to her mother, "I took your place out of love for you." And to her father "I did it out of love for my mother." This helps her to come back to the position of a child, who is innocent and acts out of love for her parents and in this way she can leave all feelings of responsibility to them.

This is typical of dynamics in Family Constellation sessions dealing with issues of sexual abuse and shows why a daughter enters into an incestuous relationship: the representative for the father feels sexual attraction towards the daughter, while the representative for the mother looks the other way. Since we are using stand-ins who are not related to the client and who have no personal investment in the way a session develops, we can conclude that this indicates a general pattern in such cases, implying, as already noted, an unstated mutual contract between the parents, in which the daughter is offered as substitute for the mother.

So both parents are equally responsible: the father being the obviously guilty party and the mother being the undercover guilty party. Usually, the father is the one who is condemned for acts of incestuous child abuse and the less obvious role played by the mother and her degree of guilt is too often ignored.

By way of resolving the situation, we need to bring to light how the child became involved out of love for the mother and when this happens it usually re-establishes contact between mother and daughter. In this way, the daughter is relieved of her burden of replacing the mother and she can again become a child. Usually, at this point, the interest of the father in her as a sexual partner also subsides. After all, the father really wanted the mother as a sexual partner and the daughter was serving as a substitute.

When these dynamics are revealed, it becomes easier for the client to move beyond the anger, hurt and guilt that she feels towards her father and she can leave the responsibility and guilt with him for having wronged his own daughter. If the client remains locked in anger, or in a feeling of guilt, she is in fact carrying negative consequences for something that was not her doing - it was something her father did.

To remain angry will create more difficulties for the client and ultimately prevent any solution. First of all, anger is a very binding attachment between two people and secondly it will prevent acknowledgment of the sexual bonding that happened with the father, making future sexual relationships difficult.

As we said before, the first sexual connection creates a strong bond, which needs to be acknowledged if later sexual relationships are going to succeed. If an abused daughter stays locked in her negative attitude towards her father and continues to blame him, there can be no acknowledgment of this bond and no resolution. Ultimately, this means she will be unable to get over the trauma and move to another partner. This is often the reason why, where clients have suffered incest or other sexual abuse, they have difficulty with later relationships.

Another point to consider is that, in spite of the obvious wrong that has been done to her, the daughter may have derived some form of pleasure from the incestuous relationship with her father and there may also have been a quality of love involved, however distorted. When the client stays in an attitude of blame and condemnation towards the perpetrator, she cannot allow herself to recognise this, which again makes it difficult for her to fully enjoy other sexual relationships.

Initially, a client may even be offended by the suggestion that there could have been anything pleasurable in the experience. However, it is a dynamic that has been observed in many constellation sessions dealing with this issue and should not be avoided.

Therapy that validates a client's anger, that sympathises and supports this emotion as the rightful response to an incestuous paedophilic perpetrator, the father, may prevent the client from arriving at a solution. An angry catharsis, releasing emotions that have long been held back, may be helpful as an initial step, but cannot be seen as a final resolution.

The solution in a constellation session may lie in inviting the daughter to tell her mother, "I did it out of love for you," and to tell her father, "I did it out of love for my mother." And then to say to both the parents, "I am only a child. I am innocent. I leave the responsibility and the guilt for what happened with you."

The abused child's innocence has to be restored and her position as a child in the affair needs to be reaffirmed.

When this has been clarified and resolved, the client is free to leave behind any residual anger she feels towards her father.

Another way for the client to address her father would be to say to him, "What you did was wrong. I am only a child. Now I will leave the responsibility and the guilt for what you did with you and I let you carry the consequences of it." It is important, however, that this is said in a calm and neutral way, without anger or blame and without thinking of oneself as a victim. If this equanimity is not present, it means there is still something incomplete to be addressed and understood.

For a therapist, the challenge in such cases is to avoid falling into the role of a sympathetic ally in the client's hostility towards the perpetrator. If he lets this happen, the therapist loses any possibility of helping his client. While always having the client's best interests at heart, a therapist nevertheless has to resist taking sides in his client's problems. When we suspend judgment, stay neutral and observe a situation with the client's true welfare at heart, solutions appear more easily and clearly.

The therapist also needs to recognise that a child deep down wants to belong to both parents, no matter what and instances like these show us the enormous power of this family bond. We may consider the parents to be cruel, or violent, or unworthy to bring up a child, but from the child's viewpoint it doesn't matter what her parents are like; they are her parents.

Abortion

It is not an abortion itself that creates after-effects, but how a woman deals with it. As we have seen in Family Constellation generally, it is never the event in itself - whether abortion, crime, or early death - that creates entanglement in a family system, but a person's unconscious way of dealing with it, or, rather, trying to avoid dealing with it. Typically, this means not fully acknowledging and taking responsibility for an event, for the pain of separation and this creates a hangover - something left incomplete

In constellation sessions where abortion is an issue, it is apparent from the responses of those representing the unborn child that he is usually in agreement with his fate and is not so much concerned about being not allowed to come into life, but wants to be recognised as a child of these parents.

This demand for recognition is a basic theme in Family Constellation dynamics: just as it is important to honour all our sexual partners, whoever they may have been, it is important to honour all the children we have conceived, including those who died at an early age, children sent for adoption, unborn children, those aborted or stillborn. All conceptions need to be recognised.

In order to create resolution and healing, Bert Hellinger has suggested a simple, but powerful ritual to acknowledge what happens in the case of abortion. A representative for the aborted child is asked to sit in front of the mother and the mother looks at him, puts her hand on his head and says something like, "I am your mother, you are my child. I took everything, you gave everything. Now I give you a big place in my heart." Usually, this brings the mother in touch with her grief, which most likely she has not felt before in a conscious and deliberate way. The father can also do this ritual.

During the session, it will become obvious whether or not the mother can take responsibility for what has occurred, or whether she remains frozen, or tries to find excuses, or behaves in some way like a child herself - any of these reactions is a way of not taking responsibility. Sometimes we can find a way to give the mother sufficient strength to face her child and acknowledge his fate, by placing her own mother behind her.

Once the mother has acknowledged her child, she can look at her partner and together they can acknowledge each other's responsibility. Then, after a period of grieving, which may last some time, the mother needs to let go of the child and allow him to find his peace.

An important aspect of this kind of session is to check whether the mother, or father, is sincere. As a facilitator, one can feel this from the quality of a parents' grief and from the response of the stand-in who is representing the child. As I mentioned in an earlier chapter, when we work with parents, we test the truth of what they say, or do, through the response of their children. If the child feels relief, it is usually genuine; if the child doesn't feel anything, then the parents are not being honest, or are not able to take responsibility as a parent at this moment.

What we see from sessions of this kind is that abortions are significant events in the family system and need to be acknowledged as such. Healing can occur through a client feeling love for the unborn child and recognising its sacrifice. A client, who, out of guilt, tries to explain why there was no other choice, is refusing to recognise her part in the affair. Rationalising is a subtle way of not wanting to take responsibility, not wanting to feel the pain of loss.

Hellinger's opinion on this issue used to be that abortions are a private matter concerning the two adult partners and do not affect their children. Later, he reversed his opinion, saying that other children of the couple are also affected. In my opinion, the impact on other children will depend on how many abortions a couple has had, in which month of pregnancy a termination took place and how painful or traumatic the experience was for the woman.

When one or other of the partners favours having an abortion, at a biological level he, or she, is saying 'no' to the fulfilment of the sexual relationship and in some way this means he, or she, is a saying 'no' to the other partner. This is the reason why, in the majority of cases where abortion occurs, the relationship does not pick up where it was before and often comes to an end. Usually, one can see that an abortion was the point where the relationship actually ended, even if partners stay together after it.

Abortion is always a discontinuation of a relationship. If partners stay together afterwards, they are beginning a new relationship and, as we discussed earlier, a new relationship can work only if what went on between the partners previously has been successfully resolved.

In Family Constellation, we see that all decisions regarding pregnancy have consequences of one kind or another. For example, people who oppose abortion often recommend adoption as the favoured solution to an unwanted birth, but, as we will shortly discuss, for a mother to give away her child is also a very significant event that is likely to create suffering for the child, disturb the family system and create a burden for later arrivals. Another option, that of giving birth to and raising, an unwanted offspring, is also likely to create misery and suffering for the unfortunate child.

The point here is not that one course of action is better than another, but that each action has to be examined for its consequences.

Adoption

In the case of adoption, a child is taken away from her mother and father and hence from her roots. The decision to give her for adoption can be either the choice of her parents, because they don't want the child, or because both parents have died - in an accident, for example. The latter situation is usually easier for the child to deal with in later life.

From the perspective of Family Constellation, if a child has to be parted from her natural parents, usually the best option for her is to be given to her closest relatives, such as her grandparents, aunts, or uncles. Staying with these close relatives is likely to be the least disturbing situation for the child, as she remains close to her biological roots. If this is not possible, the next best option will be for her to be given to foster parents, because in this situation she usually keeps her own name, knows who her real parents are and remains somehow connected to them.

In adoption, however, the child loses her original identity and may never know her birth parents. What we often see is that adoptions are not carried out in the interest of the child, but in the interest of the parents, biological or adoptive, who refuse to accept their responsibilities or their destiny. For example, a couple may want a child, but cannot have one of their own, maybe because they are infertile, or for some other reason and they are unwilling to accept being childless. A child is therefore adopted and treated by her new parents as if they are her birth parents and sometimes is not even told that she is adopted.

Coming to terms with having lost one's birth parents, or being given away by them, is always difficult for a child, who may feel deeply unwanted. What we see in constellation sessions dealing with this issue is that an adopted person frequently remains angry with the original parents, especially when they have given the child away without any clear necessity - for example, simply because she is a girl, as is often done in China or India.

However, as we have seen in previous situations, to remain angry with the birth parents is to remain involved with them and, unconsciously, can also be a way for a client to hold onto the hope that one day the blood parents will return and take her back. It is very difficult for a child to accept as final and irreversible the fact that she, or he, has been given away by the parents... unconsciously, there always seems to be some element of hope that the situation may change.

The fact that your mother carried you for nine months in her womb, delivered you into the world and then sent you away can be heartbreaking. It is an ultimate farewell that is extremely painful, but facing and agreeing to this reality is the only way for a client to have the strength to leave the past behind and move forward in life.

One possible solution to the adoption issue in a constellation is to invite the client to look at her birth parents and say, "Thank you for giving me life. That is all I got from you, but I take it from you as a big gift. And now I will go to my new parents, as you have decreed for me. You have given me away forever and I let you go now from my heart." This often feels the best to all involved.

When a client is able to accept the decision of the birth parents and its finality, she may for the first time be able to connect deeply with her adoptive parents and express gratitude for having been raised by them. Such a client may say, "Thank you, you helped me to survive." Or, "Now I take you as my new parents."

It is important to remember that these sentences cannot be taken as a fixed formula, because each case is unique and it is not possible to say exactly what the best solution will be in all cases. The most important element is that the client needs to remain in the position of a child in her response both to her birth parents and her adopted parents, which includes agreeing to the decision of her birth parents to give her away.

In addition, it is important to be clear for whom the session is being conducted: whether for a child who was adopted, or for those adults who have done the adopting. Clarity about this will dictate precisely how to proceed. As a general rule, a child has to regain her innocence by leaving responsibility to the parents and a parent needs to regain his dignity by accepting responsibility for what has happened.

One of the issues which may arise in a constellation session is that adoptive parents may be feeling guilty for having taken the child away from her natural parents. Or they may be having a misplaced sense of arrogance, especially when they are from a wealthy, technologically-advanced country and have taken a child from a poor environment in a Third World country. What is needed is for the adoptive parents to honour the birth parents for having brought the child into the world. They are not to replace them, but only to continue what they could not or were not willing to do. In a similar way the birth parents would need to respect what the adoptive parents have done for the child and agree to the fact that they took an ultimate decision in giving away the child.

The collective conscience is not interested in our good intentions, nor in our ideas about global charity and compassion for the poor, but in whether we take full responsibility for our decisions and for its consequences.

Homosexuality

Family Constellation finds that there is often a particular family dynamic behind instances of homosexuality. A homosexual can be looked at in two ways: first, as someone who has difficulty in identifying with his biological sex; second, as an outsider, since homosexuality lies outside the heterosexual norm. As we have seen, the roots of family entanglement have to do with identification - someone in the present family identifies with someone from the family of origin. The same is the case with a homosexual; he, or she, often identifies with someone from the former family and it is this identification that leads to a homosexual tendency.

Hellinger describes three main reasons for a child becoming homosexual:

1) In the case of a gay man, a boy has to represent a female figure from his former family and, because there is no girl in the family, the boy has to stand in for her and as a result becomes homosexual.

2) The mother does not allow her son to get close to the father; the father is then rejected and the boy stays under the influence of his mother.

3) The child has to represent an earlier family member who is an outcast, or an outsider in some other way and by becoming homosexual he makes himself an outsider, too.

The first situation is the most deep-rooted of the three possibilities and is most likely to create an unwavering, lifelong sexual identity as a homosexual, while the others are less fixed. In chapter six, Sebastian from Barcelona was not allowed by his mother to come close to his father and at the same time he was identifying with an excluded grandfather, who was in a concentration camp. Sebastian therefore had two motivating factors for becoming a homosexual, although, in this particular instance, the client's issue in his constellation session was not his homosexuality.

Homosexuality is rarely reversible, even if the client does uncover the family dynamic involved and in any case homosexuals do not often wish to reverse their sexual preference. Generally speaking, it is more important to consider the issue the client brings into the session and find a good solution for that, rather than dwelling on any homosexuality that might show up during a session. Homosexuality is no more than one destiny among many others that each of us carries, arising from the family into which we were born.

Multiple Partners and Love Triangles

What does it mean for a married man or woman to have another partner outside their marriage? Triangles are nothing new. Kings have always had concubines, politicians and artists have always had mistresses and society has responded to this in varying ways, depending on the moral climate of the country and the times in which they occurred.

In modern Taiwan, for example, it is not unusual for partners to remain married while both have another love partner; it may even be someone they both know, who may himself be married to someone else. In European countries and the United States, although it may be kept secret, it is quite common for couples to have extra-marital affairs from time to time.

Looking at this phenomenon from the Family Constellation perspective, it means that the person who is having affairs is not a stable and reliable partner. He, or she, keeps other avenues open and is always ready to escape. Similarly, choosing a partner who is already in a relationship may be an indication that one is not really available for a committed relationship oneself.

There may be many reasons behind the behaviour pattern of an unfaithful husband. One of the most common is that, rather than being connected to his father, he remains under the influence of his mother. So, when this man meets a love partner, he will at first see her as a desirable, sexual woman, but once a relationship is established he starts seeing her as his mother. When she has become his mother, she will lose her sexual attractiveness to him and the man will need another woman to fill that role.

The same is the case for a woman if she is her father's girl, is not close to her mother and is missing her feminine strength. Desiring the man reflects the desire for her father and not being fully available to him reflects her feeling of inadequacy as a partner to her father, so she needs someone else. As Hellinger says, mother's son and father's daughter can have a passionate love affair, but are not committed to a relationship.

A relationship is a risk, in the sense that you can never be certain about the next moment and whether or not a love affair will continue. One common fear is that without a back-up partner you may find yourself totally on your own, hence it feels safer to have more than one lover. However, if you lack the strength, or the capacity to be alone, you are likely to feel you cannot live without the first partner regardless of who else you are with. Your first partner represents a parent, from whom you did not separate. Couples who remain married even after they have new partners largely fall into this category.

According to family dynamics, when a man who is already in a relationship creates another relationship and has a child by this second woman, the best outcome occurs when he leaves the first partner and moves in with the new one. He needs to respect his former wife by honouring what they had together and by acknowledging that this relationship has now ended and this will make him more capable to commit himself fully to his new partner and especially to his new child. It is the most adult way of taking responsibility for the situation.

In family system therapy, a new system has precedence over an earlier one. So if the man does not leave his existing family for his new one, it is the child who will pay the price. A child in the new family will have to represent one of his parent's earlier partners and this is because the parent's first partner has not been fully honoured – and honouring does not occur when somehow the man remains entangled with this previous partner.

So, contrary to what one may normally assume, leaving an earlier partner may not be unkind or disrespectful to her, but on the contrary, may be a suitable and caring resolution. In most cases, the real difficulty for the client is to give up clinging to the first family and everything it represents and to pass through the pain of separation.

Within a single family system, according to the law of the Sacred Order, earlier family members have precedence over later ones. But between two family systems, the reverse is the case: a new family has precedence over an earlier one. So if a man has a child with another woman he needs to leave his former wife and be with his new woman and child.

This is similar to the way in which we move away from our original family: a young woman falls in love with a man; she creates a family of her own and gives up the bonding to her original family. Her new family and her children have priority over her love for her original family. In the same way, starting a new relationship and maybe even having a child together, pulls one away from one's present family into a new situation which takes priority over the first.

In both instances, we can see, deep down, how nature takes care of the survival of the species by giving priority to the new family arrangement.

Part Three

Facilitating Family Constellations

This section of the book is primarily for people who want to learn to facilitate Family Constellation sessions, but will also be interesting to anyone who wants to understand this new and innovative form of therapy more profoundly.

Chapter Sixteen

Steps of Setting up a Constellation

At the beginning of a session, both the therapist and the client need to take time to settle. Here, haste may be the worst enemy. Some facilitators are in too much of a hurry and ask the client immediately, "What is your issue?" or "What is your problem?" as if this person is a defective machine and the therapist is some kind of mechanic who can immediately fix it. Sometimes, too, a client is impatient to get started and begins talking as if from a premeditated script, offering preconceived ideas about what is going on in his life without opening to deeper layers of perception.

The intellectual and rational layers of the human mind are relatively superficial and want to jump to quick conclusions, while the deeper layers have a much slower rhythm and are more difficult to penetrate - at this deep level, many issues have remained unchanged all our lives. So it is important for both the client and the therapist to connect with each other and "arrive" in the present moment, without immediately galloping into action. Sometimes nothing is said in the beginning, but an inner process of perception begins, just by being present and giving enough time.

After a while, the therapist may ask the client why he came, what is his interest, if he has a question, or if he is bringing some issue that bothers him. As the client responds, it is important that the therapist does not allow him to embark on long stories - just a few simple sentences will do. Hellinger has said that he allows a client only three sentences by way of explanation; anything more is likely to be a smokescreen intended to confuse the therapist and is not required for a solution. My personal approach is less strict, but I see the point that Hellinger is making: many

205

clients wish only to talk about their issues; they don't really want to change and are accustomed to reiterating their "problems" to themselves and to others again and again, precisely as a way of not dealing with them. Starting with a long story is often the prelude to lengthy analysis, during which the therapist's energy may be diverted into 'talking about' and thus little is left for resolution.

There are many ways of working and every facilitator has his own style, or perhaps a variety of styles. Here, I will simply give some general principles of how a session may develop.

Identifying the Real Issue

It is significant whether or not a client can formulate his question in a clear and straightforward way; for example, "I have a difficulty with my father," or, "My daughter doesn't want to talk to me," or "I have a problem in creating a relationship." These initial responses indicate how much a person is already in touch with an issue and will determine whether a session can begin immediately, or whether more time has to be spent with the therapist identifying the real issue.

Just recently, I worked with a middle-aged woman in Taiwan who was eager to experience a constellation session with me and had written down her whole line of family members and all the things that had happened to them. She was talking so rapidly that she could hardly pause to gain breath. Intuitively, I resisted her desire to work with what she was telling me and instead I asked her to stop talking and close her eyes. Whenever she opened her eyes to begin speaking again, I gently insisted that we should remain in silence. After several minutes, during which nothing was said, something shifted in her and without me doing anything at all, tears started flowing from her eyes. One could see that she had touched some deep feeling inside, which had been prevented from surfacing by all her talking. Bowing her head slightly, she started to relax and, when she opened her eyes again, she looked changed. She told me she was satisfied. We didn't do anything else at this time. I didn't ask her anything. It was enough.

This case is an exception. Usually, the therapist will ask the client for information about his, or her, original and present family. One has to be very attentive while this information is being given, because any change in the tone of the client's voice, or sign of emotion being stirred while he speaks, will help to indicate where the real issue lies. With these clues, an experienced therapist can begin the session at the right point and will not need to know the whole family history.

At other times, the situation may be not so clear and the therapist will need to ask a client in more detail who belongs to the family system and what important events took place in this family. In his more recent approach, which he calls 'movements of the soul,' Hellinger has changed much of his procedure and may not even ask a person for details about his family. Hellinger has learned to trust his intuitive reading of the client's general disposition, body posture and energy, rather than what the client is saying. We will discuss this further in Chapter 21.

Which Family First?

After the interview, the therapist, or facilitator, has to make a decision: which system to put up, the family of origin or the present family. Sometimes, one begins with one family system and then later adds people from the other system - this is possible. It all depends on the client's issue, or issues and which aspect is going to be tackled first. Generally speaking, we deal first with things that are closest to the present moment in a client's personal history and only when this cannot be resolved do we go back into the past. So, as a general rule, we look first at the present family, especially if there are children and only later look at the original family, even if the client's problems have their origins there.

This emphasis on the present reflects the importance of taking responsibility for whatever life decisions a client has made. For example, the moment a person decides to have children, it doesn't matter what burdens he carries from his past; he is fully responsible for his decision, for his choice and no 'excuses' can be allowed. Family dynamics demand that we live up to what we have chosen to do in our lives, even if we made those decisions in an unconscious or careless way, without considering the consequences. To put it another way: even if we *feel* like a child, the moment we have a child of our own, we *are* a grown up and a parent. As I've said before, what matters in family dynamics is the actual act, not what we feel about it. Very often people are confused about this important dimension of family system therapy and want to give more importance to a personal feeling rather than acknowledging what has become manifest.

So, generally speaking, we begin with the present family, but it needs to be stressed that this is only a guideline and in certain cases may not apply. For example, if some major event from the original system demands immediate attention. Each client is unique and with each new client the therapist has to decide from where to begin and with which family system to work.

Who Needs to be Represented?

Having made his decision, the therapist then needs to decide who are the important members of the system that need to be represented in the constellation, which ones are essential for the purpose of coming to a solution for the client. Something that may seem obvious, but which needs to be remembered throughout a session is that we are working for a particular client in order to bring more understanding and healing into this person's life and not for anyone else within this family system.

As a general principle, we work with the minimum number of family representatives - it is better to use too few than too many. For example, a client may have many brothers and sisters, all of whom, of course, belong to his system, but some of whom may not be needed in this particular constellation. Too many representatives may diminish the impact of a constellation and create unnecessary confusion. It is always possible to add representatives later, if one finds that someone is missing.

As a personal preference, I often like to bring in excluded family members, who I know from the start will be important, at a later moment. In this way, everyone can see and feel the impact of this key figure when he or she appears in the constellation picture. If there is no impact, this will also be a useful indication, because it will tell me that my original hypothesis may be wrong.

When the facilitator has decided who should be placed in the constellation, he can ask the client to choose representatives for these family members from a group of participants: somebody to represent his father, mother and sister, for example. Sometimes, I choose the representatives myself as the facilitator.

It's not important that a representative looks similar to the family member that he, or she, is representing. In fact, it's better when the client does not look for similarities in the people he chooses, because then he is in touch with something more essential, which is not related to the character, or physical appearance, of a particular family member.

If a constellation requires many representatives then, before placing them, it is usually a good idea to arrange them all in their natural order - the earliest members standing first in line - and then repeat each one's role as a family member to avoid confusion. Now, the facilitator invites the client to take both hands of each representative and lead this person to a place in the room following his own personal intuition, not according to any preconceived plan. The client places each representative in relation to the others without giving any instructions or saying anything to them. Also, the client needs to place them without requesting any special body posture or gesture. When this process has been completed, the constellation has been created and the client sits down. The client and therapist then look together at this visual picture of a family, which gives a certain impression and has a certain impact on any observer.

Sometimes, there are deviations from this classical way of doing a constellation, which will be discussed in more detail in chapter 21. In such cases, the client may not place the representatives himself and the representatives may be asked to follow their own inner impulses and move accordingly, without saying anything.

Gathering Feedback

In the classic method of doing constellations, after receiving his own impression of this family portrait and what it may indicate, the therapist will go from representative to representative, asking each one how he feels in the position in which he has been placed and whether he is aware of any body sensations, moods, or feelings towards other members of the family.

This feedback process is effective because each representative is connected to the energy field of the family system and to his, or her, unique position in this field.

Feedback is not related to what we normally call the 'character' of a person; in fact we avoid gathering information that relates to a family member's personality. We don't want to know what kind of person he may be like, because we are looking for something that motivates people from a deeper place.

An experienced facilitator usually has some idea how each person must be feeling in a constellation and this may be enough to guide him as to how to proceed. But sometimes more detailed and subtle information can be obtained by asking each representative directly. Of course, the representative's response is bound to be slightly coloured by his own personality, but this is not important. What is important are the sensations he receives as a result of standing in a particular position and this is why different stand-ins representing the same family member will observe something similar - they are in touch with the 'knowing field.'

In a way, everybody, the facilitator and the representatives, are exploring together, cooperating in solving a puzzle. The representatives are identifying with certain family members and the facilitator, as the outsider, has the general overview. He should not identify with any member of the family, nor with the client. He has to be in a neutral position, while at the same time keeping the client's best interests at heart. We will discuss this in more detail in the next chapter.

From Diagnosis to Solution

At this stage of the session, the therapist, through his own insights, or through the feedback he receives from the representatives, may arrive at a first 'diagnosis' of what is going on in this family system and can begin to work towards a solution. This work includes changing the positions of the representatives or allowing them to move according to their own feelings, bringing in 'missing' people, gathering more information from the client when necessary and suggesting solution sentences to the representatives to say to each other.

Each move is guided by the facilitator's observations and by the feedback he receives from the representatives, either verbally or non-verbally. At each step, different layers of the hidden reality of a family system, plus the client's entanglements, may come to light. The aim of the work is to find a more harmonious place within the family system for everyone, following the principles of Sacred Order, the laws of belonging and balance, all of which we have previously discussed.

Chapter Seventeen

The Attitude of the Facilitator

What are the qualities required of a person who wishes to facilitate a Family Constellation session? What is the best state of mind for a therapist to be in? In this chapter, we discuss factors of which a facilitator needs to be aware when he begins to give sessions and the personal qualities that will enable him, or her, to be comfortable in the work and bring satisfactory solutions.

There are two main qualities a therapist needs to have if she wants to help people: first of all, she has to develop a quality of "lovingness" when she works with a client and second, she needs a certain presence. These two qualities combine to create an approach that is best described as an attitude of 'cool love.'

Cool love is not something we are generally familiar with; most of us know only a 'hot' kind of love which has to do with passion and mutual attraction between men and women, or the binding type of love that exists between parents and children, created by nature to keep the family together. Cool love is more like compassion, while presence is the quality of being available in the present moment and being alert to whatever is happening here-and-now, without being distracted by accumulated knowledge, theory, or by thinking about the past or future. Many mystics have described this quality of 'being present' as a state of meditation.

Qualities of Presence

Presence for a therapist means two things:

1) She is ready to give up any pre-conceived ideas she may have developed during the course of her work experience with previous clients and their problems and is able to look at each new person with fresh eyes, addressing the situation as if she has never seen a case like this before. In other words, while working with a deep understanding based on past experience as a Family Constellation therapist, she also needs to continuously let go of this past.

2) The therapist also needs to give up any plan, any pre-formulated idea and any notion about what may be 'good' for the client. What is good for a client is not something the therapist can know; in fact, like the rest of us, she cannot really know what is good for anybody, other than perhaps herself. She can have ideas about it and all therapists usually do, but ultimately there is no way to know ahead of time what will work, or not work, for other people. Moreover, nobody *needs* to know because no client, or indeed anybody, needs to be protected or saved by anybody else - the desire or intention to save anyone is essentially an arrogant attitude. In Family Constellation, a good therapist needs to drop any idea of what should be the outcome of a particular session and relax into a state of open inquiry, a willingness to explore and experiment and above all an attitude of "not knowing."

If a facilitator is able to do these two things - forget about the past and future and relax into not-knowing - a quality of presence arises naturally. In this state, the therapist does not need anything from the client and, once she has no expectations, she can relax and accept the situation simply as it is. Love is then experienced in a new way. Presence and lovingness go hand in hand, they occur at the same time, they are either absent together or present together.

Working Without Prejudice

In my training courses I have found that to be simple and unprejudiced is often more easy for those who are not already in the helping professions and are not practicing therapists, because "amateurs" have no preconceived concepts and are therefore free to simply observe whatever shows up in a constellation session. They have no special understanding of psychological theory and other types of specialised knowledge, which tend to create unnecessary theories and conclusions about what is happening.

For example, let's imagine a constellation set-up in which all the family members are looking in one direction. It will probably be obvious to any observer that they are looking somewhere, or at something. If we allow this picture to have an impact on us, without having any theory in mind, one conclusion we may reach is that someone in the family is missing - this will be self-evident for a facilitator who looks at such a picture innocently. But if people's minds are full of psychological theories, they may not be able to see such a simple and obvious thing. Rather, they may try to interpret the state of mind of the client, that he may be suffering from depression or neurosis. I give this example because it happened in one of my training courses and is typical of the kind of difficulty faced by a professional.

The best approach for any Family Constellation therapist is to observe with as little prejudice as possible, asking herself what such a picture could indicate and then introduce a hypothesis from past experience with which to start working. It is, however, important to test whether the hypothesis is valid in this situation and if it is not, to remain flexible enough to try something else.

The more open-minded a therapist can be, the more she can allow the actual picture to have an impact, just as it is, in this moment. Pure observation is not easy for most people, including many therapists; they usually respond to a request for observation with an interpretation of what is going on and sometimes cannot even distinguish between the two. Their educational system trains them to label things and quickly arrive at conclusions, which prevents the unusual or improbable from emerging.

In my training courses, I introduce exercises for people so they can practice the art of observation, such as noticing a client's body language and reflecting it back to him without judgment, thereby creating resonance between client and facilitator. Neuro-Linguistic Programming (NLP) - which calls this process 'rapport' - has investigated this field of mirroring in detail and has observed how it creates a special quality of trust in the client.

The Art of Self-Observation

The art of observing others is not the only quality a therapist needs to develop. What is more fundamental is being able to observe oneself. Strangely, in most therapy trainings, this essential ability is barely mentioned, let alone taught. The majority of trainings focus on how to deal with clients and rarely provide any instruction on how to remain in touch with oneself. People may go through intensive personal therapy as part of a training and get to know personal issues, blind spots and unresolved problems which, as a therapist, they may project onto a client, yet they are not taught the art of staying alert to their inner thought processes and emotions, which is the only way to prevent oneself from falling into this trap.

This form of self-observation, watching one's own internal process moment-to-moment, can be called "centered," and is a vital ingredient to therapy practice because it enables a facilitator to approach a situation without prejudice, expectations, or preconceived ideas. Centered means staying alert at critical moments when a therapist may otherwise lose touch with herself and get caught up in "helping," or "saving" the client, or assuming a personal point of view. It means remaining aware of one's own state of consciousness and thereby not getting lost in the client and the client's issues.

There are many ways to help people develop the quality of centered, which can also be described as a state of "resting in oneself" and I'll talk more about this in part four of this book.

One important benefit of being able to practice self-observation is that it helps a facilitator not to fall into the habit of being a 'professional therapist,' which, at its worst, is a mixture of routine and repetition of a certain psychological method. Identification with the role of therapist is perhaps one of the greatest difficulties facing a person who wants to be a good therapist, because she is likely to identify with the client's suffering, categorise his problems and prescribe formula solutions, thus preventing her from seeing with fresh, innocent eyes what is actually happening, here and now, with this client.

In Family Constellation, we see how a client's identification with other family members creates pain and this suffering is a powerful force. Suffering tends to preoccupy people, filling up their lives and giving them a sense of purpose and motivation: to find a way to get out of suffering. It also brings a feeling of self-importance and power and one of the therapist's main tasks is to avoid supporting the client's investment in this feeling of power and significance through suffering.

If the therapist can avoid being pulled into her client's suffering, if she can avoid becoming emotionally engaged on any level, remaining centered and undisturbed - which doesn't mean being cold and aloof - then in some way she has dethroned the client's problem and taken away some of its power. This ability of a therapist to remain unengaged is one of the most effective ways to bring a client in touch with his deeper reality.

Face to Face with Fear

A therapist's work is to help the client get in tune with his life as it is now, as it is unfolding in the present and to accept the consequences of it. This requires a certain maturity on the therapist's part, a trust in life which, in turn, requires a certain depth of life experience that cannot be taught. So there will always be different facilitators, each operating in their own way, according to their own levels of personal experiences.

It is this process of growth and maturity that eliminates the element of fear when working with Family Constellation. If she is in accord with life as it is, the therapist grows in courage and becomes more able to see what *is*, without fear. Then she doesn't need to protect the client, not even from death - if that is the direction in which the client is heading.

It requires courage to see what is happening in a constellation, to say it out loud and allow its consequences. As Bert Hellinger said in his book *Der Austausch*, "Exchange", which I paraphrase here, in my own translation: "If one has the courage to look at reality as it is and speak it out, nothing bad can happen because reality itself can never be bad. Only the fear of looking at reality can be bad, because in that moment something gets suppressed into the unconscious part of the mind and works against us from there."

Clients are more resilient than we imagine and the therapist can trust them to deal with situations as they really are. Often, it is the therapist who is afraid, not the client. Whenever the therapist can trust her intuition and say what she sees as true in a certain moment, even though it may seem hard on the client, it usually has a positive effect and often the client will thank the therapist for it afterwards. There is power in telling someone, "You want to die", if this is what a constellation reveals. But if the therapist tries to soften this message by saying, for example, "it looks as if you may want to die", or by playing the saviour, or by helping the client avoid doing what the constellation shows he really wants to do. For example, lie down next to a dead father - then the client cannot be helped or healed and the opportunity for change is lost.

Our work as Family Constellation therapists is to help clients face a certain reality; it is not our job to rescue people. It is reality that gives strength and grounding and the opportunity for the client to save himself. It's the truth of *this* moment that illuminates any constellation.

The Need for Sincerity

Both courage and sincerity are needed on the part of the therapist. We have already spoken about courage, but sincerity has a particular part to play, too. Sincerity, in this case, means to see and consent to personal limitations as a facilitator, to know what one can handle and what one cannot. If there is an issue that brings up fear in the facilitator, she should respect that, too, and acknowledge that this is something with which she cannot work.

It doesn't matter whether it's because a therapist doesn't have enough experience, or simply because it makes her afraid – there doesn't need to be a reason for it.

Personally, I would have more trust in a facilitator who says directly that she cannot work with a certain problem, than in someone who says she can, then pretends to be what she is not.

This, in turn, is an invitation for a therapist to study and explore an unknown or taboo area within herself, becoming familiar with it as a prelude to making it part of her work. In meeting such challenges, it is helpful, of course, if the therapist has faced similar situations in her own life. But this doesn't mean that she can deal only with those problems she has faced herself - she can deal with childhood abuse, for example, only if she has been abused as a child herself. Certainly, however, she will need to have the humility to learn from an abused person's life and understand the family situation in which he or she has lived.

Everyone can grow beyond personal limits. Whenever a therapist is empathetically available, she can learn from her clients and in this way transforms herself, too. She becomes aware of other lives, other motivations, other sacrifices, ambitions, anxieties, other ways that people have acted, which may be very different from her own life experience.

The basic approach of a Family Constellation facilitator should be to continuously confront her own limitations and be open to new possibilities. That is to say, she cannot give up her work because she happens to come across one of her own personal blind spots. When a therapist comes up against one of her limitations - something that happens all the time - she needs to recognise this and see how to go beyond it, for example, under supervision from someone who is more experienced in this field.

When a Family Constellation therapist is committed to growth, which all therapists must essentially be, she may at some point come to a barrier where she feels she can go no further. But even though it may feel like knocking her head against a wall, again and again, she needs to keep learning until she understands something about it. Sessions that are not going well, or are difficult in some way, usually turn out to be more important for the therapist than successful ones and should be honoured as such. When a session goes well, she may gain confidence and may feel satisfaction, but she won't learn much. When a session is a failure, the therapist has a chance to learn a lot - and, in particular, she learns humility.

Beyond Personal Conscience

In the context of Family Constellation, a therapist with blind spots is probably being constrained by her personal conscience, binding her to her original family and making it difficult for her to acknowledge, or even see, certain situations or certain people. If, for example, a female therapist's mother has been beaten by her husband, the therapist's father, it may be difficult for this therapist to open her heart and acknowledge the violent husband of her client, because it could make her feel disloyal to her mother.

A more extreme example: imagine that a therapist who has been raped in the past has a client who comes to see her with the same issue. On the one hand, she may be able to understand the client well, but on the other may find it difficult to help her client make peace with her rapist, if she herself has not been fully able to do that with the man who raped her.

In the first example, a therapist whose mother has been beaten will probably be carrying her mother's anger towards men and the question arises: how can someone who is angry with men help someone else become open to them? In a situation like this, an excluded husband of the client may be overlooked entirely without anyone noticing it. One can understand that identification with a client can prevent resolution and that it is important to be able to distinguish between empathy with the client and identification with the client's issues.

Identification is where there is no distinction between the therapist and the client. Her pain is the therapist's pain. Her anxieties are the therapist's anxieties. Identification is largely unconscious and applies to whatever issue causes the therapist to invest a large amount of feeling or emotion in the constellation and its outcome.

Empathy, on the other hand, is more like a conscious feeling, akin to sympathy but without the need to re-make or change the client in some way. Empathy is a parallel feeling, in which the mind, heart and even the body can resonate with the pain of the client without the therapist believing it to be her own. She can sense it, feel it, understand it deeply and existentially for as long as she is exposed to it, or as long as she wishes, without feeling caught up in it as if it is her own.

Identification is like an extra skin. Empathy is like a hat: the therapist can put it on and she can also take it off.

So, in the case of a female therapist whose mother has been beaten by her husband, she would need to have a certain distance from her mother - a distance from her mother's personal prejudices and preferences and from the outcome of her life. In other words, this therapist will need to be able to accept a certain amount of guilt in relation to her mother. If she is able to do this, she will have the strength to deal with the issue that her client brings, without taking sides or being blinded by preconceived ideas.

The main point here is that a facilitator needs to have worked on her own family system in some depth and gone beyond the limitations of her personal conscience. It would be difficult to imagine how a therapist can help a client overcome the consequences of a rape, if she is still in rage against an ex-husband who was violent with her. This may seem obvious, yet I have often come across clients who are themselves working as therapists with Family Constellation, who fervently reject one of their parents.

Connecting to One's Parents

A Family Constellation facilitator needs to be connected to her own parents in a healthy way; she needs to have her parents in her heart. Only then does she have the necessary strength and emotional resources to find a place in her heart for the client's parents as well. The real help for a client comes when the therapist can honour and respect the client's parents for whoever they are, whatever they may have done and this can happen only if she has done the same with her own parents.

Hellinger, on many occasions, has refused to work with people who insistently reject their parents. However, the respect Hellinger requires for parents is not directed towards anything they may have done, but towards who they intrinsically are, *towards the very fact that they are simply parents.* This is an important discrimination that many people find difficult to resolve: being able to make an emotional distinction between the ugliness of an act and the essential humanity of the person who commits it.

When the therapist can honour the client's parents simply for who they are, on a deep level, she honours her client, too. If she does this regardless of whether or not her client rejects his parents himself, she falls deeply in tune with the unfolding of her client's life. Then she has the power to work in whatever way feels appropriate, which may even include such "non-therapeutic" decisions as choosing not to facilitate a particular constellation, or even to 'abort' a session half way through, both of which are valid interventions in their own way.

Discouraging Transference

In Family Constellation, we do not work with the concept of transference, whereby a client's love for his parents is projected onto the therapist. In fact, rather than encouraging transference, we do the opposite and discourage transference from the very beginning.

Transference usually involves the client turning his therapist into the ideal parent and in some schools of psychoanalysis an analyst may allow and encourage this as an appropriate method through which to try and solve the client's problems. In Family Constellation, we don't replace the parents; instead, from the very beginning, we help the client connect directly with his real parents and, as a result, transference is minimal. With minimal transference, the Family Constellation facilitator doesn't need to treat her client as a child and from the very beginning she leaves all responsibility for the client's life in his own hands.

Not taking responsibility for the client means the facilitator need not be involved in solving problems or finding solutions. Her job is to accompany the client and help him find a deep and healthy connection with his parents. In this sense, she needs to adopt a humble approach and not allow any dependency to develop.

The idea of 'working through' an issue is not appropriate in Family Constellation, which is one of the reasons why each session is complete in itself. Instead, something quite different occurs: the facilitator or therapist sets up a constellation, creating the systemic field - or knowing field – of a client's family and supervising the positioning of the stand-ins. As the therapist enters this field and exposes herself to it, she gains insights, which she then reflects back to the client. Having done this, she leaves the new understanding to have its impact on the client and withdraws herself; she doesn't even need to know what happens afterwards.

In other words, the facilitator's role is to connect with a force larger than herself and function as an instrument of that force - one could say she becomes a vehicle or channel. In this way, a facilitator cannot claim to have done something herself; she has only made herself available. Often, she herself may be surprised by the turn of events that occurs in a session. Indeed, a good therapist frequently learns as much from a constellation as the client and thereby expands her understanding of the work.

So, what a therapist can do in a session and how far it goes, is not really in her own hands. She looks at a family constellation portrait and moves with the underlying dynamic until there comes a point when it stops of its own accord. At this point, the therapist also needs to stop and withdraw, because she can go only as far as the movement for reconciliation within this family system is ready to go at this stage. Equally, she goes as far as she herself can stay in contact with this movement, or force and the more experience she has, the more she will be able to step out of the way and allow that force to move.

A novice therapist may try too hard, may feel too much of an urge to help, may be too determined to create harmony in a family system, thereby putting pressure on the client. A good therapist learns when to move forward and when to retreat and to not be afraid of either. Patience is needed and the ability to wait receptively. When a facilitator can stay in a passive waiting state, very often a new impulse or insight comes of its own accord. She needs to be able to trust that this moment will arrive and then trust again when it departs, so that she knows instinctively how to proceed and when to stop.

In short, the basic approach to Family Constellation involves seeing what is the case, relaxing with this understanding, resting in a space of acceptance and allowing the natural dynamics of the session to make the next step visible - which is really nothing more, nor less, than allowing life itself to be the therapist's guide.

Unpredictable Solutions

A real solution is always a 'happening;' it is unplanned, unexpected. The therapist has no way of knowing where a constellation will lead. Even though a particular constellation may look to the therapist like a dozen others she has previously facilitated, fundamentally no two situations are alike and during the work each one will turn out to be different.

In one case, the family dynamic may come to a resolution and everyone will be deeply touched, whereas in a seemingly identical situation nothing will move and everyone will feel drained. It is important to allow this unpredictable quality, this mystery, without trying to figure it out, or "fix" the outcome. This may feel uncomfortable in the beginning, especially at moments when the therapist has seen a possible solution, a hypothesis, which, when tested in the constellation does not in fact work... and no new insights have arrived to replace it.

Many times in a constellation session such a gap appears and the therapist doesn't know how to proceed. To rest in this gap and wait until something becomes manifest can be uncomfortable, because, essentially, the therapist is waiting for an insight that is not part of her book-learning, or training, or related to any preconceived notions of what she may think should happen in this case, yet this is one of the most important things a facilitator can learn. Real insights always arise out of such gaps.

Having emphasised the need to embrace the mysterious and the intuitive, I should perhaps balance my approach in this book by stating that I am not against rational explanations, or an intellectual understanding of what happens in the dynamics of a family system. After all, this

226

book is itself a rational explanation of those rules and dynamics. But I need to point out the importance of a therapist remaining aware of the presence of greater forces involved in Family Constellation therapy, before which we are and probably always will be, ignorant. Life, in its essence, is mysterious and Family Constellation reflects this reality.

Respecting Energy Fields

Each family system has its own energy field and this is something that emerges spontaneously whenever a new constellation is created. It is via this energy field, or knowing field, that the stand-ins are able to sense what is going on within a particular family system and reflect it back to the client and the therapist. Personally speaking, when I work as a facilitator, I am very aware of this energy field and show my respect by moving around the room with as much sensitivity as I can manage. For example, if there is a conflict developing between two people in the family system, I don't stand directly in front of them, or walk between them. I am aware that I am an outsider and need to respect their relationship. Sometimes, if I am not clear how a certain position feels, I may put myself next to the stand-in in order to feel it for myself, but in general I trust what the stand-ins report about their inner observations.

I do not allow any unnecessary movement in the room during a constellation session as it may disturb what is happening in the middle of the room, or interfere with the movements of the stand-ins. I ask people not to move around, or leave the room when a constellation is taking place. Once the process has begun, everybody should stay put. Sometimes very subtle energies surface and anything from outside can be a disturbance.

As I have said before, the therapist works in the best interests of her client and this, in turn, means she is working mainly on behalf of those who have been excluded from a family system, because these are the people who are affecting the client - we will discuss this more in the following chapter. She needs to work out who has been misjudged, ignored, not honoured in some way and then take that person's interests to heart, not in a biased way, out of prejudice, but with an understanding that the main source of energy in any family system is always found with the excluded members - it is this energy that gives the therapist her power to create movement towards resolution.

Let us say there has been a murder in a family and the murderer was subsequently condemned by other family members and excluded from it. This would mean that, in order to find a good solution for the client, the therapist will need to create a place in her heart for this murderer, as she would for any past perpetrator. Now, if the therapist herself has a moral judgment or condemnatory attitude towards the murderer, she will not be able to help the client come out of family entanglement. This capacity to embrace the perpetrator is not easy at times, as it often means that the therapist has to stand alone against the judgments of a whole group, or society, as it manifests through this particular family. Yet, if she is to successfully lead the client to a realistic solution, it is essential for her to be able to let go of any moral prejudices or social values that in subtle ways may be colouring her perception.

Supporting Healing Movements

A therapist's work is to allow a movement to happen in whichever way it wants to go and on occasion this will take the client to the extreme of death. For example, if it is revealed in a constellation that a client unconsciously wants to follow his father, who died when he was a child, the therapist needs to allow it, however much she may dislike the idea herself. In a case like this, she may invite the client

228

to lie down on the floor next to his dead father. The therapist must be aware not to try and save the client from the inclination to follow his father but to trust this movement, even though it may seem to take him towards something with which the therapist herself feels uncomfortable.

If the therapist allows this movement to go to its extreme, there may come a point where the son himself feels that this is not right; he has started to get an insight into the law of Sacred Order and understands that it is inappropriate for him to follow his father. Indeed, this is the whole point of allowing the constellation to go this far: so that a natural turning point can spontaneously arise, because when a constellation has moved to such an extreme the client's revelation that it is not right can occur more easily. In addition, the client may receive feedback from the one representing his father that he would prefer his son to be alive, well and happy.

In Family Constellation, a therapist deals with two kinds of movements: healing movements and entangled movements (we will discuss movements in chapter 21). First, the therapist helps the entangled movement come to light and then supports the emergence of a healing movement as it manifests within the family system. For example, the client who wants to follow his father into death is caught up in an entangled movement and once he deeply experiences this and its implications, he may be ready to get up, bow to his dead parent, turn around and go forward into his own life.

This would be the manifestation of the natural healing movement. But, just as possibly, he may remain lying on the ground next to his father. The therapist cannot know the outcome when she begins a session and she needs to respect whatever the stand-in feels to do. Typically, in such a case, the stand-in will feel the entangled movement first and then, after a while, the healing movement reveals itself.

Looking at the bigger picture, each system wants to heal itself and has a built-in urge for health, continuity and survival, just as all living organisms do. But how and in what way this will happen and over which time period, a Family Constellation therapist has no way of knowing.

Chapter Eighteen

Guidelines for the Facilitator

When conducting a Family Constellation session, Bert Hellinger asserts that his priority is to gain a view of the whole family picture. "I look first at those who are missing in the system, those who have been denied recognition or love," Hellinger explains. "My heart is with the excluded and because my heart is with them, I can bring them back in. It is not siding with any individual, but standing with the entirety. When I stand by the excluded, the others are forced into a new orientation and as I hold the whole, the others come into relationship with those who have been excluded."

We have already mentioned that a facilitator has to be on the side of an excluded person in a family system. But it may not be clear from the beginning who that excluded person will be. Usually, the facilitator begins with a certain hypothesis, or theory, a kind of intelligent guess, based on the information she gathers from studying the constellation portrait in front of her and from the pre-session interview with the client. The excluded one is usually a person with a difficult destiny, or somebody whose remembrance may stir up painful memories in other family members.

The search for an excluded person takes priority because - as has already been noted – exclusion as such creates painful consequences for later family members, who become entangled by trying to represent this person, driven to do so by a collective conscience which demands that each member of a family system has the same right to belong and be recognised.

The main reason why the therapist asks for information about certain events in the family history is because she is searching for the excluded or the missing. If she finds evidence that indicates exclusion then, on this basis, she builds her hypothesis, which has to be verified through the actual dynamics of the constellation session. She observes if the introduction of this person into the system has the expected effect, which is measured by the response of the representatives of other family members, when such a person is brought into the picture.

Two Basic Questions

This is one way to proceed. The other way is to simply create a constellation with all the family members who may be important and then, looking at the picture that unfolds, the therapist asks two basic questions:

1) Who is missing?
   Who has been excluded, forgotten, or in some way disregarded in this family system?

2) Who wants to go?
   Who wants to leave this family - whose energy is going out of the system?

An excluded family member usually stands at the side of a constellation picture, apart from the others, or in the back... and nobody is looking at him. He will usually feel like an outsider, not seen, lonely, not loved, or respected. When the facilitator changes his position so that he is seen, or turns the others, so they can see him, there is usually a noticeable change in the attitude of the other family members. Everyone feels more alive, or becomes interested in what is happening, or starts feeling touched in some way; in addition, the excluded member himself feels more at ease and less burdened.

A person who wants to leave the family system may have her eyes focused on something, or someone, far away, or she may be looking at the ground, as if looking at a dead person, or she may simply feel like going away from other family members. Sometimes, letting this person follow her impulse to move away will bring relief to the rest of the family; at other times, there may be a child who wants to follow this person, or who stands in her way to prevent her from leaving.

Of course, looking far away, or to the ground, may be an indication that there is a missing person who is not yet in the picture and the facilitator may ask the client what happened in this part of the family, or she may simply place a person in the direction where the representative is looking. Often, this intervention will bring relief to the one who wants to go and love for some missing person will come to light. It shows why somebody wanted to leave the family in the first place - out of love for those who are missing - and sometimes the one who wanted to leave is now ready to stay with the family, when being placed next to the excluded one, who is now given an honourable place in the family system.

Sometimes, this dynamic is illustrated very dramatically, when all members of a particular family are looking in one direction. Almost always, this indicates that there is someone, or perhaps many people, missing from the system. This picture often occurs in the case of Holocaust survivors, where later members of a family are together looking in the same direction - at the ones who died. When these victims are placed within the system, there is usually great relief, as it becomes clear that this is where the attention of the rest of the family was being drawn.

Of course, there are so many possible scenarios in Family Constellation that guidelines for conducting a session cannot be exact. Each case has its own unique dynamic. But, generally speaking, it is a good approach for a facilitator to let herself be guided by these two basic questions: finding out who is missing and who wants to leave. Then it becomes clear who needs to be included, who needs to be recognised and honoured; who needs to be allowed to go, who needs to be left to his own destiny.

Sometimes, for example, a parent may want to go to a family relative who carries guilt, or to someone who died early and the child has to respect this desire and allow the parent to go. In such cases, it means that the child needs to respect the wishes of the parent and no longer interfere in his, or her, destiny; this kind of respect being a more mature and higher form of love than trying to cling to the parent, trying to stay close, or making demands.

The healing movement in a constellation is usually connected to these basic issues: coming closer to a certain family member, or allowing some distance, taking someone more into the heart, or letting someone go.

Often, for example, a client is too close to one of his parents and in order to find peace and create reconciliation he needs to give up that closeness and move closer to the other parent. This will not only be relieving for him, but also for his parents.

Of course, it is entirely another question whether or not the client is ready to step away from a particular parent to whom he is attached. In many cases, the client wants to remain entangled, which to him may seem easier and more innocent, because giving up the closeness to a parent often creates guilt in a child. To renounce this closeness and be ready to be alone is a difficult challenge for many people and here the therapist can only offer the client the opportunity to change; she cannot compel the client to step away.

However, there is an important consideration that may help the client: reminding him about the Sacred Order of the system, according to which everyone has his rightful place in the family; the children have to be children and the parents, parents.

Three Principles

As conscience follows three laws, belonging, balance and order, so the facilitator needs to consider three principles: she includes the excluded, allows those to leave who want to go and affirms the right order. These principles can guide a facilitator and help her follow the movement of a particular constellation, remaining focused without getting lost in side-issues.

Using her skills, the therapist goes with the movement that wants to happen. For example, if she sees that somebody wants to leave the family - perhaps one of the parents - she may help this person by asking him to take a few more steps in the direction in which he is facing and then observe the effect this has on other family representatives. Or, if the therapist sees that someone needs to be included, she may help this person by bringing him more closely into the family picture and again watch the effect.

One movement may lead to another and, step by step, the energy of the constellation guides the therapist in a certain direction. After each movement, somebody may feel touched, someone may want to come closer... many possibilities arise and can be followed, while always keeping the three main principles in mind.

Chapter Nineteen

Three Elements: Order, Reality, Energy

When conducting a Family Constellation session, a facilitator will find it useful to bear in mind three elements that support the success of a constellation. Bertold Ulsamer, a German Family Constellation therapist, called these elements "order, reality and energy," and they are helpful in analysing why a session does not go deeper or reaches an impasse. In this chapter, I will discuss their relevance and how they can be used in constellations.

Order

'Order' refers to the fact that the therapist should always keep in mind the position and place of each person in the family hierarchy. The order of a family system is determined by how long each member has been part of it and we discussed this in detail in chapter four.

In a constellation, order or disorder finds expression in the way representatives are placed, so a facilitator needs to remember who is the father, who is the son, who is the "big one," who is the "small one," who was here first, who came later. Then she will be able to understand whether the representatives are behaving appropriately. For example, if a child is actually behaving like a child, or more like a parent; if a parent acts like one, or more like a child; if a statement made by one family member to another is in accordance with the Sacred Order.

A woman places herself next to her father in a constellation and her mother to the side. From this constellation picture the therapist can guess that she is taking her mother's place, standing like a wife with her

237

father and looking at her mother as if she is a child. The order is distorted and secretly this woman will punish herself for usurping the mother's rightful place. The therapist exchanges the positions of mother and daughter, placing the mother next to the father and the daughter opposite. Both parents feel this new positioning is 'right' and after initial resistance the daughter concedes it, too. The therapist invites the daughter to bow to the mother, saying to her, "I am only a child. I will never be able to take your place. I am sorry. I was a little stupid. You are big and I am small." In this way, the order is re-established, which brings relaxation and peace to the whole family.

A constellation reveals that a child carries his father's pain. The child is asked to say to his father, "I want to do everything for you, even it costs me my happiness." After the representatives confirm the truth of this sentence, the therapist then introduces a sentence that is in accordance with the natural order: "Dear father, I leave your pain to you, with love, because I am only your child. I thank you for what you did for me. Now, in my own life, I will do something in your honour... I will be happy." According to the order, a later member, a child, is not allowed to interfere or carry anything on behalf of an earlier member of the family.

In order to help a client, a facilitator may sometimes need to insist that he respects the order. She may ask the client - as a child in the original family - to bow before his parents, even if the client does not feel like doing it. This kind of intervention can lead to a deep insight for some people, who suddenly find themselves feeling lighter and realise that they have been carrying a burden for another family member, without even noticing it.

Of course, the therapist needs to be able to determine whether the client's gesture of respect is superficial or whether it touches a deep place in his psyche. If there is resistance, then some other aspect of the client's family dynamics, such as identification with a former family member, will need to be considered first and this will be revealed by following the movement of the representatives in the system.

As a general guideline, the therapist first observes where the energy in the system wants to go - I'll say more about this in a moment - and, as the session proceeds, she introduces more elements that have to do with acknowledging order. However, the balance between imposing order and allowing energy to move of its own accord is very delicate and can be mastered only with experience.

To insist on acknowledging the order is a more "directorial" approach to a facilitator's work, but if it is relied on too much the work is likely to become mechanistic and superficial and may well bring up resistance in a client. Also, it can lead to a feeling that everything depends on the therapist and her capacity to re-position the representatives and do the 'right' thing, which of course is not the truth.

On the other hand, sometimes it is important for the therapist to use her authority. To depend only on watching the representatives, where they want to move and how they feel in relation to other members of the family, can lead to an impasse and no solution will be found, as everyone remains within the original entanglement. The therapist, as an outsider, can see things that are overlooked by people within the system and therefore she needs to make use of her insights and trust her intuition in a determined way, without hesitation.

When in a session the therapist noticed a client's identification with a Nazi perpetrator, she asked the client to stand next to the perpetrator. After initial resistance, the client did so and actually felt better standing next to this person. He was asked to say to the perpetrator, "I feel for you," which proved true.

The danger of relying too much on a directorial approach is that a therapist may follow her own preconceived ideas without really connecting to the energy of the system with which she is working. This is sometimes felt by representatives, who follow the therapist's suggestions unwillingly and any solution found in this way is bound to be superficial and feels enforced. This happens to facilitators who lack experience and is usually a consequence of a therapist trying to cover up her own insecurity. In such cases, it is good to watch closely the responses of representatives to any directive and to slow down the proceedings. Less intervention is often better than too much. Another disadvantage of the directorial approach is that more subtle energies and hidden entanglements tend to be overlooked.

A constellation is a process in which the therapist is also a learner and her interventions should be guided by the responses of the representatives. By watching the interaction of the representatives and receiving feedback from them, the therapist gradually penetrates and understands the underlying family dynamic, including entanglements that are very complex.

So, as we have seen, knowing the sequential order - who has precedence over whom - functions as a general guideline. It helps the therapist to be rooted in the basic laws of Family Constellation, keeping a certain overview and direction and prevents her from getting lost in feelings and energy movements among the representatives. From this perspective, she can usually understand why there is disorder in a family system and what is needed to bring it into harmony and balance.

Facilitators who are used to working with structure find it easy to establish the natural order in the family system, whereas those who are more intuitive and accustomed to working with energy may need to remind themselves who is actually the parent in this system and who is the child. It is good to acknowledge what various family members feel about each other, but ultimately what matters more is to recognise the Sacred Order.

For example, when a therapist is faced with the situation in which a child in the system keeps feeling superior to her mother, it will be helpful to invite the child to say to her mother, "I feel big, but I *am* small." Or in the case of a father, who feels like a child, to say to his children, "Even if I feel small, I *am* your father." This shows that what really matters in Family Constellation are the facts of life - in other words the right family order - not what we feel about them.

Reality

This brings us to the second element, which we may call "the reality." Reality refers to the events that happened in a family - we can also call it "the facts" -including who belongs to the system and what they did. These facts are usually gathered in an interview with a client before the start of a session, but further information can also be collected from a client after a session has begun.

Gathering Facts

As we know, family members who are deceased are part of the system, so the therapist can ask if there has been any early death - "early" in this context means that the client lost a parent or sister in childhood. If one of the client's grandparents dies when he is a child, this would not be considered early. Other significant family events include sickness, accidents, somebody leaving or being sent away, somebody participating in a war or related wartime experiences. Crimes of family members, or victims of a crime, are also important events, as well as early separation of the parents, or whether one of the parents had an earlier love partner. It may also be important to know whether the client's parents come from two different countries, or were forced to leave a country.

A facilitator will gather these facts in her pre-session interview, but will often only discover in the constellation session itself which of these events are really relevant. In the work of Family Constellation, a bare minimum of information is needed; there is no need to go into the details of family stories.

Naturally, most clients will have feelings, sometimes very strong feelings, about such events and sometimes, too, it may be difficult for a client to simply report the facts without immediately evaluating them. It may also be that a specific event was so overwhelming that the client may not want to acknowledge what happened.

If a client begins to talk about non-relevant information, such as "my father was always angry," or "my mother was never happy," or wants to relate a long story about what happened in his family, perhaps offering analysis about why he has a certain difficulty, the facilitator can interrupt him and explain the type of information that is useful in Family Constellation.

One way to help a client focus on essentials, as has been mentioned earlier in the book, is to ask him to describe his issue and family in only a few sentences. Offering an interpretation of events can be an unconscious way of trying to lead the therapist on to a wrong track, thereby avoiding the real issue. In allowing a client only few sentences, the therapist protects himself from getting distracted.

It is typical of clients who talk a lot that they are trying to avoid deep pain. Allowing them to mention only essentials takes away their usual strategy and brings them directly in touch with the main issue. Asking a person to slow down or take a deep breath between sentences, or just asking him to be silent for a while, serves the same purpose. Other clients may give a flood of information as "facts," in which case the therapist needs to select what is important for this particular session and what events have had the strongest impact.

It is possible to work with very little information, for example, in cases where the client does not know much about his previous family. Here, one has to rely more on feedback or movements from the representatives standing in the constellation itself. Many times, it also happens that a client remembers important events only later, especially if these events concern an excluded family member.

Often, clients don't know what information is relevant and in such cases it can be helpful to explain, in the beginning, how Family Constellation works. If a client is unable to provide any information, the therapist can guide him to realise what is important, or, in a group situation, he can be asked to watch the constellations of others first.

There are so many different scenarios that it is difficult to cover all the possibilities, but it is always relevant to find out who belongs to a family system and with whom the client has been experiencing difficulty.

Besides gathering information, the pre-interview can also be a way for the therapist to gauge how "in touch" a client is with himself, with his feelings, with his understanding of what has been happening in his family. This will give the therapist an idea of what is possible for this client in a constellation session.

Some therapists use questionnaires for gathering information and this can help clients to remember events and people, but personally I never allow a client to just read to me what he has written. I want to hear the client talk about these things, because then I will be able to detect which events and which family members trigger feelings and carry emotions and these will be useful indicators of where to look for imbalances in this family system.

Using Facts in a Session

Working with reality in a constellation session means remembering facts about a family system and including them in the work, for example, by inviting a murderer to say to his victim, "I killed you," or a wife to the husband who left her, "I have two children with you," or a child to parents who gave him for adoption, "You gave me away."

These facts are not directly visible through the constellation, so the therapist has to find ways to include them, for example, by giving a particular sentence to one family member to say to another - just short, direct and factual statements without any emotional or moral undertone. For example, it may happen that a woman is still in love with a former partner, but the reality is that she is now married to someone else, with whom she has children. This has to be acknowledged openly and directly.

Or a father, who died early because of sickness, may need to say to his child that it was not his choice to leave the family in this way. If he had committed suicide, it would be different and he may need to say, "I wanted to leave." Through such statements, family members are obliged to come to terms with what they did, or with what happened and face reality.

The function of the therapist is to give reality its full importance, so she needs to remain objective, neutral and unafraid to call things by their real names - for example, to call a murderer a murderer, or to help a person with advanced cancer face death. If a therapist wants to make things "look good" and is afraid to see the naked truth, or is

244

unable to confront people with their responsibilities, then the reality of the situation cannot have its full impact in a constellation and the result may be indecisive, without a clear resolution.

For example, it is important to ask a client exactly what happened in a certain situation and not to leave it vague. Rather than using the expression 'abuse' as a general term, it is often better to describe what actually happened. As a general rule, clients do not need to be protected from the reality of their life and will find it more relaxing if things are made clear. For a man who didn't love his partner, it may be more helpful for him to say, "I used you," rather than "I felt attracted to you in the beginning, but this faded with time." It will be stronger to say "I want to kill you," rather than "I feel violent."

Generally, abstract expressions are less powerful than directly communicating the actual fact. It may be easy for a client to say to his parent, "I honour you", but difficult to say, "I respect your love for your mother and let you carry your pain." Similarly, a client may say he is at peace with his ex-partner, but when it comes to acknowledging this partner's right as a parent of their common children, a very different reality may be revealed.

The therapist also needs to be able to distinguish between feelings that arise in the client through denying reality and feelings that result from acknowledging reality. This distinction is important, as the aim is to help people face the truth of what happened rather than supporting fantasies that lead nowhere. Facing reality is the only way to have strength and integrity and so the therapist's job is to help the client agree to reality, as it is, which will often bring the client out of an unreal situation.

A client, who lost her father very early in her life, tearfully tells the therapist that if she doesn't cling to her father's memory, she feels that she will be unable to go on with her life. The therapist reminds the client that she has been living without her father for most of her life, being now over 40 years old and having a child of her own. The client immediately comes out of her feeling and smiles.

Many therapists support clients to go into feelings without distinguishing whether the feeling comes from a 'yes' to life as it really is, or from a desire to have things different. Of course, after realising a painful event, a client may go through a strong emotion, but this usually lasts only a short time. Generally, the moment a person agrees to a reality, he feels a certain strength and at the same time relaxes.

A woman who lost her mother early in her life, remains angry with this parent, as if her mother had betrayed her by dying. After facing and fully confronting her mother's death and feeling the pain of this loss, the client feels refreshed and is able to stand in front of her mother, face her and say that now she will be happy in her life, out of respect and love for her mother.

Energy

The third element to remember is energy and how it influences a constellation session. Energy is movement, sensation, impulse, aliveness; it is dynamic, vital and always changing, something that everyone can feel, but which sometimes gets lost or forgotten when people get involved in theories, ideas and concepts. As a session progresses, the facilitator watches the representatives... their body language, how they move, to where they feel drawn, any feelings or sensations they report. These indicators guide the facilitator throughout her work and help her find the next step.

Energy always has to do with this present moment; it is manifesting right now and is something to which everyone in the room responds. Sometimes an energy dynamic within a system is obvious from the beginning, such as a strong attraction between two representatives, but it can be also very subtle and may require alertness on the part of the therapist to detect. Energy decides if there is life in a constellation or not, if it is exciting to follow what is happening, or if it is becoming boring, stale and tiring.

A facilitator has to be connected to the energy of a client, to the energy of each representative in the constellation, to the family as a whole and also to the energy of the people who are present as observers, because even the behaviour of passive spectators may give clues about what is happening in a constellation. For example, if they look bored and are checking their watches, it may indicate that a constellation needs to be interrupted, or continued in a different direction.

In the course of a session, the therapist may move people around in the constellation, or ask them to say sentences to one another, keeping a close watch on how everyone is affected by each development. For example, if a missing person is brought into the picture and everyone in the constellation turns spontaneously around to face that person, or the client gives a deep sigh of relief, it is usually an indication to the therapist that she has introduced the right person.

From the first moment, when meeting a client, the therapist is dealing with him on an energy level. This energy expresses itself in a mental way, through words, but is also communicated in deeper ways, such as through emotions and body language. A client can and often does, exhibit contradictory attitudes, saying one thing on a verbal level and indicating something entirely different by the way he sits, gestures and generally behaves and it is the therapist's job to decode what the client is really trying to communicate. Working with a client only on an intellectual level often misses depth, while working only on an emotional or physical level may lack direction and clarity.

The therapist needs to be continuously aware whether a client's communication is touching her in some way, not in the sense that she identifies with what is being expressed, but in the sense that she can recognise it as true.

Therapists who use a theoretical or academic approach to Family Constellation usually give too much importance to what a client is communicating verbally. Others, who are more intuitive and sensitive to energy, may tune in to a client's actual feelings beneath the words, but may get lost in the ups and downs of emotional expression without giving the session a clear direction.

A constellation exposes the energy hidden in a family system, including the love between family members. It makes these qualities visible through the positions in which the representatives are standing, through their physical reactions, facial and verbal expressions and in more subtle ways that may become apparent when the therapist asks representatives to report what they are feeling or experiencing.

It is, of course, an art to notice and feel energy and the therapist usually develops this ability through experience. For example, if a son bows to his father, a skilled therapist will know immediately if the bow is being done reluctantly, with resistance, or if it is a genuine expression of love and respect. Or, observing a hug between a child and her mother, the therapist can notice if the client is really hugging his mother as a child would, allowing himself to be held by his mother, or if he remains in the position of an adult, hugging his mother as if she is the "small" one. There are many subtle and significant differences like these to be noticed in a constellation.

What may be even more important is to notice which part of the family system contains the most energy: the side of the mother and her previous family, or the side of the father and his family. In addition, the facilitator needs to keep an overview of the whole system, seeing what needs to be dealt with right away and what is a side issue, embracing the entire picture without getting lost in details and especially keeping the client's best interests at heart.

No solution can be found if the facilitator does not respect the energy of a system. She may move people around according to the 'right' order, but will soon encounter so much resistance from the representatives that she will have to give up. It can be an important indicator for a therapist to notice when she is getting tired, or making too much effort and it often means that she is not going with the energy. So, rather than telling representatives where to move, the therapist may ask them if they feel any impulse and where they would like to stand, allowing them to move according to their own feelings. This can indicate where family entanglements lie.

It is rather like team work: the representatives feel the family members they are representing and what is going on inside them and the facilitator is like a coordinator, helping these dynamics to become manifest.

There are, of course, many levels of energy. Usually, the energy that finds expression at the beginning of a constellation is an entanglement, connected to 'blind' or 'bonded' love. For example, a son wants to lie down next to his dead father, indicating that he doesn't want to continue living without his father. Later in the session, a deeper layer of energy may be revealed through which family members become aware of a more conscious form of love. For example, the son may decide to say goodbye to his dead father, with tears and wants to stand up and turn towards his own life.

We will discuss movements of energy in more detail in the chapter on "movements of the soul;" what is important for us to remember here is that following the energy in a

249

constellation has limits. Allowing people to follow their impulses may not lead to a resolution, as these movements can just indicate the 'blind love' of the child. In order to have a positive and healing influence, the client's love has to become more conscious, more mature, more rooted in reality and introducing an element of order into the system, such as reminding someone that he is only a child - can also be seen as a way to bring more consciousness into the situation.

All Three are Needed

We can see that all three elements, energy, order and reality, need to be brought into play in a single session. Usually, if a constellation doesn't move, it is because one of these elements is not taken into account. It means that the facilitator has forgotten to respect the order, or has overlooked an important fact about what happened in the family, or is insensitive to the energy of the system. The moment a missing element is brought in, further movement towards reconciliation is usually possible.

Chapter Twenty

Sentences that Heal

In a Family Constellation session, the therapist does not usually allow the representatives to talk to one another directly, but instead acts as a channel between their communications, asking them to report to her about what they feel in relation to other family members and then suggesting sentences to say to one another. The reason for this is clear: in our usual way of talking to each other we often do not take responsibility for what we feel; rather, we tend to blame others and talk more about what people have been doing to us, instead of exposing our true feelings.

Moreover, we are often out of touch with what is happening at a deeper level of our psyche. For example, we may say to someone that we are angry with her, while the deeper truth may be that we miss her. In this way, a secondary feeling will cover up the primary feeling. So, in our normal way of talking, it is often the case that we perpetuate difficulties rather than solving them, keeping personal conflicts alive instead of healing them, defending ourselves and perhaps even hardening our positions, thereby making resolution more difficult. Often, people feel more hurt after participating in this kind of "communication" than they were before.

In Family Constellation, we avoid this tendency by channelling communication through the therapist, who introduces a sense of responsibility, a neutral perspective and more accurate statements. She can do this because she has no investment in supporting any particular member of the family system. Moreover, she will get immediate feedback from the person to whom she has given a particular sentence, whether it feels true, half true or not true at all, and can adjust her interventions accordingly.

In this way, a constellation slowly gains depth and what the family members say to each other begins to resonate with truthfulness rather then moving in circles of blame, excuse and justification. An experienced therapist quickly brings everyone to the essential point of a relationship issue.

For example, rather than allowing the client to blame another family member for what he did, the therapist may suggest the sentence, "I feel angry that you left me." After acknowledging this feeling, the client may then be invited to experience a deeper truth by saying, "I miss you a lot." In addition, by recognising that these feelings are stronger than can be explained by what actually happened, the client may remember the early loss of a parent and can be invited to say something like, "I miss my mother, she died very early. This has nothing to do with you; you are not responsible; you are not my mother." Or, understanding that he has been incapable of sustaining a love relationship as an adult, due to his mother's early departure when he was a child, he may be able to say to an ex-partner, "I chose you as a partner because I knew you would leave me."

Through these sentences, more awareness of the basic entanglements in this family is being introduced and the client can begin to take responsibility for his own behaviour. By knowing something about the client's life-history, perhaps from the pre-session interview and by watching the energy of the constellation develop, the therapist can formulate a hypothesis about the client's problem, which she then can verify in the sentences that she suggests.

If a facilitator doesn't have much information about her client's history, she can rely on her general understanding of Family Constellation dynamics - for example, that partners are usually responsible in equal measure for the outcome of their relationship - or on her knowledge of the Sacred Order in a family system. We often see, for example, that a client chooses a partner who later leaves him, precisely because he unconsciously needs this to happen and when the underlying cause is brought to light, the blame for the one who leaves dissolves and the client relaxes. However, any hypothesis like this has to be tested for its truth in the actual constellation.

Many times in constellation sessions the therapist uses sentences that have a certain pattern, like, "You are big and I am small," or, "I honour you," or, "You give and I receive," and so on. We have seen these kinds of sentences appearing again and again. They are what some facilitators call "sentences of the soul," but it is more accurate to say that they resonate in a deep, collective level of the human mind, where they are recognised and accepted as true. They are not sentences we would normally say to anyone in day-to-day life, but they refer to the natural order of a family system, which is influencing our behaviour in an invisible way.

If they are introduced too early in a constellation session, such sentences may feel awkward or superficial, but when the surface layers of entanglement have become obvious, these statements can have a profound effect on people, creating deep insights into the causes of personal suffering. So, if these sentences are to touch the heart and heal the client, the timing of introducing them is very important.

In general, sentences relate to the three basic aspects of a Family Constellation session: the order in a family system, the energy in that system and the reality of what happened in this family. Examples of sentences that reflect order include, "You were first, I came later," and "I am only the child." Sentences that reflect the energy in a system often include the expression of feelings, such as, "I am angry with you" or, "I feel very big," or they may indicate that a person wants to move. For example, "I want to follow you," or, "I cannot stand up anymore, I want to lie down." Sentences that reflect reality are plainly describing, without evaluation or judgment, some specific event that happened in the family, such as, "You killed me," or, "I left you and married someone else," or, "I had an accident and died."

In order to have power and be effective, sentences need to be kept simple, short and plain; they should carry no blame or judgment and they need to be expressed with a loud and clear voice. It may be that the representative needs to repeat a sentence a few times in order to help him feel how it affects him. If a sentence is not appropriate, the person usually refuses to say it, or utters the words without any sign of being touched by them.

A sentence that contains truth immediately empowers the person who says it. Truth, as such, gives strength; it doesn't matter what it is; facing and stating it is enough. For example, if it is revealed that a client wants to follow an earlier family member who died, the facilitator needs to expose this reality by inviting the client to say clearly, "I want to follow you into death," without trying to soften the statement.

Sometimes, the therapist can introduce sentences to show a client what consequences his, or her, acts will have towards others. For example, in a case where a mother wants to leave her present family, her daughter may be invited to say to the mother, "If you leave, I will take your place with father, out of love for you." The bold assertion of the consequences of certain acts can sometimes lead to a turning point in which the mother may change her mind.

In order to provoke strength in such people, the facilitator must not be afraid to clearly expose those consequences and this can mean going to an extreme. For example, a murderer may be confronted by another family member who says, "You deserve to die." A father, who wants to follow his own father into death, is confronted by his son with the sentence, "If you leave, I will follow you."

Usually, in the beginning of a session, sentences refer to things that are obvious to everyone involved and then move towards deeper truths. Sometimes it is good to begin without sentences, allowing the energy of movement within the system to expose a certain reality and then later on introduce healing statements.

Penetrating the deeper realities of any family system is rather like peeling an onion, going layer by layer and much depends on the experience of the facilitator to see through situations and events without being deceived. If the therapist stays in contact with the energy of the system, avoids interpretation and has no specific goal, the truth will usually reveal itself.

Sometimes, as was mentioned in the previous chapter, it is good to combine two elements in one sentence, such as "Even if I feel like a child, I am your father," which contains the energy of feeling, while respecting the family order; or, "I left you and now I feel very sorry to have hurt you. I will carry the consequence," which contains the reality of the situation and the feeling of the person who left; or, "I respect your love for your brother, who died early and I leave this pain to you," which contains the statement of reality and acknowledgment of order.

The main danger of working with sentences is that they can be used merely as routine formulas, in which case they will not touch the hearts of those involved or have a deep effect. The same will be true if the therapist is in a hurry and does not allow the movement of the energy in the system to reach to a point where the introduction of sentences is appropriate and effective. Even a 'right' sentence given in a 'wrong' moment may prove ineffective and so a therapist needs to remain closely tuned to the energy field of a system, because this 'tuning' will create unexpected insights, out of which sentences may arise that are both unique and appropriate - as we have said before, each Family Constellation session is different and unique, however similar it may appear in the beginning.

The power of a sentence lies in its ability to create a response in everyone, expressing a truth so clearly that no one in the family system is likely to remain the same once it has been uttered. Sometimes, too, exaggerating an entanglement may be effective, thereby making it obvious to all who are involved. For example, a son whose mother does not want him to meet his father, is given the sentence to say to her, "I will always remain with you." Or, the therapist may deliberately ask a person to say the opposite of the truth, such as, "It's all your fault!" which may provoke a client to recognise the untruth of it.

Hellinger himself works a lot with these paradoxical interventions, suggesting sentences that appear to keep the problem in place, but which effectively plant a seed of transformation.

Sentences can also exaggerate an energy, or a movement, that is manifesting in a constellation. For example, rather than inviting a client or representative to say, "I want to go," the therapist may give the sentence, "I want to die." Or, a male child is invited to face a line of men in the family and say, "I am stronger than all of you." Suddenly, the client may see the ridiculousness of such a statement and understand the consequences of his actions, which may lead to a transformation of his attitude. As mentioned earlier, the effect of a sentence and its healing power, or its power to transform, can be seen by the responses of everyone involved in the constellation. A sentence that contains both power and truth can permanently change a client's perception of his relationship with his family.

Chapter Twenty One

Movements of the Soul

A few years ago, Hellinger further developed and changed his work into what he calls "Movements of the Soul," in which there is significantly less intervention by a therapist during a constellation session and less instruction to representatives to move in a specific way or say things to each other. In this new style of working, the facilitator relies more on the energy that manifests spontaneously during a constellation session and on how this energy expresses itself through movements and body language.

Earlier in this book, I cautioned against the use of the word "soul" because it is a vague term that includes both the deeper layers of the human mind and the consciousness that exists beyond mind, but I will allow its use here because it has been given by Hellinger as the name of a specific method.

In Movements of the Soul, the work depends more on the capacity of each representative to put aside any preconceived ideas and intentions and be able to observe and follow impulses that arise spontaneously from inside, as a result of having entered the systemic field of a family.

The facilitator gives freedom to these representatives to follow any direction in which their bodies wish to move; for example, away from a certain family member, or towards another member, or lie down on the floor, or leave the system, or allow some other form of expression, such as trembling and to do all this without speaking.

The therapist needs to limit the number of people who are allowed to move in this way – usually no more than three - otherwise many representatives moving at the same time can lead to confusion and chaos. Sometimes it will be only two people and sometimes even one. The other members of the family system are imagined as present and the ones who are placed are also representing the whole system.

As the representatives are being moved by the energy of the systemic field, it is no longer so important that a client personally chooses and positions them in a constellation, as described earlier in the book. It is sometimes sufficient if a therapist chooses two representatives for certain roles and places them opposite each other and then observes their subtle non-verbal interaction.

After a while, certain movements or bodily expressions start to manifest. For example, one representative may start trembling, or step back, or look at the floor, or gaze far away, indicating an entanglement with another member of this family system. The therapist may then add the missing person to the constellation and observe how this affects the way the representatives move. Later, he may suggest certain movements; for example, that someone should look at another person, or lie down. Or, he may give representatives words to say to each other, but always keeping his interventions to a minimum.

At times, the healing movement will emerge by itself and no intervention from the therapist will be needed. However, the therapist's attentive presence is a major contributing factor; he is the catalyst, effecting change through the Taoist approach of 'doing through non-doing.'

Even though this method looks very different from the classical style of working, it is based on the same family laws of order, balance and belonging.

A Continuous Flow

The name "Movements of the Soul" acknowledges the fact that life is a constant flux in which nothing remains static or fixed and that human beings are connected to a bigger reality - we may call it 'existence' or "universal nature" - that constantly influences us, whether we are aware of it or not. In contrast, the word 'constellation' and the idea of a 'solution' give the impression that a particular family situation is static and that changes can occur only in the form of shifting from an 'entangled constellation' to a more 'healthy' one, which is then regarded as the 'solution,' after which the family order is 'in place.'

This is not so; life moves on and within its continuous flow the individual discovers there is no end to personal growth. To find a final 'solution' or 'answer' to our life's quest would in fact be the end of personal development and learning.

Seen from this perspective, a family constellation is like a momentary picture of a relating dynamic that is in continuous movement. It is like taking a picture of a river: the picture may look static, but the river itself is always moving and changing; if another picture is taken at a later time the same river may look very different; it may have changed its course, it may be deeper or shallower, flowing faster or more slowly.

In Movements of the Soul, this dynamic reality is being reflected and it also shows that it is not the therapist who brings change into a system; she is, in fact, simply creating a space in which a particular movement can show and express itself. Therefore, the therapist is less active in this type of session.

Entangled Movements, Healing Movements

Movements of the Soul have different layers: there are movements that arise out of entanglement and there are healing movements. Entangled movements lead to suffering, healing movements lead to reconciliation and in order to be able to work with this method a therapist needs to be able to recognise the difference between the two.

For example, a hug between a child and a parent can arise out of an entanglement, or can be a reconciliation, depending on who is supporting whom. The movement of reconciliation has to come from the child towards his parents and parents should have the strength to wait until their child approaches them - the exception being the interrupted movement described in chapter eight. If a parent moves towards his child to hug him, it usually indicates the need of the parent and often one can observe a certain hesitation in the child. The child probably represents someone from the parents' original family and is not really seen as a child at all. In such a situation, a therapist intervenes to protect the child from being burdened by the parent.

A facilitator has to be able to recognise this distinction and will usually intervene once an entangled movement has become manifest, or, on occasion, wait to allow the love underneath this entanglement to surface, so that a healing movement can then begin.

Entangled movements can be seen as attempt to complete something in an unsuccessful way - it is rather like repeating a traumatic event again and again. Healing movements lead to a successful completion, in which a past event is brought to closure and the love that has been entangled is free to flow in a new direction. This completion can be a sequence with several steps. For example, 'honouring' an earlier family member may take the form of bowing down, but it is only complete when the client stands up again. First, he comes close and bows to the one that came before him, then he stands up, turns around and moves into his own life.

People who wish to separate from their parents need to bow down to them first; otherwise they can never really move away. Without acknowledging the parents, the client tends to stay in a frozen position and this usually means he will never truly be able to achieve separation. Others have no problem bowing down, but then find they don't want to stand up again - they don't want to let go. Mostly, when a client desires a particular outcome, such as to separate from his parents, he needs to do the opposite first; that is to say, come closer and show gratitude for the place of his parents in his life. Only then can the client go his own way without carrying any burdens from the past.

Sometimes to work with a movement can lead to more depth in a constellation than work based only on acknowledgment of the order:

A client, a woman, lost her father soon after she was born. The therapist simply places father and client in a constellation and then invites the representatives to follow any inner feelings and move accordingly. At first, the client's representative does not want to look at the father and turns away, but then she becomes curious and starts looking at him; after some time, she gets in touch with a deep pain and starts sobbing and, finally, after a long time, she can come closer to the father. All this happens over a long period of time in which nothing is spoken and the therapist does not do anything, but just provides a space for these movements to manifest, one after another.

In a more conventional approach to the same situation, the therapist might ask the client to look at her father and bow down to him, thereby acknowledging him as her father according to the Sacred Order in her family, but in comparison this seems superficial and will not touch the heart. Allowing energies to surface slowly creates a totally different depth. In Movements of the Soul, many subtle energies and movements that no one can anticipate reveal themselves and these are essential to give the resolution depth and meaning.

Working with Movements of the Soul requires a therapist to wait patiently, even if it seems that nothing is happening. She is trusting a bigger force that is becoming manifest through the representatives, without knowing where it is going to lead. This takes courage and a certain self-discipline to refrain from giving solution sentences to the representatives as a way of taking control and trying to push the dynamic in a certain direction. Any words spoken while these subtle movements take place may be a disturbance. It is like asking someone who is feeling deeply emotional and who is about to start weeping, "How do you feel now?" To find the right moment to intervene as a facilitator takes experience and sensitivity.

Generally speaking, one can say that working with Sacred Order in the 'classic' constellation method will tend to be more superficial and touch the heart less, even though it may be 'right,' while on the other hand, the "non-doing" approach of Movements of the Soul can reach deep layers of our psyche that lie beyond our normal perception. In addition, a truth may reveal itself that is beyond our ideas of what is right or good.

A Greater Wisdom

The approach of Movements of the Soul acknowledges that there is a greater wisdom in life than we can logically or intellectually comprehend and it is not the therapist, nor the client, nor the representatives, who are responsible for healing, but this greater force. It is rather like having an injury to one's body; we can clean the wound and apply ointment and band-aids and this will help, but there is a power within the body that mends the wound and this is really the healing force. We are not really doing much.

In the same way, one can say there is a greater life force - Hellinger calls it the 'greater soul' - at the root of all healing and it is my personal experience, over many constellation sessions, that there is a deep movement in every one of us towards reconciliation and resolution. If, in

262

a constellation, we reach to this depth and through our parents are able to love the wholeness of life, healing has happened. Seeing Family Constellation in this way, honouring our parents is a spiritual act; it is saying "yes" to life as it comes to us, without complaint, without any idea that things would have been better if our parents had been different. Instead, we look beyond our parents at the life that comes to us through them. In this sense, all parents are perfect; they all give life and are therefore equally 'good' and 'right.'

Family Constellation therapy offers a client the opportunity to develop sufficient sensitivity and awareness to be able to fall in tune with life and live in harmony with its flow and movements. Healing occurs when we are in this state of harmony, or oneness and the main work in Family Constellation, in any spiritual therapy, is to remove whatever obstacles may be in the way, recognising that our problems are actually coming out of our resistance to life. This process may also bring an insight that there are things in life that are not only bigger than us but beyond our comprehension and it is important to trust and respect this mystery.

For a therapist who is just beginning to work with Family Constellation, it is good to first learn the classic way of doing constellation sessions, before exploring Movements of the Soul. The latter method may look simple - to allow representatives to move as they feel - but it is a delicate task to detect whether a particular representative is deeply in touch with a greater movement, or is simply following a personal idea of his own. Only when one knows how to use the basic tools of the classic method, such as family order, can a therapist start working effectively without them.

The more experience one has, the more one can trust and allow energies in a family system to move of their own accord. But, even then, it is good to limit the number of representatives who are invited to follow their movements, not only to avoid confusion but also to keep the focus of the session on the client. We do a constellation for a particular client and the therapist needs to keep this in mind and not get distracted by trying to find a solution for every member of a family.

For example, if one sees a client's mother wanting to follow a dead person from her original family, the work should be to find a solution for the client - perhaps by supporting him to connect with his father - rather than trying to help the mother remain alive. This may seem obvious, yet many constellation facilitators are misled on this important point.

Past and Present

It is sometimes difficult for a therapist to decide when to explore past events and when to keep the focus in the present. An important guideline is to make sure the client does not look for excuses in past events to avoid honouring his parents and continue to blame them - that they did this, or that and therefore he is justified in looking down on them. If remembrance of past events helps a client to understand an entanglement it is helpful to explore it, but it is the client, as a child, who needs to change and acknowledge his parents - it is not the parents who need to change.

For example, if a client's father is an adopted child and keeps being drawn towards his birth parents, then his son, the client, may be feeling that "my father was not there for me." But the therapist does not support this view of the situation. In fact, the opposite is true: the father did not repeat what his parents did, he did not give away his child, which shows a certain strength. In order to acknowledge this positive outcome, a son might be invited to say to his father, "Thank you for keeping me."

It is also important to understand what is healing for a child to know about his family of origin and what is not; for example, in the case of family secrets. There are secrets that deserve to be protected, because it is not the business of the child to know about them, such as a past event that created guilt in the parents and there are secrets that a child should know about, for example, an event concerning a forgotten sibling.

Generally speaking, going into the past can be considered meaningful if it helps a client to feel more love and understanding for his parents and gives him strength to take responsibility for his present life.

Some people want to look into the past with the intention to find excuses for their unwillingness to take responsibility for their lives right now. A therapist should not support this if he wants to help a client actively change his life. Looking into the past needs to be done with the intention of completing something that has remained as a hangover, so that the client's energy can fully turn to the present. So, both these things are needed: living fully in the present and understanding what hangovers from the past are preventing us from fully experiencing this moment.

Different Emotions

Another important point is to be able to distinguish between different kinds of emotions. There are emotions that are simply draining and apparently endless, never leading to completion. Hellinger calls them 'secondary' emotions, in contrast to 'primary' emotions, which are usually short, empowering and an appropriate response to a certain event. Secondary emotions usually help a person not to face a painful reality and tend to cover up a deeper feeling. For example, the client may become angry instead of feeling hurt, or he may start crying when he is really angry. Sometimes secondary emotions feel like a demand, in which case they are designed to manipulate another family member - children frequently do this with their mother.

Primary emotions are a direct response to an event, they last a short time and when the client can allow them fully he immediately feels refreshed, strengthened and is able to act. As a therapist, one has to learn to distinguish between the two and discourage secondary emotional expression. For example, if a client is crying, the therapist needs to ask herself whether this expression is helping her client become more integrated and stronger, or whether it is simply exhausting. The answer may not always be immediately clear, but if an emotion continues for a long time without any sign of coming to completion, most probably it is the secondary type. Primary emotions are always relieving for a client, they don't last long and leave a person with more strength than before.

There are other kinds of emotions that we often see in constellation sessions, which we may call "systemic." They are taken over by the client from another person in the family system and there is relief when these are given back - the client feels unburdened.

Generally, the therapist has to be able to distinguish between an expression that is a client's defence against feeling an uncomfortable emotion and an expression that is a healthy release of the emotion itself. For example, by expressing anger we often deny our own helplessness, or try to avoid the pain of love.

Allowing Energy to Build

As I have said before, even though many family systems look alike it is good to remember that each system is unique. Two persons may have had a similar destiny in their respective families, but in one case everything may fall into place easily and everyone will be deeply moved, while in the other nothing is really resolved and no solution can be found. There can be many reasons for this; for example, it may be that essential facts about a family have not yet come to light, or the client is avoiding the real issue in some way, but basically the therapist will have to accept that this is the case. Of course, a therapist's skills are also an important factor; it may be that she has the capacity to intervene and easily resolve entanglements of a certain kind, while finding it more difficult with others.

In order to allow a certain energy to build - for example, for a quality of love or a rage come to light – the timing in a constellation session is important. The therapist needs to be patient, without forcing the situation to move and always be ready to let go of her previous ideas. Movements happen in their own time and a client may need to stand facing one of his parents for a long time without intervention, before any movement arises. Through waiting, more can be accomplished than through doing, but it needs to be an intelligent kind of waiting: centred and attentive, ready to act at any moment. If, after some time, nothing happens, the therapist needs to be able to sense that the energy is finished and stop the constellation. The ability to tune into energy is important in this type of work, while, at the same time, knowing the right order will give direction and clarity.

Both styles of working, the 'classic' Family Constellation and Movements of the Soul have their intrinsic advantages and disadvantages. Using sentences too frequently can be superficial, or become a stereotype, while giving a sentence at exactly the right moment brings clarity. Allowing a spontaneous movement can touch a deep inner space, but the meaning can remain vague if not complemented by a healing sentence.

There is no doubt that of the two styles, Movements of the Soul is more controversial, even among Family Constellation therapists, and this may be because Hellinger, the creative genius behind both methods, is content to be more mysterious and indefinable in working with Movement of the Soul.

Part Four

The Role of Meditation in Family Constellation

In this section, I describe the work of Family Constellation in the context of meditation, showing how the added dimension of meditation can deepen understanding of family dynamics, both in terms of knowing oneself and seeing the unconscious nature of the ties that bind us to others.

In my personal experience, as far as being a Family Constellation therapist is concerned, I have found that it is not so much the therapeutic method, or technique, that is important in helping people, but the degree of awareness or consciousness of the facilitator who is guiding the process. Since meditation is basically a method of heightening self-awareness, its significance lies in the fact that it can assist therapists, as well as clients, to be as conscious as possible.

Chapter 22

The Art of Meditation

In this chapter, I discuss in more detail what is meditation and how it can contribute to Family Constellation and, indeed, to therapy in general.

Traditionally, the word meditation has been used in two ways:

1) To refer to methods of meditation that can help a person look within his own psyche and explore his interior reality. In this context, the word refers to a particular technique that is being used for the purpose of observing the workings of the mind and accessing states of consciousness that lie beyond it.

2) To refer to an enlightened state of consciousness, a continuing state in which the thinking process has ceased, in which there is only silence, peace and stillness. This state has been called many things: Zen monks refer to it as "No Mind," or, more colourfully, as "the Roaring Silence;" Indian mystics have called it "Samadhi," or "Moksha;" Christian mystics have called it "the peace that passes understanding."

The two definitions are closely linked, since the aim of meditation methods is to eventually arrive at a continuing and permanent state of meditation.

In this chapter, I use the word meditation in the first sense, referring to methods that help people touch a deeper truth inside themselves, which in turn often leads to an experience of relaxation and silence. Perhaps I should mention here that during the past 28 years I have explored

271

many different types of meditation techniques, mostly under the guidance of the Indian mystic Osho and have been using them in conjunction with a wide variety of therapeutic methods for most of that period.

In meditation, as in Family Constellation, we are trying to contact something within us that is deeper than our thoughts, desires and hopes. Mystics have called this "something" our being, self, essence, spirit, or God. Hellinger calls it "soul." The name does not really matter, since anyway the experience is essentially indefinable, but I prefer the expression 'inner being,' as it seems to be the least contaminated by any ideology.

Usually, in our normal, day to day, waking consciousness, we are not aware of our inner being. We are too preoccupied with the outer world of activity, of things to be done, of schedules to keep, people to meet and also too caught up in our moods, feelings, ideas, attitudes and beliefs – in other words, absorbed by external events and our ongoing mental and emotional activity.

We are not aware of the one who is behind all this, the one who is aware of all these happenings, the one who, in a sense, is simply watching these activities as they occur. This state of watching, or witnessing, applies not only to the world around us, but also to our reactions to it – in other words, to how we are feeling in any given moment.

For example, there is a difference between saying, "I am angry," and "I am aware that anger is arising in me." It may appear to be the same, but experientially and existentially it is not. Meditation is concerned with this difference, with this small gap, it makes us aware of our capacity to watch events; it brings us in contact with the one within us who is witnessing everything that happens to us. Mystics of all ages have asserted that this is who we really are - the one who witnesses everything but who is not touched by anything.

One of the contributions made by Osho to making meditation a more accessible and contemporary phenomenon is to draw attention to the fact that witnessing is the root of all authentic meditation techniques. For example, in his commentaries on Vigyan Bhairav Tantra, an ancient Indian text containing no less than 108 different techniques, Osho repeatedly draws attention to the subtle undercurrent – present in all of them – of a continuing, inner state of awareness.

One can compare it with sitting in a movie theatre and watching a film. On the screen, all kinds of things are happening and if the movie is well produced we are likely to become identified with one or more of the characters. We will find ourselves crying, or laughing, or anxiously waiting to see if the hero and heroine are going to survive whatever perilous situation they find themselves in.

At the same time, some part of our consciousness is aware that all of this is just a drama; we are sitting in a chair, watching a story that has been fabricated for our entertainment and which has nothing to do with us. The moment we remember that we are not really involved in this drama, we can relax, but when we forget, we tend to become tense, involved, emotional, excited.

Meditation is similar. It gives us the understanding that throughout our lives, no matter what happens, no matter how we feel, there is a silent witness at the deepest core of our consciousness who is simply sitting in a chair, watching the dramas that unfold. Nothing ever happens to this watcher, only to the one who is acting in the movie.

In reality we are both: on the surface, we are the one who is acting, and at the core, we are the one who is watching. The one who is watching is our deeper reality, but most of us lack the meditative awareness needed to penetrate this far into our inner being, so we tend to be much more identified and involved with the one who is playing in the drama.

273

One of the most significant qualities that arises through discovering our inner being is a state of self-acceptance, or self-love, because it gives us a profound realisation that the peace and fulfilment we were searching for outside ourselves has always been an intrinsic part of our nature. Immediately, all self-judgment, self-doubt and self-criticism ceases. We accept who we are, and we can say "yes" to life as it is, without trying to improve or alter anything.

Family Constellation is related to meditation in this sense: in both cases we are trying to discover how things are, not how we would like them to be. Hellinger gave a very appropriate title to one of his books, which he called, "Acknowledging What Is," and this is what also meditation offers: looking inside oneself, seeing what is, and saying 'yes' to it.

In my courses, I sometimes use an exercise that gives participants a taste of how it feels when we say 'yes' to ourselves and to events in our lives. It is a simple but effective technique developed by Sagarpriya Delong Miller, an American psychotherapist who has spent many years exploring ways to bridge therapy and meditation.

In this exercise, people are asked to move around a room, allowing their bodies to do whatever they want, without being controlled or guided in any way. As they do so, they are invited to speak aloud to themselves, saying sentences that begin with the words, "If I say yes to my body, I would…" adding at the end whatever the body spontaneously wants to do in each moment. For example, a person moving around the room with her right arm raised in the air will say, "If I say yes to my body, my arm will move upwards;" another, who has begun to run, will say, "If I say yes to my body, it will run around the room…" and so on.

At each moment, participants announce to themselves whatever the body is spontaneously doing, and in this way they witness what is happening, while at the same time paying attention to any changes to the quality of their inner state. After a while, they are asked to describe this state with simple words and this usually reflects a positive experience such as "expanded," "relaxed," "light," "joyous," "alive."

Meditation techniques offer similar experiences. For example, the Buddhist method called "Vipassana," which has been used for hundreds of years, consists essentially of sitting silently, doing nothing, paying attention to one's breathing and also to sensations arising in the body and thoughts arising in the mind. There is no attempt to evaluate or judge any feeling, thought or idea that arises while sitting. The meditator simply notices, or watches, everything that occurs and through this method arrives at a state of inner tranquillity, a sense of harmony with life and a feeling of self-acceptance.

In meditation, people don't try to change or fix anything, but rather become aware of their inner being, their witnessing state of consciousness. The moment this happens, all fight and struggle ceases. Hence, many mystics have taught relaxation and effortlessness as a path to experiencing self-nature.

In Family Constellation, people are looking at how they are related to their own families, learning to accept and embrace these roots and in this way coming into contact with a universal life force that moves us all. When people feel grateful to their parents, in the same moment they experience a wider feeling of self-acceptance, falling in tune with the whole of life.

By seeing and understanding the ways they are tied to their families, people also understand why they behave in a certain way. When they accept that this is how they are, something else shines through, something of the inner being, soul, or essence, which is eternal and not part of the superficial layers of human personality.

Really, it is a spiritual quality that comes through in such moments. Imagine, for a moment, a disabled or handicapped person, who is unable to perform and experience many things in life that ordinary people do. Most "normal" people would look at this person with the attitude that he has a disadvantage and, indeed, he may feel this way himself. But if he is able to fully agree with his fate and fall in tune with it, he is likely to develop a certain strength and well-being that others will not have.

In a way, our objections or disagreements to life function like a handicap. We may think, for example, that it would have been better if our childhood was different, or if our parents had behaved differently, or if we had behaved differently in our relationships. The opportunities for regret when reviewing our personal life history are endless. But in doing this we are in fact taking away something from ourselves, because the reality of events will not change; all we are doing is denying ourselves the positive experiences that arise out of accepting ourselves and our past.

In meditation, as in Family Constellation, we are trying to come into harmony with something bigger than ourselves. Hellinger calls it 'the Greater Soul," I prefer the word 'Existence.' Personal growth and maturity, in my view, is the process of becoming more and more in tune with this greater force and giving up the idea of being separate.

Applied to family dynamics, this means giving our parents and all members of our family a place in our hearts and agreeing to whatever happened in the past without judging it as 'good' or 'bad' - in fact, without having any opinion about it.

To do this is a considerable personal achievement. It is never easy. Imagine, for example, what this requires from a person whose parents were killed. He will need to drop any hateful attitude towards their murderer and understand that to agree to the fate of his parents is the only way to truly honour them. The moment a person is able to do this, he is going beyond both personal and collective conscience.

Paradoxically, the moment one wants to go beyond the prison of conscience one cannot. The moment one feels, "I want to leave behind the burdens of my family" one is trapped by those burdens. To really attain liberation, one needs to accept and carry the destiny of one's family. In other words, one has to leave behind the idea of wanting to get rid of whatever we may be carrying for our predecessors. When we agree to this, in the very same moment, the past loses its power over us and we find ourselves blessed with a feeling of strength and freedom.

Meditation offers the same experience. By approaching the centre of our being and dis-identifying with the personality, the same state of self-acceptance is achieved. The desire to change anything about ourselves is replaced by a profound acceptance of whatever life has given to us.

Every desire is a barrier, including the desire to leave behind a particular burden. As Osho has pointed out: "Transcendence comes through experience. You cannot manage it. It is not something that you have to do. You simply pass through many experiences and those experiences make you more and more mature."

One or two more things to be noted about meditation: regularly practicing meditation techniques helps us become accustomed to noticing our inner world – the world of bodily sensations, thoughts, feelings, moods – and therefore enhances the individual's sensitivity. This in turn, makes it easier and more accurate, for representatives to notice changes in moods when standing in for family members. At the same time, the practice of witnessing and dis-identifying from personal attitudes and beliefs makes it easier for the client to let go of burdens that are being carried for earlier members of the family system

Chapter 23

Individual Sessions and Seminars

Individual Sessions

Usually, Family Constellation is done in a group setting, but when no representatives are available it is also possible to conduct sessions with individuals. In order to mark the positions of the client's family members in a constellation, one has to use symbols to represent them and these symbols need to be able to indicate the direction in which each of the placed family members is looking.

Some practitioners use shoes to mark the positions, some use pieces of paper with symbols on them. I normally use cushions, to which I give a direction by placing a tissue on top. This, for me, is the most convenient method, as I tend not to carry large amounts of shoes around with me and I like it better than paper as you can see the positions easily from a distance. One can be inventive how to represent family members in such sessions, but it is always important to know in which direction a placed person is facing.

After identifying the family member represented by each symbol, the therapist can invite the client to place the symbols in a constellation. Or, as I prefer to do it, the therapist can ask the client to pick up one symbol and hand it to the therapist, then – while visualising this particular family member – guide the therapist to a place in the room where this family member should be standing. The therapist then leaves the symbol there, making sure the direction is clear. In this way, positioning continues until all relevant members have been placed.

The advantage of doing it this way, even though it may take a longer time, is that the therapist gets a direct feeling of each family member while holding and placing each cushion.

After each family member has been placed, the therapist can ask the client to look at the picture and describe what he sees, saying what strikes him about this family portrait. Then the therapist can tell the client his own perception of the relationships in the constellation. Or the therapist may stand in one, or perhaps all positions, stepping onto each cushion and reporting to the client what he notices, how he feels as this person.

Sometimes the client can be invited to do the same, imagining, in turn, how each person feels. This, of course, requires a certain capacity in the client to tune into other family members, but it is usually productive. It can be interesting for the client to experience how each of his close family members may feel, but the therapist needs to be watchful that the client is sensing and reporting the actual feeling in that very moment, rather than relying on preconceived ideas about certain family members.

In some sessions, work can begin by asking the client to say a sentence to another family member, addressing the cushion that represents this person. Or the therapist can give feedback from the places of other family members. Each session will develop differently and the therapist needs to rely on his perception about what may be helpful or possible.

Working with symbols can be similar to working with actual people: changing positions, giving sentences, asking the client to notice any changes in mood or feeling that may happen as the session proceeds. Of course, the therapist does not see energy changes in representatives directly, such as occur in constellations using actual persons – this is a disadvantage of having no people available - but it is a practical alternative to working with a group and outcomes are similar.

Difficulties may arise if it becomes necessary to go back to earlier generations where there is not much information available, because without representatives it may be too problematic to decide how each family member feels, merely from the arrangement of cushions or other symbols.

Here, the therapist will need to focus more on the present and limit the work to this aspect of family dynamics. In general, it is good to keep the number of symbols to a minimum. Sometimes placing the client opposite one parent is sufficient in the beginning, allowing the client to stand for a long time in front of his mother or father, while the therapist watches changes in energy and body language, which may then lead to a suggestion for the client to say something to the parent, or make a move, or gesture.

In group work, the therapist can begin to work with a particular client and then decide to interrupt the constellation, in order to continue at a later moment, allowing this participant to take a back seat and observe while other members of the group explore their own family systems. But this is not possible in individual work – this person has booked a session and is here for a certain time period – so more talking may be needed in the beginning to create the right approach and perhaps a short meditation to help a client get in touch with deeper issues and feelings.

Seminars: Working in Groups

The beauty and uniqueness of Family Constellation becomes most apparent when working with groups. Representatives are placed by the client and, from that moment onwards, the client is basically an observer while the inter-play of relationships in the constellation unfolds in front of him. He remains free to receive it or not.

For most of the time, the client simply sits and allows himself to be touched by what is taking place in front of him. Even without much information about the client's family system, the work unfolds as the representatives become part of the energetic field of a particular family. It is an elegant and effective way to bypass any resistance in a client, as the therapist can work on the client in an indirect way through the representatives.

In the seminar format, I usually work with a minimum of 15 participants and a maximum of 50. In smaller groups, I try to ensure that there is a good balance of men and women.

In these seminars, I give no guarantee that all participants will get their personal constellation done. Much benefit can be derived from either observing or participating as a representative in a succession of different constellations, which provide insights for everyone present. In my experience, people who try to insist on receiving their own constellation are usually not in touch with what really matters in the work. In practice, it is not essential whose constellation is being performed; anybody's constellation can touch a participant and create a movement towards healing and resolution. In general, I trust the energy of the moment, which means that the 'right' person will get a constellation at the 'right' time. It is important for participants to develop trust that resolutions will happen in their own time and cannot be forced by making contracts or agreements.

Concerning the set up, wherever possible I invite people to sit on chairs, as this helps everyone to see the constellation better and avoids slouching and sleepiness that sometimes happens when people sit on cushions on the floor. Mostly, the chairs are placed in a circle with a free chair next to me, where the current client will sit and the constellation sessions take place within the circle.

At the beginning of a seminar, I usually say a few words about Family Constellation and then do an introductory "round," which I will shortly explain. A typical workshop consists of individual constellations, rounds, exercises and various meditations.

Rounds

This is a way of sharing in groups that has been embraced by Bert Hellinger and I use it in the same way, sometimes with slight variations. In a round, everyone present is asked to say a few words about how he is feeling, or what is happening for him at this moment. In the very first round of a seminar, I ask people to introduce themselves briefly, saying why they have come and in the last round I invite them to say what has been important for them after participating.

The sharing is usually short. I don't want people to indulge in lengthy story-telling, or interpretations of events in their lives; sometimes I ask everyone to say only one word about how they are feeling at a particular moment, as a quick check to see where the group energy is focused.

In rounds, nobody is allowed to comment on anyone else, everyone has the same right to talk and the talk has to be personal – each person talks only about himself, or herself. It is important that any facilitator conducting a Family Constellation seminar takes care that this rule is respected.

I will use rounds at any moment in a seminar to get a feeling for the group as a whole and to know who is most ready to receive a constellation, or whose issue is most interesting at this time. It can be helpful, after an intense constellation, to use a round to give participants time to integrate what has affected them, or to bring the energy of the group together for continuing the work.

Sometimes, I may interrupt a round to work with someone immediately, only to come back to the round later.

Exercises

In my workshops I use exercises from time to time, in which everyone is invited to participate. This prepares people for working with constellations as it triggers a certain inner process of energy movement. It also helps to move physical energy, as people need to be active when they are otherwise just sitting and watching. The body and mind are one unit and if there is a lot of 'inner movement,' or psychological work, as in Family Constellation sessions, it is helpful to balance this with some physical movement as well, so I use active meditations, dancing and exercises on a daily basis.

I never insist that everyone should follow these exercises exactly as instructed, since the nature and type of participants in any seminar is bound to vary widely and some people will really enjoy an exercise while others will feel less motivated.

After the first introductory round, I usually ask people to sit with a partner and then lead them into a guided meditation to recall their original family and the earlier families of their mother and father, including who belonged to these systems and what events took place. I give examples of the kinds of events that are considered relevant in Family Constellation and then invite them to talk with their partner about their families, while the partner listens quietly, noticing what touches him about the events being shared. This is a good preparation for bringing people in touch with their family system and the important events that have occurred within it.

Another exercise I may use at any time during the workshop is again done in pairs, with partners standing opposite each other; one plays himself as a child, while the other plays the role of parent to this person.

The parent partner functions only as a presence. The one who is the child faces the parent and becomes aware how it feels to stand in this position, in this relationship, noting if he feels 'bigger' or 'smaller' than this parent, or if he feels like coming closer or retreating back. After some time, I may ask the child to bow in front of the parent, in his own way and timing, then the roles are reversed and in the end the two partners share what they noticed in themselves and in the other person. This helps people get in touch with the reality of their relationships with their parents, which is often quite different than they thought.

Sometimes, dividing a big group into small units of four or five people, I introduce an exercise in which one participant acts as the client and one as the facilitator, with the rest as representatives. The facilitator helps the client place his father, mother and a representative for himself, in a mini-constellation. No deep work is done with this constellation; it is just a family portrait to get people involved in the process. The representatives may be asked to report what they perceive in their positions, but apart from coordinating these responses, the person acting as facilitator is not really doing anything, although in training courses this will be developed further.

In another exercise that I use in longer courses - already described in chapter four - I ask people to bring symbols, little objects that have a certain shape and can be easily arranged. In groups of three, each participant creates a constellation with his symbols, either on the floor or on a table, with each symbol representing a person from his original family. Each participant assembles his family portrait in turn, while the others watch and comment on what they observe in the picture. The participant is invited to go from one symbol to the next, asking himself how each family member in this position might be feeling.

285

There are many other structures and exercises that I use, for example, to demonstrate how conscience works, or how it feels to relate to a love partner when a parent stands behind you, but there is no need to describe them all here. The above examples will suffice to give the general idea.

Meditations

I have already described what I mean by meditation in the previous chapter.

Family Constellation work helps a person to move more deeply into meditation, as it clears the mind of unresolved conflicts and encourages the habit of noticing one's own feelings, thoughts and behaviour.

Meditation, on the other hand, helps a person go more deeply into a constellation, as it makes him aware of his interior reality and inner movements - it works both ways.

In my workshops, I do both structured meditations and guided meditations. For example, in the morning and at the end of the day we do active meditations that follow a fixed structure, leading from physical activity to stillness and watchfulness. Mostly, I use two active techniques developed by Osho: Dynamic Meditation in the morning and Kundalini Meditation in the evening. Both last one hour and help people integrate whatever has been touched, provoked or moved during the constellation sessions.

Guided meditations are usually shorter and can happen at any time during the day, preparing people for further work - for example after a break, or before the first session - and also to help people absorb and process their emotions after a particularly intense constellation.

These meditations are guided by the therapist and are a spontaneous response to what is required in a certain moment for the whole group. Here are some examples of guided meditations that I may use in my seminars. The instructions that you see below are given over a period of time, with gaps that allow participants to integrate each suggestion. Participants are either standing or sitting.

1. Receiving Strength from Family Predecessors

Close your eyes. Imagine that your father is standing behind your right shoulder and your mother is standing behind your left shoulder. Notice how it feels. Notice if you feel that one parent is standing closer than the other.

Now imagine that behind your parents stand their parents; your grandparents are standing exactly in the same way - your father's parents behind him, your mother's parents behind her.

Then imagine behind them are their parents, your great-grandparents... and behind them their parents... The number of people is growing as you go back in time, but not a single one can be left out; each one was needed; each one contributed to your existence; each one passed on the life that he, or she, received.

Now imagine that you are leaning against all of them and receiving their support from behind. Feel the strength that flows into you from this long line of your family predecessors.

2. Feeling Your Roots

Stand with your knees slightly bent and imagine that your legs are roots, reaching deep into the earth beneath you.

As you breathe in, imagine that you are reaching down into the earth with these roots to receive its nourishment. Allow your knees to bend more with your in-breath.

As you breathe out, allow your knees to straighten, as if you are pushing down into the earth in order to rise up, like a tree that wants to grow out of the earth towards the sky.

Connected to the rhythm of your in-breath and out-breath, allow your knees to bend and straighten, so there is continuous movement between being nourished by your roots and reaching towards the sky.

Do this for a while.

Now imagine that these two roots, your legs, come from your parents - one from your mother, the other from your father. Imagine how deep these roots go into the earth, how far back they go in your family line. Most of these ancestors you never knew, you will never be able to see them, yet they all support and nourish you. Now feel how these two family lines connect in you, with the two roots meeting in your sex centre. Each cell of your body comes out of this meeting of your father and mother, both contributed equally.

3. Watching in a Movie House

With your eyes closed, become aware of your body and any tensions that may be present in any part of it... in a leg, a hand, the neck, shoulders and so on. Allow them to be there without trying to change anything. Notice where in your body you feel at ease, expanded, light or joyful.

Watch the pattern of your breathing, the rhythm of your in-breath and out-breath. Be aware of any movements that want to happen, arising from inside your body and any feelings that may arise. Allow these sensations without needing to do anything. In the same way, become aware of the continuous stream of thoughts passing through your mind.

Now, imagine you are sitting relaxed in a seat in a movie house, watching these thoughts, images, movements and feelings, as if they are happening on the screen in front of you. Let everything happen on its own, without doing anything, without judging or wanting to interfere or change anything in the movie that is unfolding.

As in any film, you will experience beautiful moments, moments of love, moments of pain, joy, fear... they all come and go, everything changes and you are simply watching...

These are some examples of how a guided meditation can look. Usually, they are responses to the energy of the group at a particular moment and are not pre-planned; they are aimed mostly at helping people get in touch with deeper layers of their personality and preparing them for an actual constellation.

Such exercises may seem simple, but they usually have a profound effect. Our mother and father and their predecessors, are our connection to life itself and the way we feel about them reflects the way we feel about life. On a physical, material level, they represent our origin and everyone will feel this in some way. Deep down, everyone is moved by this understanding, either negatively or positively.

In addition to guided meditations and structured techniques, meditation can also take us a step beyond therapy and this we discuss in the next chapter.

Chapter 24

The Context of the Work

Therapy and Meditation

By definition, therapy is a way of healing, a way of supporting our intrinsic capacity to come into balance. In this sense, therapy attempts to change our present state into one that is imagined as healthier, or 'better,' and this in turn requires an understanding of what a healthier state may be.

Concerning the body and its sicknesses, the orientation towards better health seems clear, but when we try to apply the same concept to our normal, day-to-day lifestyle, with all its challenges and difficulties, the task gets harder and we find that it's almost impossible to define any objective standard.

For example, we can assume that any general concept of human health is going to include a feeling of happiness, well-being and fulfilment, but upon investigation we soon find that what one person desires to make him content is the opposite of what someone else considers as 'happiness.'

One person may want to be more self-assertive, dynamic and confident at work, with a view to mapping out a career and climbing higher on the corporate ladder, while another may be looking for ways to be more relaxed, quiet and less driven by competition. One person may be looking for the strength to be alone, while another may want to learn basic skills of enhancing intimacy with others.

Therapy that works on these kinds of issues can be loosely bracketed under the title of "self-improvement" or "self-help," and aims to help an individual fulfil his, or her, ideas about what will produce a desired state of well-being. However, the problem is that unless these desires are in accord with the deeper forces of life, such as we have seen in Family Constellation sessions, they are unlikely to produce the desired state for very long.

In this kind of self-improvement work, rather than helping a person to come in touch with his being and be more accepting of reality, a therapist may be supporting a client's dreams or fantasies about who he wants to be. These dreams may not even be his own; they may be collectively-held social values or fashions that have been absorbed from the media and culture.

After such therapy, a client may say that he is 'happier,' but if he looks deeply inside himself he may find that he is more tense and fearful, since really he has learned only to suppress certain parts of his personality and project other types of behaviour that have been learned or added. At any moment, the social mask that has been so recently acquired may slip, exposing a different reality underneath.

Really, there can be only one criterion for lasting happiness: Does my happiness depend on the outside, on external circumstances, on getting what I want, or is it rooted within me? If it needs to be supported from outside, it is a fleeting phenomenon; if it is a natural quality of my being, it is authentically mine.

Seen from this perspective, a truly helpful way of doing therapy is one that leads a person towards his interiority, rather than supporting dreams and the therapist who offers it will need to be someone who has personal understanding and experience of meditation. Why? Because, as we have seen, meditation is nothing more nor less than the art of becoming familiar with one's own interiority.

Therapy based in meditation will help a person develop a profound trust in what is, rather than what is desired and will lead a person towards an inner state of relaxation that exists independently from the daily ups and downs of life.

Two Kinds of Happiness

We need to distinguish between two kinds of happiness:

One type arises from the human mind, with all its desires, fantasies and dreams about what will make us happy, focusing on getting what we want from the social environment surrounding us. There is nothing wrong with this kind of happiness, it is not to be condemned, but it has a basic flaw that is often ignored: it does not last and is periodically followed by frustration and discontent. You may have noticed that, even when you attain to a certain goal you have been desiring, within a relatively short time you again find yourself hankering for something more. As Osho and other mystics have pointed out, it is a chronic habit of the human mind never to be satisfied, so any kind of happiness that depends on external circumstances is bound to be momentary.

The other kind of happiness comes from deep inside and is the result of being in touch with one's inner being and this will be more lasting, since it does not depend on outer events. It is an undercurrent that is constantly present, more like a state than an experience and usually manifests in moments of deep relaxation and when one is able to be fully present without mental preoccupation.

We all know the first kind of happiness and to some degree many of us have had glimpses of the second and a therapist has to be able to clearly distinguish these two states when working with his client.

Also, in our discussion of Family Constellation, we have described two kinds of love, the blind one and the conscious one and two kinds of joy, one that arises because the child is close to his parents and the other as a result of seeing one's parents in their totality. In the first case, the child is 'happy' and feels innocent, because he is entangled and bonded with his parents, even though he may carry a burden of pain for them. In the second, he feels alone and

293

maybe even guilty, as he leaves any pain that belongs to his parents, but he is less burdened and experiences happiness in a totally new and different way. It is the happiness of a mature and adult outlook on life and of not being controlled by the past.

It is important for a therapist to be able to detect these two states in his client - the childish love and the mature one.

Two Ways of Doing Family Constellation

As I've already indicated in earlier chapters, Family Constellation can be approached in two ways, both of which are of value to the client.

First, as a therapeutic method that leads to understanding family entanglements and helps an individual overcome any problems related to his family system. In this way it functions more or less like any other therapy, providing insights into human nature that are becoming mainstream psychological knowledge in many countries throughout the world.

Second, one can approach Family Constellation as a way to come in touch with what moves us deeply in life, as a preparation to contact our inner being beyond personal and collective conscience. This approach has a more spiritual dimension and perhaps this is the reason why Bert Hellinger called this aspect of his work 'applied philosophy.' We may also call it a 'meditative approach.'

In general, therapy works with our body, mind and emotions and tries to bring harmony into how they function together, thereby attempting to free the individual from conflict, stress and tension. Meditation, on the other hand, is the realisation that we are something else, something that lies altogether beyond the body-mind structure. In this sense, one might describe meditation as the ultimate form of therapy, since only when we are rooted deeply in meditation can we truly be free from stress.

Even a so-called 'peaceful mind' will have tensions, even a harmonised system is likely to become unstable again and revert to a state of conflict or tension. The real solution is brought by the insight that we are neither body nor mind, that life's drama is just an existential play and the only difficulty is that we have forgotten that we are actors in it. We take it as real.

Authentic therapy, in my view, is a preparation that leads a person towards the spiritual quest, since any interest in self-improvement, if it is authentic, will lead one steadily deeper into oneself, deeper into the inquiry "Who am I?"

Therapy is a useful first step, clearing the ground of debris so that we can make the inner journey more easily. If we are full of tension and stress, there will be no energy left for meditation, so most people will find that therapy unburdens them of psychological baggage and allows them to see the essential nature of the spiritual quest.

A Model of Reality

In Family Constellation we learn that the individual is part of a collectivity, a family, that forms him and this explains much of his behaviour. In this way, we are looking not only at an individual history, but at a bigger system and seeing its affect on a client. However, it would be wrong to take the view that an individual is merely the product of his family's past. In a sense, he is his parents, but he is also something more - a unique human being with many dimensions.

One model is not enough to explain the whole complexity of how each person functions. A tree can be looked at from many angles and will always appear different, depending where we stand, even though it is the same tree. In the same way, we may need to look at ourselves from many different standpoints and get insights with the help of different therapeutic models, so we may finally be able to see ourselves directly. As Hellinger says, "The fullness of life cannot be reduced to one path."

Let's consider, for a moment, the man-woman relationship, where Family Constellation offers many insights, including the need for balance between giving and taking, which we discussed in chapter ten. Looking at a love relationship only from this angle may lead some people to conclude that a love relationship is a business deal, in which one must continuously calculate how much to give, or what one should receive. This not only destroys the spontaneity of love, it is also contrary to the ultimate experience of love in which two people find themselves dissolving into one – if only for a few fleeting moments – and entering into a transpersonal state of ecstasy where thinking stops.

Such a misunderstanding might occur if one focuses too much on the map of love and too little on the actual terrain. A model, map, or another person's insight may be a help to open one's vision, but it cannot be a substitute for personal experience and exploration. The love relationship between men and women is too vast a phenomenon to be encapsulated by a single concept, or even many concepts. In order to know what love really is, one has to enter into it oneself.

Perhaps this is the reason why many mystics do not teach a specific philosophical system. Zen Masters, for example, are known to be very contradictory, saying one thing in one moment and the opposite the next, as a provocation to abandon linear, logical thinking and trust in a deeper layer of awareness that is beyond the realm of fixed ideas and beliefs.

Coming back to the issue of love relationship, we can say that if love is conscious then there is bound to be a certain balance in giving and taking, but without having to think about it, or calculate gain and loss. Similarly, if love towards our parents has reached a certain level of awareness and understanding, it will include what we learned about the Sacred Order and bowing down to our predecessors, while at the same time transcending it. Real gratitude, or respect, happens when we do not need to remember them; they are just part of our natural, spontaneous behaviour.

The Transcendental Standpoint

When we embrace a transcendental standpoint, all truths appear relative. For example, we have understood that parents need to give and children receive, which is true for the biological dimension of their relationship. However, if we consider the spiritual dimension, it is also true to say that a person with more awareness is more able to give, in terms of overflowing with love and compassion, than a person with less awareness. On this level, it is possible for children to give to their parents, but this will not be a material giving, or imply any form of hierarchical acknowledgment; it will be giving without action, without 'doing.' It will be the presence, or being, of the child that will constitute the gift, providing, of course, that the parent is open to receive it.

On a biological level, giving birth is the greatest possible creativity, since it is through this act that the survival of both the tribe and the species is ensured. Seen from a spiritual perspective, however, the same act is quite ordinary and mundane, as every animal is doing the same thing. Instead, becoming more conscious, giving birth to oneself, to one's inner being, is now regarded as the greatest possible creative act. Both perspectives are true; it depends from which standpoint you are looking.

Another example concerns respect and honour. In Family Constellation, we take the view that our parents deserve our respect for no other reason than because they gave birth to us – simply because they are our parents. If this is taken as an absolute truth it starts to create problems, especially in terms of placing tremendous social emphasis on blind respect and obedience to authority, a disease which has plagued humanity for thousands of years.

Today, we are more aware of the implications of such attitudes and it is now a more commonly accepted social understanding that a person should be respected not for who he is, or how old he is, but for what he does and says. In other words, a parent should be respected only if he deserves respect, not because he is a father, not because she is a mother. Both viewpoints seem to be right and are contradictory in appearance only, each pointing to a different truth.

Respecting a father, irrespective of what he does, does not mean that the child has to approve all of his father's actions. In the same way, if the child does not approve of some of his father's actions, this does not mean that he lacks respect for the person who is his father - it does not need to be a judgment about the person at all.

In the past, a father was likely to know more about work, craft and professional skills than his son, who out of necessity was always a newcomer in the type of work in which his father was engaged. In such circumstances, respect for the father was natural and easy. But nowadays the flexibility of social status and the rapid rate of change in work skills, especially in areas like technology and computers, means that a father's knowledge is very likely to be either useless to his son – he chose another type of work - or out of date. In such a situation, a son may be more knowledgeable than his father and may look down on his father.

So respecting a father does not mean one needs to follow his advice. Respect and gratefulness do not imply obedience, as so often understood in the past. Following someone and being grateful are contrary phenomena; indeed, as history often shows, followers tend not to be grateful but rather resentful.

To really understand the meaning of respect and honour is not easy. When we assume the attitude that a person should be respected only if he deserves it, we may prevent ourselves from becoming blind followers, but we may simultaneously fall into the trap of judging or condemning our parents, as many have done. Then it becomes difficult to understand the Family Constellation perspective that parents deserve respect just because they are parents.

Beyond Belief Systems

Any model or system that reflects the workings of the human psyche can help people grow in awareness, be it Family Constellation, Reichian body types, Enneagram personality types, or the Jungian psychology of inner male and female archetypes, but the same system can easily become knowledge - something we believe to be true without having tested it ourselves, something passed on to us from others. With this in mind, the orientation should always be to use a system to deepen one's own understanding, or to question an old attitude or assumption about ourselves and our beliefs.

Many times it happens that people who gain a deeper understanding with the help of a particular model become fascinated and overly identified with it. It becomes a kind of faith, a fixed perspective through which to view the whole of life. They may be clients, they may be teachers, it doesn't matter; any teaching can become an ideology and then it is dangerous, because it can give the idea of knowing without self-inquiry and self-experience. On many occasions, Hellinger reminded his students that what he said was relevant only in a certain context and at a certain moment and should not be regarded as more than that.

Here the difference can be seen between an ordinary teacher and a great one. The ordinary teacher conveys a model, a method, or a system, passing on knowledge in a consistent way and making his students feel more at ease and secure. A great teacher conveys a vision, but at the same time challenges the intelligence and alertness of his students, destroying belief systems without creating fixed replacements. With a teacher we feel comfortable and safe, with a visionary we tend to feel insecure and uneasy, as he leaves us alone to find things out for ourselves.

Many people are attracted to a certain model or methodology because it gives them the feeling of knowing what to do, or how to look at life and saves them from the uncertainty of confronting life afresh, moment to moment, in a spontaneous and innocent way. However, I personally would not want Family Constellation to be adopted as a guideline for 'right' behaviour. Rather, I would like the ideas presented in this book, including those of Hellinger and Osho, to be understood as a working hypothesis that needs to be verified by each reader individually.

I have noticed that there are clients who have had several sessions and participated as representatives in other constellations, seem to go through the motions of looking inside, rather than making the effort to actually do so. They already know the 'right' solution sentence and to whom to 'bow,' but the feeling is automatic and sometimes reminds one of a formal ritual in a church.

Similarly, some facilitators suggest solution sentences and ask questions in a routine way that indicates a predetermined outlook; they have not taken the trouble to see each situation and each client as new. For example, in a particular circumstance, it may be more authentic for the client to express his anger towards the father rather than bowing down to him, especially if the bow is done out of knowledge of what one is supposed to do. Or as a facilitator, it may be more sincere, in a particular situation, to admit that one doesn't know how to proceed.

What is important is to remain open, to question and to trust one's own experience. At this point, I wish to acknowledge the flexibility of Hellinger himself, who has repeatedly changed his views, even to the point of contradicting things he said earlier. By the same token, I wish to acknowledge Osho as a mystic who insists on individual responsibility as the foundation of self inquiry – the understanding that truth cannot be borrowed or transferred from anyone else. Everyone needs to evolve and grow in his own unique way and theory should always follow personal experience, not vice versa.

Learning Family Constellation

A constellation is a process of learning, not only for the client, but also for the representatives and facilitator. This learning has several levels:

A representative, standing in for a member of a family, comes in touch with the feelings of that person and as a result may have an experience he never had before in his life. Likewise, a facilitator may have new experiences when connecting to each person in a system through his openness and empathy. In this way, representatives and facilitators gain life experiences without having been through them personally.

Learning Family Constellation as a therapeutic tool brings a deeper understanding of the function of conscience, the 'order of love' that exists in every family and of the laws that rule a family system.

Moreover, it is important for facilitators to realise that there are additional skills required to master the art of helping people that are not directly related to Family Constellation. For example, a facilitator needs basic counselling and communication skills, knowing how to stay centred in oneself, understanding the phenomenon of projection... to mention only a few.

In addition, it is helpful to understand the significance of body language, recognising that what the body expresses may be very different from what the client is saying. Often, in constellations, we look at subtle movements and gestures of the body rather than relying on what is being said. Experience in emotional release work is also helpful, learning to distinguish between those kinds of emotional expressions that deserve to be supported and those that do not.

Deeper Significance of Family Constellation Laws

As discussed earlier, in Family Constellations we are coming in touch with laws that move us deeply in life and, if we apply them in a wider context, they can provide us with some valuable principles that go far beyond therapy.

The Law of Belonging

The law of belonging points to the fact that we all have a place in existence. No one has more or less right to be here, regardless of whether he is a sinner or saint. As the mystics say, the smallest grass leaf is as much needed as the biggest star, nothing is excluded and there is no question of comparison. It is the human mind that excludes, makes divisions of better or worse, higher or lower, good or bad, but nothing can in fact be excluded because the existence that surrounds us is universal, all-encompassing and all-inclusive; everything will remain present and will continue to have influence.

The Law of Order

The law of order points to the fact that each one of us is unique, no two human beings are alike, so each individual has a special place in existence that cannot be taken by anyone else. Here we see an expanded version of what we have called the Sacred Order, in which our place is assured by our very uniqueness.

The Law of Balance

The law of balance reminds us that whatever anyone does has consequences; it doesn't go unnoticed. We influence what happens around us and we are influenced by it. We are neither dependent nor independent; rather, we live in a vast network of inter-dependence. It is like a pendulum, as you push it to one side, you are in fact building momentum for it to eventually swing to the other side. There is balance in life, high tide is followed by low tide, summer by winter, day by night; if you work hard there is need for rest; if you hurt someone, in some way you also hurt yourself. Everyone is and always will be, fully responsible for what he does. Hellinger calls it 'carrying one's guilt,' which also means carrying one's own responsibility.

Honouring the Dead

Acknowledging the importance of the dead reminds us that life and death belong together, neither can exist without the other and in fact life is given value only because of death. It is a question of contrast. In a classroom, students can read white writing only because of the black board on which it is written. Similarly, the dance of life emerges from a womb of death, or nothingness, which Gautam the Buddha has called "shunyata," or emptiness. A society that does not remember the dead has no existential strength.

Victims and Perpetrators

Bringing to light the connection between victims and perpetrators shows us that polar opposites are really part of one organic whole and exist because of each other; one cannot be a victim without a perpetrator and vice versa, they mutually define each other. In fact, these polar opposites also exist within each individual: one side is visible, while the other remains hidden and comes to light only when the opportunity arises. Victims often carry hidden violence within themselves, while murderers often experience themselves as victims. It is a tendency of the human mind to try and keep apart polar opposites which in fact belong together, but the more we try to pull them apart, the stronger becomes the force that pulls them back together.

In Tune with Life

When a client opens his heart to all members of his family, he is performing a spiritual act that brings him into a deeper harmony with life. Even the so-called 'evil ones' in a family system are moved by the same fundamental forces as the so-called 'good ones,' and in this sense all are equal, no one is higher, no one is lower.

When we judge or condemn someone, we are actually trying to deny his right to belong, which is against the movement of a life force that accepts everyone unconditionally. We may not understand why people feel compelled to act in certain ways, but this does not mean we have the right to condemn them. In any case, we are able to understand only a fraction of why things happen the way they do and why people act in a certain way. The major part of life remains mysterious, beyond our comprehension and all we can do is bow down in front of the mysterious and the unexplainable.

All important events in life are happenings, not preconceived ideas that we try to put into action. Love is a good example: we cannot create love, nor do we know why it happens and this elusive and mysterious quality contributes to its beauty. We are carried by mysterious movements of life, as if by a wave; something is brought to the surface for a while then disappears again into the unknown.

Life, as we have seen, moves between polarities, between conflict and the resolution of conflict, between love and hate, between positive and negative, man and woman. In this context, it is worth remembering that if we were to experience only peace and harmony we would find life flat and boring. So there is a movement in life towards conflict and another movement towards resolution, reconciliation and healing. We see this in constellations, especially when we work with movements. If there is a conflict between partners, there is also a deep movement towards reconciliation; it may take its time to come to completion but we can always see it.

As I mentioned earlier, a constellation is like taking a momentary picture of where this movement has reached in this moment and by looking at it we may be able to help this movement make its next step.

I gave a session to Brigitte, a woman whose family came from Danzig, in former East Germany and had lost everything after the war as they fled westward to escape the Russians. Her mother subsequently married a Russian man, who later left her with their first child. Brigitte was a later child of this woman.

In the constellation we find that the grandmother, Brigitte's mother's mother, is very angry with the Russians.

We also see an unsuccessful effort by her child, the client's mother, to find reconciliation by marrying a Russian, while at the same time unconsciously remaining loyal to her mother and so repeating her mother's fate of suffering - losing her husband - and ending up feeling the same anger.

Only in the next generation, with Brigitte, do we find a certain completion of the healing movement between Germans and Russians, including recognition of the fact that the Germans were the initial aggressors. Brigitte finally says to her mother and grandmother, "I love the Russians too."

Brigitte's statement immediately proves to have a deeply healing effect on everyone participating in her constellation.

Here, as in other conflicts, one has to give up one's anger and identification, allowing the pain of what happened to surface without making accusations. Both Germans and Russians suffered immensely from the war. Acknowledging this basic truth allows the two opposing forces to meet and for reconciliation to happen, which sometimes occurs only in the heart of a later family member. It means to acknowledge that the 'other side' was also under the influence of a greater force and in this sense was helpless, too.

The Path to Freedom

Looking at things in a larger context one discovers that there is never really any opposition in life, all opposites belong to one whole. It is because we identify with only one aspect, or one side, that we experience conflict. Many mystics, from Gautam Buddha onwards, have pointed out that to be identified creates suffering and to be able to free oneself from identification is true liberation. Normally, we identify with many things: our profession, relationships, nation, faith, ethnic group and most of all our own mind and body. As I mentioned before, meditation is a way to realise that we are essentially none of these things. Family Constellation, in essence, leads to the same insight and therefore brings us close to a state of meditation.

For example, when Brigitte is able to say that she loves the Russians, she simultaneously gives up her identification with her German forefathers and their anger. She is in fact saying that Germans and Russians are equal, both suffered immensely, both are human beings, which is a deeper truth than any superficial identity. By acknowledging and respecting who we are and where we come from, we are able to go beyond national labels.

Identifying is a natural and necessary part of growing up, helping us to create a sense of personal identity, but a deeper and more mature understanding of life takes us beyond all such labels. In this way, transcendence is seen not as an act, but a side-effect that happens once we deeply respect our roots.

In the words of Osho, "There is no action after understanding. Understanding is the action itself. It is not that you bring the light inside the room, then you throw the darkness out. Understanding is light. The moment you understand, there is no suffering to be thrown out, to be dropped out, to be got rid off. Understanding simply cleanses you."

It may be helpful, to point out here the difference between identification and respect. Identification happens unconsciously, when we choose 'this' against 'that,' becoming one with the person with whom we are identifying. Respect is a conscious act that is not for or against anyone or anything. We realise our separate existence, which frees both parties, leaving behind a fragrance of love.

For Brigitte, respecting her grandmother means to face her, to see her life circumstances, to understand why she feels angry, but to leave her suffering, pain and anger to her. In this moment, Brigitte is no longer blindly identified with the grandmother and is free to see and acknowledge the other side, the Russians and is bound by neither side.

Respect and honour are easily misunderstood words. They don't mean that one needs to do something, to identify and take on a certain allegiance. True respect comes out of understanding; it is a side effect that occurs when we are fully able to acknowledge a person and all his life experiences without interference.

This may be one of the reasons why Hellinger no longer uses solution sentences like, 'I honour you', with such frequency as he once did. Love is not a doing, but a deep reverence towards someone and an acceptance of each one's aloneness.

Freedom is also a much misunderstood word. Most people think it means "doing what I want to do." But, as we have seen, true freedom comes only with great insight and awareness. When people talk about freedom, it usually serves a certain purpose, such as a child saying 'no' to a parent, or an adult leaving a love partner. The purpose is to loosen the bond of a relationship. This is a negative kind of freedom, which can be described as 'freedom from,' but in itself it has no positive or creative orientation. It is only when we discover the added dimension of 'freedom for' that our approach to life embraces a real 'yes' and becomes fulfilling.

In this sense, the function of therapy is to give us the experience of 'freedom from,' while the function of meditation, as a second step, is to create the possibility of 'freedom for.' In other words, dis-entangling ourselves from our psychological hang ups is a good first step, but fundamentally it is the spiritual dimension that gives life its true meaning. What gives Family Constellation its greater significance as a form of therapy is its potential for bridging these two kinds of freedoms. A client can feel attracted to the process as a way to solve a certain personal problem and can then feel drawn into a deeper appreciation of the way life moves and into the quest for discovering and experiencing who we really are.

Appendix

Frequently Asked Questions

How often one should do a constellation?

Family Constellation is a one-session method and, as such, is based on a different concept than therapies that 'work through' a difficulty or personality issue. You do not come once a week for a session for three years. A constellation helps a client to get deeply in touch with his reality and helps him gain new understanding of how he is entangled with other family members. Here the work ends.
It is like finding a new direction or perspective in life. An inner shift has happened and, from this point onwards, all the details will unfold by themselves. However, it is possible that not all the important dynamics have been untied in a single session, especially if there are a lot of complex relationships in the family of origin. Then it is possible to do another constellation. For similar reasons, the client may need one constellation for his present family and one for his family of origin. Or, it may be that time has passed and new insights or facts about a client's family have emerged; then, too, he may decide to have another constellation.

Usually, when a person has been deeply touched, he will not even think about whether to repeat a constellation. The process of absorption will continue long after the actual session is over.

What should I do after my constellation?

This question arises from the idea of having to manage or control the outcome of a session. Practically, it is best not think about what to do after a session, but rather trust that, having understood something profound about one's family situation, changes will naturally occur that are beyond the usual idea of 'doing.'

Therapists who insist that a person should change his attitude or lifestyle as a result of a session are interfering in the life of the client. Whatever a client does after a session should not be the concern of the therapist. So, obviously, the normal criteria for evaluating whether a session was successful cannot be applied to constellation work.

What does 'solution oriented' mean?

When we say that Family Constellation is a solution-oriented approach, we mean that the therapist looks at what is having a positive effect on the client in a constellation and then does the minimum necessary to support this shift. At times, giving a single sentence, or asking someone to turn, or open the eyes, is enough for the situation to develop.

In Family Constellation work there is a tendency to get lost in exploring the causes of entanglement, so the therapist should refrain from any kind of curiosity about a family system, or why something has happened, unless it is essential for the client to know. The facilitator is not a director, or guide, but more a coordinator - he looks for the keystone that keeps a problem in place. When this is found, everything shifts automatically.

Doing more than is necessary, such as placing more representatives in a constellation than are needed, takes attention away from the real issue and weakens the impact of a session.

How important is it to place the client in the constellation?

Generally, it does not matter whether the client himself is placed in a constellation, or whether someone else represents him, as we are working with the energy field of a whole family system. The specialty and elegance of Family Constellation is that a client can watch, as a witness and allow himself to be touched without directly participating. In a sense, the facilitator does not deal with the client directly, but indirectly, through working with the stand-ins and the systemic field, which is a non-intrusive approach and also an effective way to bypass any unwillingness in the client to face certain realities. In this way the client can absorb whatever is revealed, in his own way and time, without having to deal with any real or imagined expectations from the facilitator. He remains free. Often, a client is placed in the constellation at the end of a session to directly feel his position in the system, or to acknowledge a member of his family, but sometimes the facilitator may feel that this will be too overwhelming, or that the client is unwilling to receive the outcome. In this case, the client will remain as a witness, sitting in his chair.

When do you interrupt a constellation?

Generally, a constellation needs to be interrupted when there is no more energy to continue, when important facts are missing, or when the facilitator meets strong resistance from the client. Interrupting a constellation is not a punishment, but an important intervention in itself that can lead to a shift in the client's attitude, which may allow a constellation to be resumed at a later time.

Sometimes, it is a delicate matter to decide if a constellation is stuck, not moving and whether it should therefore be stopped, or if it is just a moment when patience is required so that some unseen issue or fresh insight can surface in its own time.

Can one do a constellation for someone else?

We have seen that all members of a family system are affected by a constellation, even if only one member is actually present. So constellations can be done for someone who is not actually present and can have a healing influence on that person. These constellations "in proxy" happen, for example, during a training session, when a person who is being trained as a facilitator presents the case of one of his clients, setting up a constellation for someone who is not actually in the room. The trainer, or supervisor, does the constellation without having met the client and the trainee may benefit by gaining new insights about how to continue working with this client.

In other cases, however, it is important to be clear if someone has asked for help in this way and has given permission for a constellation to be done while not personally present. If one is approached as a social worker or therapist by a client, this is obviously a statement of permission and the case can be presented in a training seminar. But wanting to do a constellation for a friend whom we think is in need of help, but who may not know that he, or she, is the object of a Family Constellation study, is a different matter and should not be encouraged.

What if nothing seems to change after a session?

Personal transformation is a process of gaining understanding and consciousness about oneself and one's life. Sometimes, the more we desire a certain change in our lives, the more it becomes impossible. Really, it shows that we haven't fully understood why something is happening, because the moment we do understand, the desire for getting rid of a particular habit, attitude, or situation, will disappear and simultaneously this will be the moment when change occurs by itself. But it will not be our personal doing. This is the secret of inner transformation.

The motivation for doing a constellation should not be to change something, but to gain more insight, because the work of Family Constellation is about 'acknowledging what is'.

The benefit of this can be experienced immediately, not at some time in the future, although there are likely to be lasting effects.

So, if there is no change after a session, either some truth has not yet come to light, or something has not been understood deeply – by either the client or therapist - or a person is not yet willing, or capable, to give up an attachment.

Constellations with Objects, Feelings and Abstractions

Sometimes the therapist may need to place a representative for an abstract concept in a constellation. For example, a person may be needed to represent a country, God, death, destiny, war, illness. In certain circumstances, one may even begin a session with this representative, such as someone to stand in for death in a case of a terminal illness. One may also place a person to represent an issue, such as alcohol abuse, or a feeling, such as fear.

In general, I am cautious about introducing representatives that are not actual people, because what we are really working with are relationships and our feelings are a result of these relationships. Often, we see that a stand-in for a country is actually a certain person, or a group of people, from the client's previous family. The same is true when we place a representative for abuse, or illness; they often represent excluded family members who can be identified.

Nevertheless, it can sometimes be helpful to move the energy of a session by introducing a person to represent an abstraction and then a basic problem may become clear. For example, placing a representative for war may help a client realise that there was a bigger movement involved in his family's history, far beyond any individual's control; placing a representative for destiny next to a mother who suddenly died may remind her child that we are all helpless in front of the deeper, unknown forces of life.

Except in the case of illness, or in the event of someone having to face his own death, I rarely begin a constellation by introducing an abstract concept, as this tends to lack depth and clarity. For example, when a client is angry with a woman, then to place his representative and one for the emotion of anger will probably not lead very far. Usually, it is better to place him and the woman, or find the relevant person from his original family. However, there are facilitators who use constellations in this abstract way and report successful outcomes.

Bibliography

Bader, E., Pearson, P. (1988): In Quest of the Mythical Mate (Brunner&Mazel, New York)

Franke, U. (2003): The River Never Looks Back. Historical and Practical Foundations of Bert Hellinger's Family Constellations (Carl-Auer-Systeme Verlag, Heidelberg)

Hellinger, B.(1999): Acknowledging What Is. Conversations with Bert Hellinger (Zeig Tucker & Theissen, Inc.)

Hellinger, B., G.Weber a. H.Beaumont (1998): Love's Hidden Symmetry. What Makes Love Work in Relationships (Zeig Tucker & Theissen, Inc.)

Hellinger, B. (2002): Der Austausch. Fortbildung für Familiensteller (Carl-Auer-Systeme Verlag, Heidelberg)

Hellinger, B. (2003): Farewell. Family Constellations with Descendants of Victims and Perpetrators (Carl-Auer-Systeme Verlag, Heidelberg)

Hellinger, B. (2003): To the Heart of the Matter. Brief Therapies (Carl-Auer-Systeme Verlag, Heidelberg)

Hellinger, B. (2003): Peace Begins in The Soul. Family Constellation in the Service of Reconciliation (Carl-Auer-Systeme Verlag, Heidelberg)

Neuhauser, J. (2001): Supporting Love. How Love Works in Couple Relationships (Zeig Tucker & Theissen, Monaco)

Osho: The Great Pilgrimage (Rebel Publishing House, India)

Osho: Beyond Psychology (Tao Publishing Pvt. Ltd., India)

Osho: The Rebellious Spirit (Rebel Publishing House, India)

Osho: The Invitation (Rebel Publishing House, India)

Osho: Satyam, Shivam, Sunderam (Tao Publishing Pvt. Ltd., India)

Osho: Meditation. The First and Last Freedom (St. Martin's Press, USA)

Osho: Love - Freedom – Aloneness. The Koan of Relationships (St. Martin's Press, USA)

Prekop, J. (1992) Hättest du mich festgehalten. Grundlagen und Anwendung der Festhalte- Therapie (Goldmann)

Ulsamer, B. (2001): The Art and Practice of Family Constellations (Carl-Auer-Systeme Verlag, Heidelberg)

About the Author

Svagito R. Liebermeister was born in Germany in 1957, holds a degree in psychology from Munich University and has over 25 years practical experience in working with people as a therapist. He has studied a wide range of therapeutic approaches, including Deep Tissue Bodywork, Neo-Reichian Breath and Energy Work, Psychic Massage and Counselling. Parallel to his interest in therapy, Svagito has been a disciple of the Indian mystic Osho since 1981 and has explored a wide range of meditation techniques. In 1995, he began to include Family Constellation in his work, studying with its founder, Bert Hellinger and since 2000 he leads his own training programs in this fascinating new approach to therapy. He is interested in combining therapy with meditation and has trained hundreds of practitioners worldwide in the art of working with people. He is currently the coordinator of the annual Therapist Training Program at the Osho Meditation Resort in Pune, India, one of the largest personal growth centres in the world. Every year, he travels extensively through Europe, Asia, Central America and other parts of the world, offering courses and training programs in over 15 different countries.

For further information about Svagito's courses and trainings:
www.family-constellation.net

For further information about Bert Hellinger and his work:
www.hellinger.com or www.hellingerschule.com

For further information about Osho and his approach to meditation:
www.osho.com

Lightning Source UK Ltd.
Milton Keynes UK
UKOW04f1949030315

247237UK00001B/84/P